A wargamers' guide to the
CRUSADES

Companion volumes

Napoleon's Campaigns in Miniature
A wargamers' guide to the Napoleonic Wars
1796-1815
by Bruce Quarrie

Air Battles in Miniature
A wargamers' guide to aerial combat 1939-1945
by Mike Spick

Alexander the Great's Campaigns
A guide to Ancient political and military wargaming
by Phil Barker

Sea Battles in Miniature
A guide to Naval Wargaming
by Paul Hague

In preparation

Hannibal's Campaigns
by Tony Bath

A wargamers' guide to the CRUSADES

Ian Heath

 Patrick Stephens, Cambridge

Dedication
To Nina, for vacuuming round the books

First published 1980

British Library Cataloguing in Publication Data

Heath, Ian
    A wargamers' guide to the Crusades.
    1. Crusades
    I. Title
    940.1'8   D157

    ISBN 0 85059 430 8

Photoset in 10 on 11pt English Times by
Manuset Limited, Baldock, Herts.
Printed in Great Britain on white book
wove 90 gsm Vol 18, and bound by
The Garden City Press, Letchworth, for
the publishers, Patrick Stephens Limited,
Bar Hill, Cambridge, CB3 8EL, England.

Contents

Introduction

When I was first asked to write this book, my synopsis of its contents began with the proviso that although it would be a book for wargamers, it would not be a wargaming book. I did not think it could lay serious claim to being the latter because of the absence of any playing rules from its pages, almost universal acceptance of the Wargames Research Group's *Ancient and Medieval* rules obviating the need for any attempt at rule-writing on my own part. It was envisaged instead as a vehicle for hopefully all the historical data—organisational, tactical and institutional—that a wargamer might need in order to set up a realistic Crusade campaign. All the better if, in passing, he should develop an interest in the history of the era for its own sake, and if I were to be absolutely honest I would admit that conversion of the uninitiated was often foremost in my thoughts as I wrote.

Even restricting my interpretation of 'Crusades' to those campaigns fought in the East for control of the Holy Land (ie, ignoring the Spanish *Reconquista* and the inglorious butchery of so-called pagans and heretics in Prussia and Southern France), comprehensive coverage of the subject is still way beyond the capacity of this book. In fact, when it came to putting pen to paper it was very much a matter not of what to put in, but rather of what to leave out. Originally, for example, I had hoped to include a chapter giving brief biographies of the principal leaders of the Crusade era—men like Richard *Coeur de Lion*, King of England, who instilled such dread into the Moslems that more than 50 years later Moslem horsemen, when their mounts were startled by a rustle in the undergrowth, would say, 'Do you think, then, that it is King Richard of England in that bush?'; or like his contemporary Philip II *Augustus* of France, who one chronicler described in terms of being to King Richard 'like a hammer tied to the tail of a cat'; or, on the Moslem side, like Saladin, such a man of honour that the Christians believed he must have once been secretly knighted; or, at the other end of the scale, like the ruthless Mamluk sultan Baibars, who murdered his way to the throne and died—appropriately enough—as a result of mistakenly drinking from a poisoned chalice he had prepared for another! I would have liked, too, to have had a general chapter on military command, to have extended the gazetteer considerably, or to have expanded on Byzantine and Mongol organisation and tactics. Space, however, was not on my side.

Nevertheless, I feel I can claim in relative safety that there should be enough data provided herein to satisfy all but the most demanding of military enthusiasts and wargamers. Within these pages can be found an outline chronology of Crusading warfare in the 12th and 13th centuries; a background description of the land over which so much blood was to be spilt; chapters on Christian and Moslem organisation and the Assassins; an explanation of the Byzantine role in the Crusades; surveys on communication, supply and attrition; detailed accounts of naval and siege warfare as practised in the East; an extensive gazetteer of over 200 fortified sites; and chapters on the Military Orders and on tactics, revisions of two sections from my earlier book *Armies and Enemies of the Crusades 1096-1291* (Wargames Research Group, 1978). The wargaming aspect is covered both by a closing chapter dealing with particular aspects of Crusading warfare in the context of a campaign, and by two appendices covering troop classification and the availability of wargame figures.

Names of people and places used in the text follow their simplest and/or most common forms, particularly those of the Moslems. For instance it is much easier and more usual to write Saladin than Salah ad-Din Yusef ibn Ayyub (Righteousness of the Faith, Joseph son of Job), and Baibars rather than Rukn ad-Din Baibars el-Bundukdari. Town and castle names are usually given in their Frankish form except where the Arabic form is in more widespread use—as for example with al-Marqab (Frankish Margat)—or where the modern form is prevalent (eg, Jerusalem). 'Frankish' denotes Western European throughout, although it is worth noting in passing that the vast majority of crusaders were in fact French. Occasionally I use the terms Latins or Syrian Franks to differentiate those settled in the East from European pilgrims just passing through. The former became known in time as *poulains* ('colts'). To Europeans the Frankish East was *Outrémer*, the lands over the sea, comprising the Kingdom of Jerusalem, the County of Tripoli, the Principality of Antioch and the County of Edessa (see map on page 11). Most of the information that is currently available, and on which this book is based, refers primarily to the Kingdom of Jerusalem, the borders of which are closely echoed by those of modern Israel, and as a result it is largely written from a Frankish viewpoint.

Nothing much has actually altered in the centuries that have elapsed since the Crusades. Israel, 'the cockpit of religion' as one of today's leading military historians has called it, is still a centre of conflict. Once it was Moslem and Christian who vied for control of the Holy Land, while now it is Moslem and Jew. The excuse, however, remains the same.

Ian Heath,
St Ives, Huntingdon, January 1980

Chapter 1

An outline chronology of the Crusades, 1095-1291

There are a considerable number of good general histories of the Crusade movement widely available these days, the most popular undoubtedly being *A History of the Crusades* by Sir Steven Runciman, available for a modest sum in Penguin paperbacks or in hardback, for a less modest sum (nearly £50 at the time of writing), from the Cambridge University Press. The fact that Runciman's history, and many others such as those of H.E. Mayer, Henry Treece and Joshua Prawer, are today so readily accessible inevitably means that any attempt on my part to give a comprehensive account of two centuries of Levantine political history would be superfluous to say the least.

As should be apparent from the Introduction, my purpose in this book is not to document the day to day events of Outremer's existence but rather to give as thorough an account as I can of every aspect of Crusading warfare. This introductory chapter is intended to provide no more than an outline survey of the main historical events of the Crusades, being restricted largely to those which you are likely to encounter in the course of this book. It therefore provides no more than a 'quick reference' guide to the main battles and campaigns of the era. Those of you requiring fuller details will not be disappointed by the depth of Runciman's research, and I would strongly recommend that each and every one of you should get hold of a copy of his three-volume classic if you do not already possess one.

The chronology

1095 The First Crusade was proclaimed by Pope Urban II, probably in continuance of the policy of Gregory VII who had earlier proposed the despatch of armed assistance to the Byzantines for use against the Seljuk Turks of Anatolia. At one point in 1074 Pope Gregory had even declared that 50,000 men were ready to follow him to the Byzantine Empire's aid. By the late 11th century Europe had a surplus of fighting men—younger sons with no inheritance, dispossessed tenants, brigands and mercenaries, not to mention powerful secular princes who delighted in the adventure of war—and Urban's plan for a crusade may therefore have been partly aimed at removing to foreign climes those elements likely to disrupt the 'Peace of God' in Europe.

1096 The People's Crusade, led by a fraud *extraordinnaire* named Peter the Hermit and a humble knight called Walter Sans-Avoir ('The Penniless'), was virtually wiped out by the Seljuk Turks near Nicaea. Walter and most of the leaders were killed and only some 3,000 souls out of perhaps 40,000 survived the disaster. The Crusades were off to an ignominious start.

1097 The main contingents of the First Crusade, having mustered in Constantinople, set out to march overland through Anatolia to the Holy Land. The leaders of the expedition were the papal legate Adhémar Le Puy, Godfrey de Bouillon and his brothers Eustace and Baldwin, Bohemond of Taranto and his nephew Tancred, Raymond de Saint-Gilles of Toulouse, Robert of Flanders, William the Conqueror's son Robert of Normandy, Stephen of Blois and Hugh de Vermandois. The Seljuk capital of Nicaea surrendered to their Byzantine allies after only a brief siege, and two weeks later the Franks themselves scored their first victory over the Turks at Dorylaeum. The army had split into two columns, the first of which the Turks had attacked in the mistaken belief that it represented the Franks' entire strength. This column, under Bohemond, held out until the other half of the army, under Adhémar and Raymond, came to its relief and chased the Turks from the field.

1098 Antioch, which the Franks had been besieging since October 1097, fell on June 3, Bohemond installing himself as ruler with the title of prince, Baldwin having similarly installed himself as Count of Edessa three months earlier. Several engagements against Seljuk forces attempting to raise the siege took place before Antioch's walls prior to its fall, followed by a spectacular victory over Kerbogha of Mosul only a few weeks after its capture.

1099 Resuming their march south under Adhémar, Raymond and Godfrey, the Franks finally encamped before Jerusalem on June 7, capturing the city from the Fatimids of Egypt in a concerted attack some five weeks later, the Fatimids themselves having recaptured Jerusalem from the Turks less than a year before. Godfrey de Bouillon was then elected *Advocatus Sancti Sepulchri*, Advocate of the Holy Sepulchre. He led the remaining Franks (an army of only 1,200-5,000 cavalry and 9-15,000 infantry by this time) to victory over a Fatimid counter-attack at Ascalon.

1101 Realising that the newly established crusader states were becoming weakened by the steady return of pilgrims to Europe, Pope Pascal II proclaimed a new Crusade, usually referred to now as 'The Crusade of 1101'. Its various contingents, however, individually met with disaster at Turkish hands during the overland march. The Franks under King Baldwin I (1100-1118) meanwhile came out the victors after a confused engagement against the Fatimids at First Ramla.

1102 Another Fatimid counter-attack towards Ramla by some 20,000 Arabs and Sudanese overwhelmed the tiny force which Baldwin led against them. Fortunately for the Franks the Egyptian attack petered out with only the victory of Second Ramla to its credit.

1104 Count Baldwin II of Edessa and Bohemond of Antioch were beaten at Harran by Turks from Mosul and Mardin. The Franks' losses were appalling, possibly amounting to 10-12,000 men, and Baldwin was amongst those captured. Bohemond returned to Europe towards the end of the year.

1105 Another Fatimid counter-attack from Egypt was defeated at Third Ramla.

1109 The coastal city of Tripoli, besieged by Raymond de Saint-Gilles from 1103 until his death in 1105 and by his cousin William-Jordan thereafter, was finally captured. Bertram, Raymond's son, became the first Count of Tripoli.

1113 Drawn in pursuit of a Turkish foraging party, King Baldwin was ambushed and defeated at Sennabra by Toghtekin of Damascus.

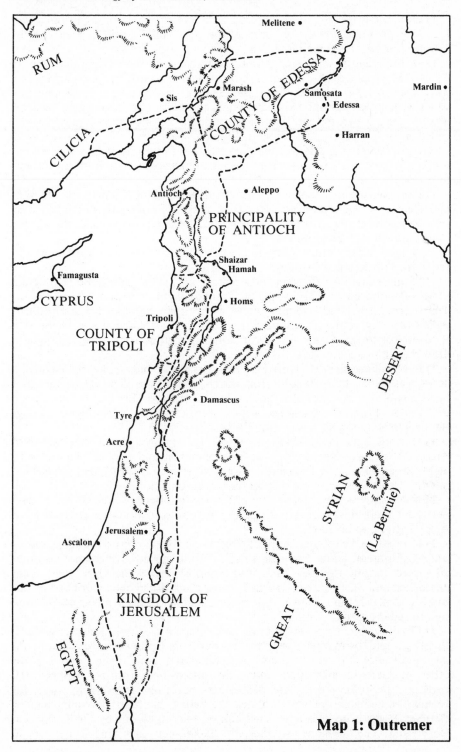

Map 1: Outremer

1115 Prince Roger of Antioch scored a notable victory over Sultan Bursuq of Hamadan in hilly, wooded country at Sarmin (Tell Danith), ambushing the Turkish army as it was making camp.

1119 Impatiently failing to await reinforcements from King Baldwin II (1118-1131) and Count Pons of Tripoli, Roger marched against an invading Turkish army led by Ilghazi of Mardin. He made the mistake of encamping in a valley, which was surrounded overnight by the Turks. In the morning his army was virtually wiped out and he himself killed in a battle that contemporaries called *Ager Sanguinus*, 'The Field of Blood'. There were possibly as few as 20 survivors. The king and Pons were then attacked in turn by Ilghazi at Hab, but the engagement was indecisive. Nevertheless, Ilghazi withdrew from Antiochene territory.

1123 Encouraged by Baldwin II's capture by Balak of Khanzit, the Fatimids launched their final large-scale offensive against the Franks. It was defeated by the Constable of the Kingdom at Ibelin, 6-7,000 Egyptians being killed in the rout. Baldwin was freed in 1124.

1124 Tyre, other than Ascalon the last coastal stronghold in Moslem hands, fell to the Franks and Venetians.

1125 Interrupted whilst besieging Zerdana, a Turkish force led by Il-Bursuqi of Mosul withdrew to Azaz, where the Franks caught up with it. Unusually, the Turks closed for hand-to-hand combat rather than standing off and utilising their firepower, and as a result they were heavily defeated. Later in the year Baldwin discomfitted the Fatimid garrison of Ascalon, using a feigned flight to draw them into an ambush.

1126 Marching against Damascus, Baldwin II was intercepted by Toghtekin at Marj es-Safar about 20 miles from the city and put to flight. However, after being chased for several miles the Franks managed to rally and in turn routed the Turks. Frankish casualties were nevertheless heavy enough to oblige Baldwin to abandon his advance on Damascus.

1132 King Fulk (1131-1143), operating in Antioch, heard that Sawar of Aleppo was mustering forces at nearby Qinnasrin and attacked his camp by night. Several Frankish detachments were wiped out in subsequent skirmishes, but the victory was complete enough for Sawar to withdraw.

1138 A combined Byzantino-Frankish force laid siege to Shaizar for 24 days but to no avail, having previously abandoned an equally unsuccessful siege of Aleppo after only six days.

1144 Imad ad-Din Zengi, ruler of Mosul and Syria, captured Edessa and its trans-Euphratean lands from the Franks. Although an Armenian conspiracy attempted to put the city back into Frankish hands in 1146, their plans miscarried and the revolt was crushed. Zengi himself had been murdered by one of his own slaves only a short while before, and it was his son Nur ed-Din who suppressed the revolt.

1147 The Second Crusade, proclaimed by Pope Eugenius as long ago as 1145, finally got underway when two armies set out from Europe for Outremer by the overland route. One was of French extraction and led by King Louis VII, the other of German extraction under the uncrowned Emperor Conrad III. Crossing the Bosporos in late September the latter, refusing to await the French, immediately set out to attack the Seljuk capital of Iconium, and on October 25 his army was ambushed and all but wiped out by the Turks near Dorylaeum. The Germans lost allegedly 30,000 men, including 90 per cent of their fighting strength, Conrad himself being badly wounded.

1148 The French crusaders fared much better, only suffering their first setback in January when they were ambushed while traversing Mount Cadmos, suffering heavy losses before nightfall put an end to hostilities. Both Louis and Conrad later met up at Acre and agreed with King Baldwin III (1143-1163) to launch an attack on Damascus, the expedition setting out in mid-July. However, dissent and treachery resulted in abandonment of the siege after only five days before Damascus' walls. Conrad quit Outremer in disgust soon after, although Louis only departed in the early summer of 1149.

1149 After relieving the fortress of Inab from a siege by Nur ed-Din of Aleppo, Prince Raymond of Antioch encamped in a hollow near Fons Muratus. The engagement that followed was virtually a re-enactment of Ager Sanguinus, Nur ed-Din's Turks surrounding the Frankish camp overnight and virtually wiping out Raymond's army in the morning. Raymond himself was killed by Nur's lieutenant, Asad ad-Din Shirkuh.

1150 The Franks abandoned the remainder of the County of Edessa, selling its major fortresses to the Byzantines, from whom the Moslems had captured them all by the middle of 1151.

1153 After a siege of nearly seven months Ascalon surrendered to the Franks.

1163 As early as 1160 Baldwin III had threatened to invade Egypt, but the Fatimid Caliph had bought him off with a promise of a 160,000-*dinar* annual tribute. This never having been paid, King Amalric I (1163-1174) made a sudden descent on Egypt in September 1163. The Fatimids, however, forced him to withdraw by breaking dykes on the Nile, which was in flood. Meanwhile Nur ed-Din had taken advantage of the king's absence to attack Tripoli, the weakest of the Frankish states, and laid siege to Krak des Chevaliers. Urgent appeals for aid brought a combined Byzantino-Frankish force to the castle's relief and Nur ed-Din's army fled in disorder after a short battle.

1164 Shawar, deposed vizier to the Fatimid Caliph, asked for and received aid from Nur ed-Din in order to regain his former position and oust his rival, Dhirgham. The force that Nur sent was commanded by his lieutenant Shirkuh and the latter's nephew, Saladin. Dhirgham, meanwhile, appealed to King Amalric for help, but Shawar and Shirkuh moved too fast for him to intercept them and by May Dhirgham was dead and Shawar reinstated as vizier. Shawar now repudiated the bargain he had made with Nur ed-Din (by which an annual tribute had been promised) and ordered Shirkuh out of the country, and when the latter refused to go Shawar in turn asked King Amalric for his help. Shawar and Amalric then laid siege to Shirkuh in Bilbeis until a truce was agreed by which Amalric and Shirkuh would both leave Egypt, Amalric hurrying back to Syria where Nur ed-Din had meanwhile inflicted a defeat on another Byzantino-Frankish force at Artah, capturing its leaders.

1167 The year of Amalric's third Egyptian expedition, the rivals again being Shirkuh and Saladin on the one hand and Shawar and Amalric on the other, Frankish assistance this time being in exchange for 400,000 *bezants*. The Franks and Fatimids succeeded in bypassing Shirkuh's forces and gaining the West Bank, catching up with Shirkuh at al-Babein ('The Two Gates') on the edge of the desert as he withdrew. Both sides hesitated in joining battle and the result was indecisive, but it was the allies who quit the field in the ensuing engagement, even though Shirkuh's own losses were heavy. Saladin, with about 1,000 men, was then besieged in Alexandria by Shawar and Amalric, Shirkuh himself slipping past the blockade with the bulk of the Syrian army. A similar treaty to that of 1164 was signed soon after and Franks and Syrians alike withdrew from Egypt in August.

1168 Following rumours that Shawar's son was negotiating with Shirkuh, Amalric himself now invaded Egypt, Shirkuh appearing on the scene soon afterwards, this time as Egypt's *ally*. Facing stiff Fatimid resistance and with Shirkuh in his rear, Amalric had no option but to abandon his invasion.

1169 With the Caliph's tacit agreement Shawar was executed, Shirkuh being proclaimed vizier and king in his place. Shirkuh's own death soon after was followed in October by yet another Frankish invasion of Egypt, where Saladin was now master, this time with the support of a large Byzantine fleet. The allies laid siege to Damietta, but discord and a failure to completely blockade the city led to the siege being raised early in December, the Byzantine fleet being smashed by a great storm as it returned to Constantinople.

1176 A large Byzantine army under Emperor Manuel I suffered a decisive defeat at the hands of the Rumi Seljuks at Myriokephalon, en route for Iconium. Byzantine military strength never fully recovered from this disaster.

1177 After having blockaded King Baldwin IV (1174-1185) in Ascalon, Saladin was marching northwards towards Jerusalem when, summoning the Templars of Gaza to his aid, Baldwin broke out of Ascalon and surprised the numerically superior Egyptian army as it negotiated a ravine near Montgisard. A complete Frankish victory ensued.

1179 Saladin inflicted a severe defeat on the Franks at Marj Ayyun on June 10, resulting largely from the impetuosity of the Templars, who outdistanced the rest of the army and failed to await the main body before attacking. Instead of following up his victory by an invasion of Palestine, Saladin attacked and razed the newly-built Templar fortress of Le Chastellet at Jacob's Ford.

1182 Reynald de Châtillon, the lord of Oultrejourdain, launched five galleys in the Gulf of Akaba in order to attack sea-going pilgrim caravans to Mecca. Moslem reaction was swift and merciless, the admiral of Egypt destroying the entire flotilla in February 1183, all prisoners being ceremoniously executed in Mecca. Reynald himself, already the perpetrator of several similar outrages, was among the few who escaped.

1183 In September Saladin invaded Palestine, but a stalemate situation in the Jezreel valley, where the Franks failed to let Saladin goad them into battle, led to his early withdrawal in October.

1187 This was Outremer's fateful year. It began when a foolhardy raid on a Moslem pilgrim caravan during a period of truce by Reynald de Châtillon sparked off another invasion by Saladin. On May 1 he despatched a reconnaissance in force (allegedly 6,000 or 7,000 men) which in the course of its travels was attacked at Cresson by a tiny Frankish force of 140 knights and 300-400 infantry, mainly Templars under their fanatic Grand Master Gerard de Ridefort, which it all but wiped out. The magnitude of this seemingly minor affray brought home to Raymond III of Tripoli, whose wife's Galilean lands the Turks had been crossing (with his permission), the very real dangers of Saladin's invasion. He therefore settled his differences with King Guy de Lusignan (1186-1192), an ineffectual and unpopular king with whom he had been at loggerheads, and joined up with the army that the latter was mustering at Acre.

On July 2 Saladin's army appeared before Raymond's fortress of Tiberias, the Frankish army having meanwhile advanced to Saphoria. Raymond advised that the Franks should remain where they were, Saphoria being amply provided with water and pasturage, but his advice was over-ruled by Gerard de Ridefort, who probably held Raymond responsible for his defeat at Cresson. On July 3 the army therefore set out towards Tiberias, its advance across the waterless Plain of Toran being dogged so persistently by Turkish skirmishers that it had to encamp again after covering barely five miles. Raymond tried to persuade the king to advance just a little further to a nearby spring but his advice went unheeded. Thirsty, demoralised and surrounded, the Frankish army was destroyed the next morning on the twin hills known as the Horns of Hattin, one source claiming that 30,000 were killed and a further 30,000 captured; certainly 1,000 knights were killed or taken captive while 200-260 Templars and Hospitallers were executed, as was Reynald de Châtillon. Other leaders taken captive included King Guy and Gerard de Ridefort. Leaderless, Outremer subsequently went down like a house of cards, Jerusalem itself being surrendered to Saladin on October 2.

1188 By the end of this year all that remained to the Franks were the cities of Antioch, Tripoli, Tyre (which was saved by the timely arrival of Conrad of Montferrat as it was about to surrender) and Tortosa, and several scattered fortresses including al-Marqab, Safita, Krak des Chevaliers, Beaufort, Belvoir and Krak de Montréal.

1189 On August 27 King Guy, released by Saladin in the spring of 1188, commenced the epic siege of Acre with a Pisan fleet and an army of 9,000 men, including 700 knights. Saladin arrived on the scene three days later, setting up his camp close to that of the Franks in order to cramp their operations and interfere with their attempts to establish a thorough blockade. On October 4 the 'Great Battle' of Acre took place, in which the Franks were heavily defeated by Saladin. Their investment of the city nevertheless continued unabated.

1190 On June 10 the Holy Roman Emperor Frederick I *Barbarossa*, leading his own army of crusaders through Cilicia, drowned while fording a river. The German crusade thereafter petered out, most of the army disbanding on reaching Antioch, but a few hundred men under Frederick of Swabia did reach Acre. The other leaders of the Third Crusade, King Richard I *Coeur de Lion* of England and King Philip II *Augustus* of France, had meanwhile only recently set out.

1191 Philip II arrived at Acre on April 20, Richard being delayed somewhat longer by his conquest of Cyprus from a Byzantine anti-Emperor between May 6 and June 5. Acre itself finally surrendered on July 12 after a series of determined assaults by the combined Frankish armies, King Philip returning to Europe only a few weeks later on July 31, leaving Richard in sole command of the Crusade. The latter achieved his signal victory over Saladin at Arsuf some five weeks later, the Moslems allegedly losing 7,000 dead compared to Richard's 700.

1192 In early January Richard decided to abandon his march on Jerusalem, realising that even if they were capable of recapturing it, the Franks of Outremer lacked the manpower to defend it after his departure. Although there were many skirmishes and *mêlées* thereafter, the only other major engagements of the Third Crusade were the capture of a great caravan on June 23 and Saladin's siege of Jaffa from July 26 to August 1, culminating in Richard's other classic victory at Jaffa on August 5. King Richard finally departed for home on October 9, his workmanlike Crusade having resurrected Outremer from the ashes of defeat. His nephew Henry de Champagne was now the uncrowned King of Jerusalem (1192-1197), Guy having been compensated with Cyprus, of which he became the first Frankish king. Conrad of Montferrat, who had been the native barons' first choice to be king in Guy's place, had been murdered by Assassins in April, an incident in which Richard himself, who supported Guy, was implicated.

1197 A German crusade planned by Emperor Henry VI collapsed following his unexpected death. German crusaders already in Outremer proclaimed Guy de Lusignan's brother Amalric II, King of Cyprus (1194-1205), as King of Jerusalem (1197-1205).

1203-1204 The Venetians and Franks of the infamous Fourth Crusade commenced their siege of Constantinople on July 6 1203, finally culminating—after a complex sequence of political manoeuvring both inside and outside the city—in its fall and sack on April 13 1204. The once-great Byzantine Empire was parcelled out amongst the crusaders that October.

1217-1221 This four-year fiasco, the Fifth Crusade, was aimed at conquering Egypt. However, although Damietta was captured on November 5 1219 it had to be surrendered back to the Moslems on September 8 1221 as part of a peace treaty following the defeat and capture of the crusading army at Bahr Ashmun. The entire Crusade had therefore achieved nothing but the loss of thousands of lives as a result of stupidity and mismanagement, for which the infamous Cardinal Pelagius was largely responsible.

1226-1229 The excommunicated Emperor Frederick II, King of Jerusalem 1225-1228, was the leader of this, the Sixth Crusade. He spent much of his time in argument with the barons of Outremer, many of whom did not recognise his claim to the throne, and certainly his lack of tact in dealing with them left much to be desired. However, he was successful in concluding a highly favourable treaty with Sultan al-Kamil in February 1229 by which Jerusalem itself was regained by the Franks.

1230 After Frederick's departure a civil war (often called the Lombard War) had broken out between his Imperialist administration, led by the Imperial Legate Richard Filangieri, and the powerful Ibelin family supported by King Henry I of Cyprus. The opposing factions for most of the war were—*Imperialists:* German troops under Filangieri, the Teutonic Knights, several barons of Outremer, and the Pisans; *Ibelins:* most of the kingdom's and Cyprus' barons including King Henry himself, the Commune of Acre, and the Genoese, later joined by the Templars, Hospitallers and Venetians.

1232 The main engagement of the civil war to take place on the mainland was at Casal Imbert, where the Ibelins were defeated. Filangieri invaded Cyprus six weeks later but this time victory went to the Ibelins, who decisively beat the Imperialists at Agridi on June 15. The surrender of Kyrenia in early April 1233 ended the Imperialist threat to Cyprus, although the civil war continued virtually unabated on the mainland for ten more years.

1237 An attempt by the Templars of Antioch under William of Montferrat, their preceptor, to recapture the fortress of Darbsaq ended in defeat when the Franks were surprised by a relief force from Aleppo.

1239 King Tibald of Navarre's Crusade arrived at Acre on September 1. A detachment which set out to attack an Egyptian force near Gaza was cut to pieces in a battle amongst the sand dunes on November 13, losing 1,000-1,800 dead and 250-500 captured.

1240 Before his departure in September, Tibald concluded favourable treaties with the rival Moslem rulers of both Damascus and Egypt which ensured the return of a considerable amount of territory to the Franks, including Jerusalem itself which had been retaken by the Moslems late in 1239. Richard of Cornwall with a force of English crusaders arrived in Outremer on October 8, confirming the treaty with Egypt prior to his own departure in May 1241.

1243 The surrender of Tyre to the Ibelin faction by its Imperialist governor, Filangieri's brother Lothair, finally ended the Lombard War.

1244 On August 23 Jerusalem was overrun and sacked by the Khwarizmians, a Turkish people driven out of Persia and then Rum by the Mongols. This disaster was followed two months later by the defeat of an allied Frankish-Syrian army at La Forbie near Gaza. The Frankish contingent, the largest army that the kingdom had mustered since 1187, was annihilated by the Egyptians and Khwarizmians, losing some 5,000 dead and 800 captured. Their Syrian allies also suffered heavily. A considerable amount of territory was lost as a result of this defeat.

1248 King Louis IX of France sailed to Cyprus and wintered there, mustering forces for the Seventh Crusade.

1249 Louis landed in Egypt in the teeth of the enemy on June 5, defending his bridgehead against fierce Moslem attacks. The crusaders captured the city of Damietta the very next day after it had been abandoned by its population. A Moslem army then began to assemble at El Mansurah (meaning 'Victorious', the site of Sultan al-Kamil's victory over the ill-starred Fifth Crusade), for which Louis finally set out on November 20 en route for Cairo. After a fierce engagement at Fariskur on December 7 the Frankish army encamped on the banks of the Bahr as-Saghir, opposite El Mansurah, on December 21.

1250 Abandoning an attempt at constructing a causeway across the river, the Franks finally crossed the Bahr as-Saghir on February 8 by a little-known ford which the Moslems had left undefended. The cavalry vanguard, under Louis' brother Count Robert d'Artois, disobeyed orders and attacked the enemy camp outside El Mansurah, catching it completely by surprise. Many Moslems were cut down including their commander, Fakhr ad-Din, but Robert then unwisely pursued the fugitives into the town itself where the mamluk troops, rallied by the future sultan Baibars, surrounded and slaughtered them in the narrow streets. Warned of this disaster in time Louis managed to draw up the main body and repulse the Egyptian attacks from El Mansurah, his engineers meanwhile completing their bridge across the river so that the Frankish bowmen could cross over. The engagement finally ended in a Pyrrhic Frankish victory. Louis had lost some 1,000-1,500 knights including 285 Templars, and his army was now too weak to continue its advance.

After being besieged in their disease-ridden camp for eight weeks the Franks were obliged to withdraw, camp being struck on April 5. The Egyptians pursued them and attacked in full force so that the next day the entire army capitulated. Many thousands of Frankish prisoners were executed, although Louis finally managed to negotiate his own release and that of some 12,000 other survivors by the surrender of Damietta and the payment of a huge ransom of 800,000 bezants.

1254 After spending a further four years in Syria, Louis finally departed for France on April 24, the disaster of El Mansurah having resulted in a loss of manpower that could never quite be recovered.

1256 The First Genoese War, often called the War of Saint Sabas, started as a squabble between the Venetians and Genoese of Acre over ownership of a local monastery. Before long it had escalated into a full-blooded civil war which was to drag on in one form or another for 32 years more, the main theatre of conflict being transferred to the Byzantine Empire after 1261. Venice and Genoa concluded a peace treaty of sorts in 1270, although Venice's Pisan allies only finally capitulated in 1288.

1260 Mongol invasions resulted in the sack of both Aleppo and Damascus, but the Mamluks (whose dynasty had come to power in Egypt in 1250) restored the balance with a decisive victory at Ain Jalut. Soon after this engagement Baibars, the Moslem commander at both La Forbie and El Mansurah (after Fakhr ad-Din's death), murdered Sultan Qalaun and himself seized the throne to become, after Saladin, the greatest Moslem leader of the Crusade era.

1261 The Byzantines succeeded in recovering Constantinople from the Franks, bringing to an end the short-lived Latin Empire of Romania.

1266 A *chevauchée* towards Tiberias under King Hugh III of Cyprus, *bailli* of Jerusalem, ended in disaster when its vanguard of Hospitallers and Teutonic Knights was ambushed at Caroublier by the Moslem garrison of Safed.

1268 After just five days of fighting the city of Antioch fell to Baibars. The Principality of Antioch, after Edessa the first Frankish state to be founded in Outremer, had lasted 171 years.

1269 The crowns of Cyprus and Jerusalem were united under King Hugh III of Cyprus (1267-1284). The same year a crusading fleet led by King James I of Aragon was smashed by a storm, only a small force under his two bastard sons reaching Acre at the end of December. The enterprise achieved nothing.

1270 After nearly three years' preparation King Louis IX launched his second expedition against the Moslems, the Eighth Crusade. This one, however, was diverted against Tunisia by the king's scheming brother Charles of Anjou who had dreams of establishing his own Mediterranean empire. Arriving off Carthage on July 18, the formidable Frankish army was almost immediately beset by disease, of which Louis himself died on August 25. Charles of Anjou finally withdrew in November.

1271 The only leader of the Eighth Crusade to actually sail on for Outremer was the English prince Edward (later King Edward I), who arrived at Acre on May 9 and remained in Palestine until September 1272. His force was insignificant, however, comprising only about 1,200 men in all although it included 300 knights, and he was unable to achieve anything more than a treaty with Baibars.

1277 The Mamluks under Baibars achieved a signal victory over the Ilkhanid Mongols at Albistan. Some sources say that it was from wounds received in this battle that Baibars died on July 1.

1281 A Mongol invasion of Syria was defeated at Homs, the Mongol army on this occasion including Knights Hospitaller from the garrison of al-Marqab, plus Cilician Armenians.

1289 On April 26 the city of Tripoli fell to Sultan Qalaun, who razed it to the ground lest the Franks should attempt to recapture it with their superior naval power.

1291 Encouraged by riots within the city, a Mamluk army under Sultan al-Ashraf, allegedly comprising 100-160,000 infantry and 60,000 cavalry, commenced the siege of Acre on April 5. The Frankish garrison, under the Constable Amalric's overall command, consisted of just 700-900 knights and

14-18,000 foot-soldiers, made up of the Military Orders, Syrian and Cypriot Franks, the French Regiment under Jean de Grailly, Pisans, Venetians, English mercenaries under Otto de Grandison and the militia of the Commune of Acre. Reinforcements of 200 knights and 500 more infantry arrived from Cyprus under Amalric's brother King Henry II (1285-1324) on May 4.

Undermined and breached by the Moslems' siege-engines, the city's outer wall fell on May 15, to be followed by the inner wall just three days later. A bitter street fight ensued, but the penetration of the Mamluks to the inner city marked the end of organised resistance. Most of the defenders and a large part of the population were massacred, although the surviving Templars and some other refugees held out in their fortress by the sea for ten days more until May 28.

The demoralised Franks had meanwhile abandoned Tyre the day after Acre's fall. Château de Mer at Sidon held out only until July 14. Haifa surrendered on July 30 and Beirut on July 31, while Château Pèlerin and Tortosa were abandoned by their Templar garrisons on August 3 and 14 respectively. Sultan al-Ashraf then systematically destroyed every port and castle along the Syrian coast so that the Franks might never again establish a foothold there. Thus within just a few short months of Acre's fall the pathetic remnants of Outremer had been obliterated.

Chapter 2

The nature of the land

Anyone who had set out on the dusty and dangerous road to the Holy Land
expecting in his innocence to find some sort of Nirvana, a land of milk and
honey such as the Bible promised, must have been sorely disappointed.
Admittedly, Syria and Palestine were less arid in mediaeval times than they are
today, and their cultivated regions were rich with orchards and gardens; but the
extremes of the climate were nevertheless punishing, there were earthquakes and
plagues of locusts, disease was widespread, and the enemy was seldom more
than a single day's ride away. All in all it would seem that many pilgrims who
settled in the newly established Frankish states of Outremer would have been
better off at home. But what was this alien land in which they chose to stay
really like? Hollywood and historical fiction have between them concocted a
rather romantic picture of rolling sand-dunes, the monotony of which is
interrupted only by the occasional cluster of tall date palms, with on the horizon
an isolated castle shimmering in the haze of summer's sweltering heat. Well,
sorry if it disappoints anyone, but in reality it was nothing like that. Oh yes,
there *were* deserts, and date palms, and even shimmering desert fortresses, but
there was much more besides.

Syria had originally derived its name from the lands around the ancient city of
Tyre (*Sur* in Arabic), although the Arabs themselves had called the land Ash
Sham, meaning 'Left' (or 'North') in ancient Arabic, referring to its position in
relation to the rising sun. The 9th-13th century Arab geographers, from whom
such information is derived, in fact provide us with virtually all that we know
about the mediaeval Levant. They invariably divide Syria up into four quite
distinct longitudinal zones (see map on page 22), comprising from west to east
(1) the Mediterranean coastal plains, extending to a maximum width of about 15
miles in the south, a mixture of sandy tracts and cultivated land together with
some woodlands; (2) the heavily-forested mountainous highlands, comprised of
the Taurus, Ammanus, Ansariyya, Lebanon and Galilean ranges, rising up
gradually on the west to some 5,000 feet in Northern Syria, 9,800 feet in
Lebanon and nearly 4,000 feet in Palestine, with many natural springs, villages
and cultivated areas, the eastern slopes falling away in a steep descent to the
third zone; (3) a relatively heavily populated region comprising a sort of long,
deep natural trench made up of the Orontes, Leontes (Litani) and Jordan
valleys and continued in the south by the Wadi el-Arabah, forming a natural
frontier beyond which the Franks penetrated only in the south and extreme
north; and (4) the highlands of Moab, the Jaulan and the Anti-Lebanon range,

a bleak plateau which nevertheless boasted forests and many fertile, well-watered spots, especially in the more northerly regions round Damascus, Homs, Hamah and Aleppo.

To these four regions should be added a fifth one, known to the Franks as *La Berruie* ('The Waste'). This was the Great Syrian Desert, a broad plateau 2-3,000 feet above sea level, part gravel-strewn, part sandy, and part hard-caked with whitish, glittering dried mud, covered with a thin layer of red-tinged, grey-green plants in most areas all the year round. Mediaeval geographers divided it into three portions called Arabia Petrarea, Arabia Deserta and Syria Deserta. Desert also bordered Syria to the south where the gently undulating and inhospitable Negev, *La Grande Berruie* or 'Great Waste', 'a country full of sand', separated her from Egypt. An Arab describing this region wrote that 'everywhere are sand-tracts, salt marshes and red sandstone hills, while occasionally palm-trees and springs of water may be met with.'

In fact these two desert regions were the real frontier that the Franks should have aimed at securing. If they could have pushed the Moslems back in the south and east until the desert had been reached then all communication between Egypt and Mesopotamia would have been cut. However, it was not to be, and the Franks' failure to achieve this requirement was a major factor in their inability to establish a more permanent occupation. In the south, in the Kingdom of Jerusalem, a narrow corridor from the Dead Sea down to the Gulf of Akaba was briefly established in Oultrejourdain between 1117 and 1182, but it stood no real chance of seriously threatening east-west Moslem communications. In the east the Franks had to be satisfied with a sort of 'no-man's land' in the Hauran district of Southern Syria, the revenue of which was spasmodically shared with Damascus during the 12th century. The Frankish domain was instead a long and on the whole extremely narrow strip of land, some 500 miles from the Euphrates in the north to the Negev in the south but in width seldom more than 50 miles and on the whole less except in the extreme north. Defence in depth was therefore impossible, and the resultant overlong frontier was to prove not only extremely vulnerable but basically indefensible.

Much of the land was uncultivated, although not wholly barren, and large tracts were designated *gastinae* or waste by the Franks, these being areas formerly inhabited or cultivated but now lying desolate, evidence of the fact that the Crusade period was one of the Levant's less prosperous times. This was largely a result of the abandonment of terrace agriculture and the subsequent careless cultivation of the soil since the Arab Conquest, resulting in serious soil erosion (2-4,000 *million* cubic metres from the Judaean hills alone since Roman times) and the abandonment of previously fertile districts.

In Galilee there are today as many as three abandoned villages to every two square kilometres, and the recurrence of the word *khirbet* or ruin, usually abbreviated to *kh*, on maps relating to the Crusade era such as that of C.N. Johns, indicates that the situation was probably little different elsewhere. An observer writing in 1241 reported that of 800 villages in the Hauran as many as 200 had been abandoned! Constant military activity was a contributory factor in the depopulation of the countryside, raiding parties from both sides indulging in the smashing of dams and water-wheels, the burning of crops, destruction of orchards and mills, and the rustling of cattle, so that the peasants, destitute and homeless, had no choice but to evacuate the district. All in all it is no surprise,

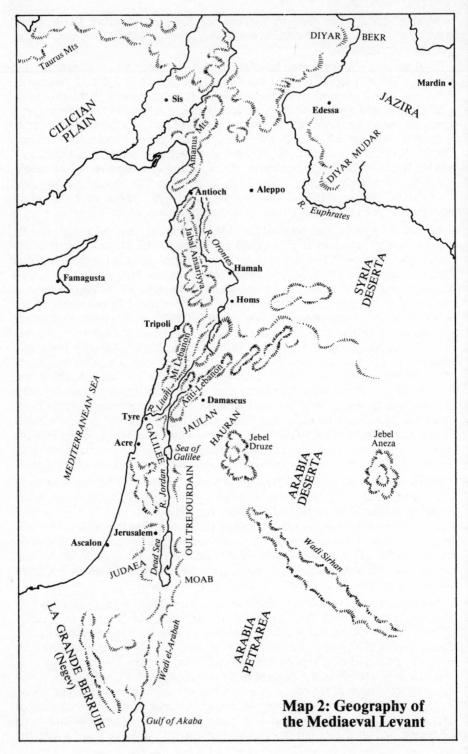

**Map 2: Geography of
the Mediaeval Levant**

then, that we frequently read of field armies encamping on the sites of derelict or ruined villages.

Some areas were completely wild and can best be described as scrubland, these including the forested regions, which were really open woodland with scattered trees and little undergrowth. Much of this Crusade-period woodland has now disappeared, but there were once fairly large forests in Judaea and the Jaulan in particular—for example the Bible records large forests in Gilead, Bashan and Lebanon, while in the 10th century a pine forest at Beirut stretched inland for some 12 miles in all directions. The cultivated areas, on the other hand, yielded a vast array of different crops, chief of which were olives, grapes and wheat, and most of the larger towns were surrounded by their own irrigated orchards and vineyards in which they cultivated olives and grapes plus as many other crops and fruits as local conditions permitted. The orchards of Tyre were reputedly so extensive that they reached to Homs, and further gardens yielding two crops of grapes a year lined the road from there all the way to Damascus. Not surprisingly, on more than one occasion we find such gardens providing sustenance for besieging armies.

The key to this agricultural bonanza, of course, was water, of which para-doxically Syria was usually noticeably short, despite having an average rainfall comparable to that of sun-soaked England (about 60 cm—nearly 24 inches), and sunshine which conversely was in abundant supply. The water problem resulted basically from the fact that in Syria the wet and dry seasons are very distinct. The wet season commences with spasmodic rainfall from the end of October when heavy showers called the 'early' or 'former rains' loosen the dry, cracked soil and open the agricultural year, these falling for a day or several days at a time and steadily increasing from November through to February, then abating to close with the 'latter rains' of March and early April. After May, when showers are rare but not entirely unknown, there is no rain—nor often even any clouds—until late October again comes round.

Most of this heavy rainfall quickly drains away from the surface through porous limestone strata to reappear in the form of countless springs and streams three to 20 feet wide and one to three feet deep at the foot of each range of hills, some of which continue to flow even through the arid dry season. The summer drought was usually overcome by artificial irrigation utilising such springs to water the orchards and ploughed fields, normally with the aid of huge water-wheels such as can still be found being used in the Near East today, windmills also being used in this capacity by the Franks. Some areas, however, such as most of Palestine (including Jerusalem, Nablus, Jaffa, Jericho, Gaza, Caesarea and Ibelin) did not require irrigation, receiving sufficient moisture in summertime from the morning dew, which was often very excessive and not uncommonly accompanied by a hazy mist.

The mean summer temperatures were probably much the same as those of modern Israel—77°F (25°C) in July and August (the hottest months, maximum daily average being 90°F, 104°F being possible at midday), with May 65°F, June 74°F, September 75°F and October 68°F, winter temperatures dropping to November 60°F, December 52°F, January 49°F, February 46°F (the coldest month, 23°F being recorded in the early morning), March 54°F and April 61°F. However, these can all fluctuate drastically under the influence of sirocco winds (called *Khamsin* in the Levant) blowing in from the desert regions to the east, south and south-east, these being hot winds which come with a cloud of fine sand 'veiling the sun, scorching vegetation, and bringing langour and fever to men'. Such winds, blowing chiefly during a 50-day period in the spring and for a day or more at a time, can raise the temperature to an amazing 95°F even in April or May, and they are quite capable of increasing a dawn temperature of 48°F to 92°F by early afternoon, shifts of one degree a minute being possible. In fact in open, sandy desert regions the sirocco and its attendant stifling clouds of sand was fully capable of overwhelming an entire caravan. By contrast it is worth noting that hail and even snow falls on the hills during most Syrian winters, as much as two feet of snow falling on the central mountain range. The fortress of Le Moinestre, for instance, 6,000 feet above sea level, is under snow for several months of the year. Hail is often intermingled with thunderstorms, particularly in the spring.

When the crusaders arrived at the end of the 11th century this land of extremes was inhabited by a mixture of peoples whose individuality resulted from their various religious convictions rather than their ethnic differences. They can basically be divided into seven distinct groups, comprising Maronites, Syrian Christians, Jews, Druzes, Assassins, Syrians and Bedouin, with the Syrian Christian elements increasing the further north one went. Considering these in turn, the Maronites of Lebanon were the most privileged group, largely because not only were they Christians and excellent soldiers but—unlike the other Eastern Christians—after 1182 they acknowledged the See of Rome; in fact the extent to which the Maronites adopted Frankish customs is quite apparent in many of their surnames, such as Salibi (Crusader), Faranjiyah (Frankish), Duryan (d'Orient) and Bardawil (Baldwin). The other Syrian Christians on the other hand—the Copts, Jacobites, Nestorians and Armenians—were not so well-respected, not least because they wore beards, largely spoke Arabic and dressed like Moslems (although this is equally true of the Maronites), but even more so because they were either Greek Orthodox or heretical in their beliefs. The Franks had also made the mistake, in the early phase of their conquests, of not distinguishing between Moslem and native Christian when it came to rape, murder and pillage, thereby ruining whatever chance they might have ever had of achieving a meaningful alliance with the Syrian Christians, who remained on the whole suspicious and distrustful of their Frankish overlords throughout Outremer's existence.

The largest individual native Christian element were the Cilician Armenians, who the Franks referred to as 'Hermins', a dour and gloomy nation of warriors with whom Frankish relations were alternately good, bad or indifferent. The Jews were a different case again; unlike the Syrian Christians, whom the Moslems had regarded as untrustworthy, the Jewish communities actually bore arms against the crusaders in defence of the towns in which they lived—notably at Jerusalem and Haifa—and as a result they were mercilessly massacred by them with no less gusto than were the Moslems. After the establishment of the Frankish states, however, no further anti-Semitic pogroms were launched and sizeable Jewish quarters arose in Ascalon, Tyre, Acre, Beirut, Sidon, Caesarea and other Galilean towns. Nevertheless, the Franks' bigotry and loathing of the Jews remained basically undiminished.

Moving on to the Moslem groups, the first thing to note is that there was a schism here comparable to that which existed between the Roman Catholic and Greek Orthodox Christian churches. Its origins are explained at the beginning of Chapter 6, but it basically resulted from a row over the election of

Mohammed's successor way back in 632, the two opposing factions being the *Sunni* and *Shia*. In the Crusade era the Abbasid Caliphs and the Turkish *amirs* of Syria were Sunnites and the Fatimids of Egypt were Shiites, the Druzes of Mount Hermon, neighbours to and bitter enemies of the Maronites of Lebanon, being adherents—after a fashion—of the latter belief. The Assassins too, who are the subject of Chapter 6, were Shiites, but of even more extreme convictions. The overwhelming majority of Syrian Moslems were Sunnites in the 10th century, although in Galilee and Transjordan the Shiites prevailed, as they did in the maritime cities at the time of the crusaders' arrival; as recently as 1098, mere months before the Franks appeared before the walls of Jerusalem, the Shiite Fatimids had successfully wrested the Holy City from its Sunni Turkish garrison.

Finally there were the Bedouin, the desert-dwelling nomads of Judaea, Sinai, the Negev, Arabia and the Great Syrian Desert, whose wandering took them regularly to and fro across the frontiers of the Frankish states. Although they were Moslems, some Bedouin, notably the Banu Darma and Banu Ruzaiq of the Negev, actually co-operated with the Franks, but on the whole their natural instinct for banditry prevailed, to the misfortune of Christian and Moslem alike. There were in addition a few Turcoman nomads in the Banyas area but their numbers remained small until the Mamluks introduced them throughout ex-Frankish Syria on a larger scale in the 13th century. Beyond the confines of the Frankish states, of course, they were always abundant.

In all there were probably about 140,000 Franks living in the Kingdom of Jerusalem at the time of Hattin (1187), together with the same number in the northern states of Tripoli and Antioch, ie, about a quarter of a million in total. The native Moslems, Jews and Christians, on the other hand, outnumbered them by about five to one, of whom some 75-80 per cent were probably Moslems. When one considers these somewhat unfavourable odds it comes as no surprise to find that the Franks sought safety in numbers by concentrating mainly in the urban centres of the coastal plain, even the nobility spending more time in their town-houses than in the castles of their *seigniories* (which were nevertheless also centres of Frankish settlement). This meant that the surrounding countryside remained almost overwhelmingly Moslem, and it has been calculated that of the 1,200 centres of population known to have existed in the Kingdom of Jerusalem itself (where there were probably about 2,000 in all) only about 80 or at the very most 100 were actually Frankish, and of these only between six and ten are known to have been rural settlements.

The villages in which the peasants of all denominations lived were referred to as either *villes* or, more commonly, *casalia* or *casiaux*. Each consisted of a cluster of one-storey, flat-roofed houses built on a hill-top or high ground, the houses being built of stone or of bricks made from straw and dry mud. Both forms of construction were considerably cheaper than timber, which was in short supply in Syria where trees were basically of insufficient size for most building requirements. The populations of such villages—which were on the whole either entirely Frankish, entirely Syrian Christian, entirely Jewish or entirely Moslem—varied from three to 200 or more family units, each of some three or four members including children. The average was about 20 families, each of which possessed one to 2½ *carrucae* of land (most commonly 1½ or two) in the immediate vicinity of the *casal*, the *carruca* being basically the amount of land required to support a single family. Officially it was some 86½ acres (35 hectares), most casals being estimated in such 'official' carrucae for taxation purposes, although in reality its size varied from place to place according to the agricultural potential of the soil.

Each casal had its own village headman or sometimes more than one; this was the *rais*, who was variously responsible for tax collection, maintenance of law and order, leadership of the local militia, and so on. Sometimes he held authority over several villages other than his own, though the latter position was more usually held by an official called a *dragoman*, a Frankish corruption of an Arabic term which basically meant 'interpreter'. He tended to act as an intermediary between rais and overlord and could administer large areas, this important office consequently becoming largely feudalised by the mid-12th century when it was usually held by a sergeant. The Military Orders had officers performing similar functions whom they called *casaliers*.

Although some sold for as much as 12-24,000 bezants (bezants being the standard form of currency—see Chapter 3), and some for as little as 600 bezants, the average casal was worth about 3-5,000, the annual revenue of such a village to its absentee overlord being about 500 bezants. This usually took the form of a tax called *terracitum* or *terrage*, made up of a proportion of the casal's produce, varying between a quarter and a half for the lucrative olive groves and vineyards and between a quarter and a third for arable lands. Additional payments also had to be made on occasion, such as a forced gift called variously *presentatica*, *nutrimenta* or *monet* payable thrice yearly, various manorial requisitions, such as on the occasion of great festivals, and a form of capitation or poll-tax on non-Christians of about 1¼ bezants per annum; the Moslems, incidentally, imposed a similar poll tax on Christians. The *presentatica* varied from one place to the next, but as an example in Tyre it involved a hen, 12 eggs, three pounds (1.36 kg) of cheese and 12 gold bezants per carruca.

Cumulatively such payments may seem extremely heavy, but the peasantry of the crusader states were nevertheless considerably better off than their counterparts in the neighbouring Moslem states, who paid even heavier taxes. Their lot was also better than that of European contemporaries in that there was only a minimum *corvée*, a system which in Europe involved giving up to three days unpaid labour ('boon-work') per week in peak seasons on the local lord's *demesne*, his own estate. Its virtual absence was for the very simple reason that in mainland Outremer most lords did not have such estates because, as we have already seen, they tended to live in the towns rather than the countryside, exploiting the casals of their seigniories instead in the role of absentee landlords. The one exception was Cyprus, where land usually was held in *demesne*, this generally comprising about one seventh of each casal's arable land. The only corvée that was exacted in the Kingdom of Jerusalem was for the repair of roads and public buildings, in which cases it involved one day a year per carruca.

In the Kingdom of Jerusalem only about 10-20,000 Franks actually lived in isolated centres such as castles, small townlets or villages, the majority of the Frankish population—120,000 or more—residing in the larger urban centres, the towns and cities, which continued in their pre-Crusade role as centres of administration and government. There were 30,000 Franks in Jerusalem, for example, and 10,000 in Ascalon, and later 30,000 each in Tyre and Acre. The proportion of town-dwellers was probably much the same in the County of Tripoli and the Principality of Antioch, but in Edessa it seems fairly certain that virtually the entire Frankish population (which was exceptionally small anyway and vastly outnumbered by Armenians and Syrian Christians) lived in the towns. Some towns also had small Jewish and Moslem communities, although neither were permitted in Jerusalem itself. Syrian Christians, on the other hand, could be found resident in most urban communities as well as in the garrisons of most fortresses.

Many towns were themselves walled against attack and had fortified citadels, while conversely small townlets grew around a number of purely military castles, the population taking refuge behind its walls in times of trouble. Even some of the very smallest settlements had simple towers erected, sometimes with curtain walls, in which the local peasants could shelter during raids, and they could be found too at agricultural storage depots, in mining centres and near abbeys and monasteries. Their castles and fortifications of all shapes and sizes, however, are representative not of how the Franks found the land in which they chose to stay, but of how they left it. Even today they remain the most lasting monument of Frankish occupation.

Chapter 3

Raising, financing and organising armies: the Christians

'Few expressions', wrote Sir Steven Runciman*, 'have done greater disservice to history than "the feudal system".' It is easy enough to say that it was through the feudal system that the Franks of Outremer raised and maintained their armies, but having once said that, it is necessary to ensure that we all understand basically what feudalism was, at least from the military viewpoint. The simplest basic definition I can come up with is that it was unpaid service in exchange for a gift of specific value, principally a grant of land. Admittedly, that leaves a lot of loopholes and as a statement of fact would be easy enough to disprove, but it gives us a starting point.

The basis of all feudal organisation was the granting of land, such a grant being called a *beneficium* or benefice, or more commonly a fief, fee or feud (all derived ultimately from the Frankish *fehu-od*, meaning in this context chattels, from which the word 'feudalism' itself evolved). By the 11th century the fief was generally granted to a retainer for the specific purpose of supporting one or more armed men who, in exchange for the grant, were to provide military service for a specified period, in 12th century Europe most commonly 40 days. Inevitably the recipients of such grants were normally of high station and therefore possessed the best equipment and fought on horseback, and the words for cavalry soldier and gentleman therefore became synonomous—English *knight*, French *chevalier*, Spanish *caballero* and German *Ritter*, for example. In feudal terminology, however, the recipient was called a vassal, and he had to swear an oath of fealty to his overlord, generally either on the hilt of a sword or on holy relics.

The tenants-in-chief, ie, the more important vassals, usually owed the service of a stipulated number of other mounted knights in addition to themselves. This was called *servicum debitum*, an obligation which they could meet either by subinfeudating parts of their fiefs to other knights or by hiring mercenaries. Either way, the number of knights such a vassal ended up with usually exceeded the size of the contingent he himself owed to the royal host, and he might only take the whole lot into action when a full muster of every able-bodied man was called; this was the *arrière-ban*. Vassals serving their own overlord (*service de chevauchée*) were apparently paid, but feudal contingents constituting a tenant-in-chief's stipulated quota for the royal or provincial army (*service d'host*)

---

* *The Families of Outremer: The Feudal Nobility of the Crusader Kingdom of Jerusalem*, The Athlone Press, 1959.

served at their own expense. They were in addition often (probably usually) accompanied by non-noble horsemen and foot-soldiers from among their lower-class retainers, these usually being camouflaged by the blanket description of 'sergeants' (*serjans, servientes*) so that cavalry and infantry are not always easy to distinguish from one another. The mounted element, called by a variety of names including *equites levis armaturae, servientes loricati* and *serjans à cheval*, are particularly difficult to find in contemporary sources, where usually only the knights are mentioned. Nevertheless, in Outremer they were of considerable importance in bolstering the ever-insufficient contingents of knights, who nevertheless seem to have generally slightly outnumbered them. However, most of what I have outlined so far applies basically to European feudalism, and in the East things were somewhat different. It is these differences we shall now examine.

The first, and possibly the principal, difference between military service in the Frankish East and Western Europe was the length of time for which it could be demanded. The western norm of 40 days was obviously totally inadequate for Outremer, with its constant excursions and alarums, and in the East there was no time-limit whatsoever on length of service; apparently only one contemporary document, for just a single fief in Tripoli, specifies a limit, and even that gives six months. It is not clear whether such prolonged service was performed at the expense of the tenant-in-chief or the vassal himself, but the latter seems more probable. John LaMonte, in his *Feudal Monarchy in the Latin Kingdom of Jerusalem 1100 to 1291*, considers that the length of the campaign was decided upon by the *Haute Cour* (High Court), and that the lord then summoned his vassals for the term agreed upon; but if the campaign should subsequently last longer than intended then the lord was thereafter responsible for the expenses of his vassals. 'But,' he adds, 'there seems to have been no limitation as to the length of time which could be demanded as the vassals' regular service at their own expense, provided it was agreed upon in advance.' Certainly that would explain a remark by Archbishop William of Tyre, who wrote in the 12th century, that when the knights had assembled at Ascalon for a campaign in 1166 they had with them food for the 'constituted days'. Either way, such service was not at the king's expense unless it took place outside the kingdom, in which case he might have to supply the rations.

In the Kingdom of Jerusalem every vassal (with the exception of church lands and the Military Orders) was a vassal of the king, irrespective of whose lands he was enfeoffed upon, and so long as he was under 60 years of age (one source mistakenly says 40) he was expected to serve mounted and fully-armed anywhere within the realm and within 15 days whenever the king summoned him; the king himself did not even need to be present except in the case of foreign expeditions. In addition the vassal would be accompanied by however many other knights, sergeants or mercenaries the terms of his enfeoffment demanded. One difference from European feudalism here was that in Jerusalem and Cyprus no vassal was allowed to subinfeudate more of his fief than he himself held, although by the mid-13th century the precise meaning of this restriction had become a bone of contention, since it could be taken to mean either that a vassal need only hold more land than was subinfeudated to his greatest tenant, or that he must retain a minimum of 51 per cent of the fief for himself.

Land being generally in short supply in Outremer, many vassals received instead money-fiefs (*fiefs-rente* or *fiefs de soudée*), these being particularly widespread in Antioch. Godfrey de Bouillon was the first to bestow money-fiefs in Outremer, as early as 1100, these taking the usual form of revenues assigned from specific trades or rents in the coastal ports and other towns. They ranged in value from 300 bezants per annum to 600 or even 1,000 in one case, but averaged 400-500 bezants, the value fluctuating according to the military situation prevailing at the time of its being granted. Some were even paid in cash and kind, a knight in 1261 receiving annually 200 bezants plus 50 measures of grain, 70 measures of barley, 50 of oil and ten of lentils! By the late 12th or 13th century money-fiefs must have been numerous, many of the nobility holding more than one each, and it has been suggested that the crown's fairly permanent financial straits resulted from its bestowal of more money-fiefs than it could actually afford. (Bezants, incidentally, were gold coins used by the Franks; crusader currency is explained in more detail further on in this chapter.)

We are very fortunate that amongst the documents to have survived from this era are several copies of a list giving the military service actually owed to the Kingdom of Jerusalem in the late 12th century, probably in the reign of Baldwin IV (1174-1185). Written *circa* 1265 by Jean d'Ibelin, the Count of Jaffa, it gives as thorough a breakdown of the knight-service due from the kingdom's vassals as we are ever likely to have, and lists the following:

Seigniorial lands

Count of Jaffa and Ascalon 100 knights comprised of: Jaffa 25, Ascalon 25, Ramla and Mirabel 40, Ibelin 10.
Prince of Galilee 100 knights comprised of: lands east of the Jordan 60 (40), lands west of the Jordan 40.
Lord of Sidon 100 knights comprised of: Sidon and Beaufort 60, Caesarea 25, Bethsan 15.
Lord of Kerak, Montréal and Hebron 60 knights comprised of: Kerak and Montréal (Oultrejourdain) 40, Hebron 20.
Count Joscelyn's fief 24 (50) knights comprised of: Château dou Rei 4, Saint George (Lydda) 10, three lesser fiefs 10.
Lord of Toron and Le Maron 18 (15) knights comprised of: Toron 15, Le Maron 3.

Ecclesiastical lands

Bishop of Saint George of Lydda 10.
Archbishop of Nazareth 6 (10).

Royal demesne

City of Jerusalem 41 (43).
City of Nablus 85 (80, 87, 102, 127).
City of Acre 80 (72).
City of Tyre 28 (25).
City of Daron 2.
City of Beirut 21.

The city contingents and some of those owed by the lords include vassals holding money-fiefs. Figures in brackets are variants that appear in alternative versions of the manuscript, and by playing with these it is possible to reduce the final total of 675 knights (which is variously, and inaccurately, given in the originals as 567, 577, 666 and 677) to 636, or to increase it to 749 at the most. In addition there are a number of fiefs not listed, Arsuf for example, and if figures for these were available it seems likely that the grand total of knights available from feudal sources could be brought up to around 1,000. This tallies with the figures of 1,300 or 1,500 knights recorded in other sources as part of an army mustered in 1183 (therefore falling within this same period), the difference being explicable by the presence of either mercenaries or contingents supplied by the Military Orders. This particular army was, in fact, the largest that the kingdom ever raised, with the inevitable exception of that destroyed at Hattin. According to one source the latter included 1,200 mercenary knights as well as 1,000 supplied by feudal contingents, a far cry from the 200 knights that were all Godfrey de Bouillon could raise in 1100, or even the 700 available to Baldwin I by 1111.

Unfortunately accurate figures such as those recorded by Jean d'Ibelin for Jerusalem do not exist for the other Frankish states. The nearest we come to it is a reference to four Edessene contingents in 1111 which provides us with the strengths of Edessa itself and three of its nine main seigniories (the others being Aintab, Birejik, Corice, Ravendel, Samosata and Tulupe): Edessa 200 knights, Marash 60, Saruj 50 and Turbessel 100. William of Tyre tells us that the Edessene lands lost between 1148 and 1150 were capable of raising 500 knights, and since these included Turbessel and Marash it would appear that the other six seigniories could between them muster the remaining 340, Edessa and Saruj having already fallen several years earlier. Altogether the County of Edessa could therefore anticipate the service of some 750 knights from feudal sources, undoubtedly including Armenians. In my own opinion the Principality of Antioch could probably muster a further 800 or so, although John Beeler* estimates Antioch's entire feudal strength somewhat lower at 700 knights, basing his figure on the army destroyed at Ager Sanguinus in 1119.

The County of Tripoli was owed the smallest feudal service of all, apparently only some 200 or 300 knights of which, Jean d'Ibelin tells us, it rendered the King of Jerusalem the service of 100. The Kingdom of Cyprus (combined with Jerusalem in 1269) could raise only about the same number of knights as Tripoli, 300 in fact, when feudal service was first established on the island following its capture in 1191, but during the 13th century this increased to 1,000. Cypriot knights, incidentally, owed service on the mainland for four months a year after 1273, although even before that date Cypriot contingents, of 100 knights on average, frequently appeared in mainland armies.

The neat 'roundness' of most of these figures, largely multiples of tens and hundreds, is no accident. Wherever possible mediaeval army units (if one can be excused for using such inappropriately formal terminology) do appear to have been established on a sort of decimal basis, or more accurately on multiples of five, ten and a hundred. Infantry as well as knights tended to be organised in such units, most commonly of 100, 500 and 1,000 men. It seems likely that in Outremer, as in France and most of Western Europe, the standard term for such a unit was *constabularia*, used both for units of a specific size and, more loosely, for any body of armed men within an army. Its size, however, could vary considerably even in its 'official' role, from five or ten men through 25, 50 and 100 to 200 or as many as 500 men, the lower figures usually being units of knights and the higher figures being infantry. The leader of such a unit was

* *Warfare in Feudal Europe 730-1200*, Cornell University Press, 1971.

called a constable—not to be confused with the baronial constables or the Constable of the Kingdom, who was a royal official and commander-in-chief of the army after the king—although in the case of knights he was usually also their feudal overlord or that lord's appointed deputy. In addition commanders of 100 men were called *centenars,* commanders of 20 were *vintenars* and commanders of ten were *dizeniers,* the latter being recorded by Jean Sire de Joinville (himself commander of a constabulary of 50 men which actually comprised 54) in his chronicle of the Seventh Crusade. On the battlefield the smaller contingents were normally grouped together under the senior barons, the number and size of such conglomerate divisions (often called *batailles* or 'battles') depending solely on the number of troops available and the number of units required.

In addition to the knights, sergeants (fairly certainly infantry) were also available from the towns and ecclesiastical establishments, although we are ignorant of the mechanism by which they were recruited. No documents relating to their obligations have survived, but most probably service was based on the individual's financial standing, as was the case with similar selective militia levies in Western Europe. Jean d'Ibelin again supplies us with a list of services owed in the Kingdom of Jerusalem:

The Patriarch of Jerusalem 500; The Chapter of the Holy Sepulchre 500; The Abbey of the Mount of Olives 50 (150); The Abbey of Mount Sion 150; The Abbey of Mount Thabor 100 (500); The Abbey of St Mary of Jehosaphat 150; The Templum Domini 50 (150); The Latina 50; The Archbishop of Caesarea 50; The Archbishop of Nazareth 150 (50); The Archbishop of Tyre 150; The Bishop of Acre 150 (550); The Bishop of Bethlehem 200; The Bishop of Hebron 50 (550); The Bishop of St George of Lydda 200; The Bishop of Sebastea 100 (150, 500); The Bishop of Sidon 50; The Bishop of Tiberias 100 (500); The City of Jerusalem 500; The City of Acre 500; The City of Tyre 100; The City of Nablus 300; The City of Caesarea 50; Ramla, Mirabel and Ibelin 150 (100); Arsuf 50; Ascalon 150 (100); Jaffa 100; Le Lyon (Legio) 100; Le Gerin (Jenin) 25; Haifa 50; Tiberias 200. This gives a total of 5,025.

Alternative versions of the same list give totals up to 7,025 sergeants, and basically there is little doubt that the actual figure should be higher than that given by d'Ibelin, since like his schedule of knight-service it is similarly incomplete. For example, Magna Mahomeria appears to have owed 65 sergeants, Gaza possibly 50, and undoubtedly other towns and abbeys also owed such service; Beirut, for instance, and Daron, Banyas, Kerak, Belvoir and Safed to name but a few. What service such towns were obliged to provide can only be guessed at, especially since it does not appear to have borne much relation to population, although a basic sergeant:population ratio of between 1:60 and 1:75 would seem to be the average. Using the population map in Meron Benvenisti's *The Crusaders in the Holy Land* as a basis, and allowing for the system's own glaring inconsistencies, this would possibly give us the following additional contingents (amongst others) for the Kingdom of Jerusalem:

The Archbishop of Bethsan 150; The Bishop of Banyas 150; The Bishop of Beirut 200; The Bishop of Gaza 50; The Bishop of Petra 50; Beaufort 50; Belvoir 100; Bethgibelin 50; Buria 50; Caco 25; Calansua 25; Casel Imbert 50; Château dou Rei 50; Daron 50; Kerak 100; Magna Mahomeria 65; Merle 25; Safed 100.

Even that undoubtedly leaves the list still incomplete. The additional

1 *12th century knight, a German from Emperor Frederick Barbarossa's contingent of the Third Crusade.* **2** *13th century Syrian Frankish knight wearing a surcoat, from a manuscript executed in Acre circa 1280; note the smaller shield, the all-enclosing 'sugar-loaf' helmet, and the more complete armour.* **3** *12th century Frankish crossbowman cocking his weapon by use of a belt-claw and stirrup.* **4** *Ilkhanid Mongol cavalryman, wearing a heavily embroidered topcoat over his lamellar armour; a quiver hangs from his belt at the right, and a bowcase hangs at the left.*

ecclesiastical contingents are particularly hypothetical, but they seem reasonable when compared with d'Ibelin's own figures for church service. The church contingents, incidentally, providing more than half of the sergeants available, were often if not usually led by their own ecclesiastical lords; for example, at the Battle of La Forbie in 1244 the Archbishop of Tyre, the Bishop of Ramla and the Abbot of St Mary of Jehosaphat were all amongst those killed. It seems likely that the church supplied a similar proportion (ie, 50 per cent or more) of sergeants in Antioch, Edessa and Tripoli, which were probably able to raise some 5,000, 4,000 and 2,000 sergeants respectively.

As already mentioned, further infantry were raised by the knights from amongst their lower-class retainers, probably at least two or three, or sometimes as many as six or ten, per knight. Certainly this is the only way that 15-20,000 'truly excellent armed foot-soldiers' recorded in 1183 can be explained when the feudal levy of sergeants, as we have just seen, could only raise 6-7,000 men. Obviously some would have been mercenaries, but at the most only 1,500 or so are likely to have been raised by this means. Additional foot-soldiers, considerably less well-equipped, could also be mustered in emergencies through the arrière-ban, which you will remember was a levy of all able-bodied freemen. This was mustered either locally (usually to raise a siege) or on a national level to face a large-scale incursion, such as in the Hattin campaign of 1187. In most

Frankish armies the usual ratio of foot-soldiers to horsemen (both knights and mounted sergeants) was 10:1.

Crusading knights and soldiers on pilgrimage contributed additional manpower to Outremer's armies, particularly those of the Kingdom of Jerusalem itself, arriving in a fairly constant stream throughout the spring and summer months to participate in a campaign or two before returning home to Europe. Indeed, on occasion their arrival even prompted campaigns so as to utilise such reinforcements while they were available. Some stayed on indefinitely, but such newcomers were more often than not hostile to the poulains, those Franks who had been born and raised in Outremer, with whose luxury, religious tolerance and political diplomacy they found themselves unable to identify. Indeed it was enmity between the opposing factions of 'newcomers' such as Gerard de Ridefort and Reynald de Châtillon, and native barons such as Raymond III of Tripoli, that led to the downfall of the Kingdom of Jerusalem in 1187. Certainly the Western Franks were more fanatical in their persecution of the Holy War against the Moslems than were their Levantine cousins. When the Mamluk sultan Baibars, passing Krak des Chevaliers in 1268, asked why the castle gates were shut during a period of truce, he was told by the Hospitaller castellan that it was to protect the Mamluks 'from the Western Franks whom we have with us. For they have no fear of death.' At the time of the Third Crusade one Syrian Frank even thought King Richard of England hardly a lesser evil than Saladin, stating that if the Moslems were dogs then the Western Franks were wolves!

In addition to these various types of Frankish soldier there were also native warriors. The Moslem population remained hostile to the Franks of course, and could not be trusted with arms, but not so with the native Christians of Outremer, the Syrians, Maronites and Armenians. Many mercenaries appear to have been hired from amongst these native elements, while others served in response to general levies in desperate situations. It has even been suggested that the Franks' infantry were drawn primarily from amongst these Syrian natives (in this context including Maronites and Armenians), although this seems unlikely.

It is clear from contemporary sources that the Franks considered their native Christian subjects unwarlike, a condition which probably arose originally from the fact that they had not been allowed to bear arms under Moslem rule. William of Tyre describes the Syrians as 'a race which is regarded by us as weak and effeminate', and Bishop Jacques de Vitry of Acre, enlarging on this view in the 13th century, wrote that 'they are altogether unwarlike and in battle are as helpless as women, save for some of them who use bows and arrows but are unarmoured and ready for running away [this probably being a reference to the Syrian soldiers called Turcopoles, to whom we shall return anon]. These men are known as Syrians ... For the most part they are untrustworthy, two-faced cunning foxes just like the Greeks [ie, Byzantines], liars and turncoats, lovers of success, traitors, easily won over with bribes, men who say one thing and mean another, and think nothing of theft and robbery. For a small sum of money they become spies and tell the Christians' secrets to the Saracens*.' It seems

---

* The original Saracens were a small Arab tribe living in a district of the Sinai Peninsula which Ptolemy called 'Sarakene'. In the 3rd century AD the Sarakene tribesmen became quite powerful and subdued a number of smaller tribes, so that as time passed the Byzantines came to regard their

apparent, then, that on the whole they were not to be relied on.

Nevertheless, it is equally apparent from the sources that some 'individuals of spirit' and 'certain groups with martial qualities', as Dr R.C. Smail calls them†, did fight alongside the Franks, each contingent under its own rais. The sources contain a variety of references to them, some even being knighted and receiving fiefs (for example the knightly families of Arrabit, Qelbe Arab and Eltaffaha). Syrians helped Raymond de Saint-Gilles in his conquest of Tripoli, and a small force under his son Bertram included native Christian infantry and cavalry in 1116. However, references to Syrians performing garrison duties are more common in the sources than those recording their appearance in field armies, and it seems likely that most if not all garrisons included at least some native soldiers, even those of the Military Orders; for example the Teutonic Knights' fortress of Montfort contained large numbers of Turcopoles and Syrians at its fall in 1271, as did the Hospitaller garrison of Krak des Chevaliers the very same year, and more than a century earlier in 1164 we hear of Nur ed-Din contacting a 'Turcoman' infantryman in Krak's garrison.

In the largely Syrian garrison of the Templar castle of Safed, however, we have a perfect example of the distrust that existed between Franks and native Christians. The incident was sparked off when Sultan Baibars, besieging the fortress, offered an amnesty to any native soldier in the garrison who would surrender. The Templars were immediately suspicious of their men and recriminations ensued, resulting in most of the Syrians deserting. One native sergeant even arranged for the Templars' own surrender and falsely guaranteed them their lives; the brethren were promptly executed as they emerged and the traitor became a convert to Islam. Episodes such as this certainly do much to explain the anti-Syrian vehemence voiced by Jacques de Vitry and others.

Although in the Kingdom of Jerusalem their numbers were small (in relation to the size of the native Christian population), native soldiers increased the further north one went. In the County of Tripoli there were the Maronites, Christian Arabs with a fighting manpower variously estimated by contemporaries at 30-40,000. They are described by William of Tyre as 'a stalwart race, valiant fighters, and of great service to the Christians in the difficult engagements which they so frequently had'; de Vitry adds, 'they are numerous, use bows and arrows, and are swift and skilful in battle', and the Cilician chronicler Haithon similarly praises their valour and describes them as 'excellent soldiers'. They served in most Tripolitanian armies under their own *muqaddams* (chieftains), many of whom were granted fiefs and wore looted Moslem armour.

The Maronites' counterparts in the far north of Outremer were the warlike Armenians who, in addition to having their own principalities (later a unified kingdom) in the mountains of Cilicia, were numerous in the Principality of Antioch and comprised most of the population of the County of Edessa, where Frankish settlement never represented more than a superficial military occupation, many of the Armenian nobility staying on under the Franks.

Armenians are to be found fighting both for and against the Byzantines as well as the Franks, in the employ of the latter serving variously as allies,

name as synonymous with 'Arab'. By the Crusade era 'Saracen' had become an all-embracing generalisation for Moslems.

† *Crusading Warfare 1097-1193*, Cambridge University Press, 1956.

mercenaries or subjects (including knights). They were at their most numerous militarily under Joscelyn II of Edessa (1131-1150) but are to be encountered on a fair number of other occasions: in 1108 an Armenian prince supplied Count Baldwin II with as many as 1-2,000 cavalry and 2,000 infantry; in 1110 an allied army included about 10-15,000 Armenians under the princes of Kesoun and Birejik; in 1119 500 Armenian cavalry were with Roger of Antioch at Ager Sanguinus; and in 1144 Edessa was defended largely by Armenian mercenaries. However, after the mid-12th century Armenians are no longer often found fighting as Frankish subjects, Edessa having fallen to be joined before long by much of Antioch's northern territories, which passed into Moslem or independent Armenian hands by the end of the century. Instead we encounter them as erstwhile allies and enemies, frequently occupied in border squabbles with the Prince of Antioch. What their own internal organisation was we cannot be very sure since little is known of the mediaeval Cilician Kingdom of Armenia, but it is apparent from the sources that they utilised a militia system to raise many of their infantry while others, and the cavalry, were provided from the paid retinues of the various princes and senior nobles, of whom there were some 45 by 1198. These retinues were largely of natives but could also include Turks and Persians (probably meaning Turcomans and Seljuks) and Franks too.

Having covered the various individual native Christian elements we must now retrace our steps a little, back to the Syrians whom de Vitry describes as those 'who use bows and arrows but are unarmoured and ready for running away', which I interpret as a reference to a special type of mercenary native soldier called a Turcopole.

Anyone who has read in the past anything about the Crusades is sure to have already encountered the Turcopoles, whether it be under this name or one of its variant spellings such as Turcoples or Turkpols. In my experience, however, general books on the subject do not attempt to explain who or what they were, or if they do merely brush them aside with a nondescript phrase like 'native horsemen'. The first book to attempt a detailed assessment in English was Dr Smail's *Crusading Warfare 1097-1193,* in which he presented the view that some were bow-armed and that they included horsemen, which implies that others did not have bows and/or fought on foot. He continues: 'It has been said that they were specially used for reconnaissance, and that they employed, on behalf of the Franks, Turkish methods of mobile mounted archery. On occasions they were employed for such purposes; yet there seems to be little justification for assuming, on the basis of the scanty information normally quoted, that all Turcopoles were both horsemen and archers . . . They were recruited to supplement the ever insufficient number of Frankish knights, and were a normal part of armies which employed modified western tactics. Those who fought on horseback added to the number and weight of the Latin *milites,* with whom they were marshalled and with whom they normally went into action.'

My own view, however, is that the Turcopoles *were* all mounted archers, and there does seem a considerable amount of evidence to support this argument. Usamah ibn-Munqidh, a Syrian Arab author of the 12th century, actually calls the Turcopoles 'the archers of the Franks', while William of Tyre states specifically that they were 'light-armed horsemen'. In addition various treaties imply that they were not foot-soldiers, and in the 13th century Jacques de Vitry not only describes *Turkish* skirmishers as Turcopoles but records Egyptians at Damietta capturing knights and Turcopoles 'after they had wounded their horses'. Even their very name implies that they were horse-archers, for it is derived from the Byzantine *Turkopouloi*, meaning 'Sons of the Turks', a chronicler of the First Crusade writing that 'Turcopoles were so named because they were either reared with Turks or were the offspring of a Christian mother and a Turkish father.' In Frankish armies they comprised a mixture of converted Turks (many bearing names such as Geoffrey 'le Baptisé'), Syrian Christians and natives of mixed parentage, although certainly by the mid-12th century there is good reason to suppose that some at least may have actually been Franks who had equipped themselves to fight Turcopole-fashion; some Turcopoles may have even held sergeanties, as they did on Cyprus. Probably the majority were Turkish converts, however, Saladin executing as apostates Turcopoles in Templar employ whom he captured in 1179. As to numbers, we know that on one occasion in 1107 a single baron (William-Jordan, regent of Tripoli) had 200 in his employ, while in 1183 1,500 are recorded in a royal army led by the bailli (regent) Guy de Lusignan, and in 1187 the army defeated at Hattin may have included as many as 4,000 (undoubtedly largely in the service of the Military Orders, who employed them in considerable numbers).

Two points in closing on the subject of Turcopoles. The first is that just because they may have all *carried* bows, they did not necessarily always use them. And the second is that after reading my comments on Turcopoles in *Armies and Enemies of the Crusades*, Dr Smail told me that he nevertheless still did not believe 'that the evidence about the equipment and function of Turcopoles is quite as clear' as I would have you all believe. You have been warned.

Before moving on to consider the hiring of mercenaries in general it is necessary to first comprehend the complex monetary system extant in the mediaeval Middle East. A brief course in Levantine numismatics therefore ensues. The standard currency at the beginning of the Crusade era until well into the 13th century was the Fatimid gold dinar, comparable in stability to today's Swiss Franc, backed up by its silver counterpart the *dirham* (there was also a silver dinar). These two coins were both of basically the same weight, although the weights of coins varied immensely throughout this era. Directly comparable to the dinar were the Byzantine *nomisma* (on which it was based), and the Frankish bezant, although the latter was actually worth somewhat more than the dinar, perhaps 20 per cent more. The nomisma could be found in reasonable abundance in the northern Frankish states, particularly Antioch, but it was the bezant that became the basis of the crusaders' own currency, and it was coined throughout Outremer by royal mints, Venetian merchants, Military Orders and baronial nobility alike.

The bezant and dinar were used mainly for large business transactions, being comparable to large denomination banknotes. Everyday commerce involved smaller coins of silver, billon (base silver) or copper. Next down from the bezant came the billon or silver *denier* or penny, of which there were 240 to the pound or *livre parisis* (192 to the less valuable *livre tournois*) and 96 to the gold bezant. This was the nearest Frankish equivalent to the Moslem *qirat*, which was one twenty-fourth of a dinar, and the dirham. Smaller denominations yet were provided by the *obol* or *maille* (half-denier; there was also a half-dirham) and, after the late 12th century, the *pougeoise* (half-obol or farthing), prior to the introduction of which farthings were provided by simply cutting obols in half, the resultant coin being termed a *parti*.

In addition large numbers of European coins were in circulation throughout Outremer (particularly the livre parisis and livre tournois, French pounds minted in Paris and Tours respectively), as too were many Byzantine, Mesopotamian, Syrian and even Persian coins. All of these remained in circulation for as long as they retained their value, and since large amounts of coins were often assessed by weight rather than quantity this basically meant until they wore down below their requisite grammage. Frequently both Moslem and Frankish coins were devalued (for instance deniers of Amalric II were only half the weight of earlier coins and only a third as pure), and this could contribute towards a particular issue's lifespan or widespread acceptance, and in the 13th century in particular inflation ran riot in the Moslem states. However, for wargaming purposes it would be simplest to assume that both bezant and dinar retained their value unchanged throughout this era.

Quite what the buying power of this money was we do not know for sure, and even if we did we do not know what the majority of foodstuffs and equipment cost anyway. We *do* know that in 1262 the full equipment of a knight (excluding his horse) was worth 2,000 silver deniers, that of a cavalry sergeant being worth 1,500 deniers some 40 years later. And from what little other information we have it would appear that it cost between one and two bezants for an individual such as a common soldier to support himself for a month. A good many of the *rustici*, or peasants, had to survive on a lot less, but this led to undernourishment resulting from an unbalanced diet of too much carbohydrate and too little protein, fruit and bread being cheaper than meat. In the Third Crusade King Philip II *Augustus* of France offered the high wage of three bezants a month to his mercenary soldiers, Richard topping him by offering as much as *four* bezants. Mind you, Richard was a very rich king. Interestingly these figures of 1191 are directly comparable to the wages a Cilician Armenian princess was paying her mercenaries in 1114, where foot-soldiers received three gold dinars per month, the Armenian equivalent to the bezant and dinar, incidentally, being called a *tahegan*, coined in both gold and silver. This source provides the additional data that horsemen were paid 12 dinars per month, and the ratio of 1:4 for the pay of infantry and cavalry mercenaries appears to have been not uncommon even amongst the Moslems. Even in early 13th century England the same ratio applied; a mercenary infantryman earnt 6d (2½p) a day at the most, while a knight earnt as much as 2s (10p). Mounted sergeants earnt somewhat less, usually half as much as knights. After the fall of Damietta in 1219, for example, Turcopoles received 12 bezants apiece from the loot while knights received 24. For wargaming purposes, then, we can conjecture from this and other information the following simplified salary scale for hired soldiers:

Knights 12-25 bezants (most often about 25); Turcopoles 6-18 bezants (half to three-quarters of a knight's salary); mounted sergeants 6-12 bezants (half of a knight's salary); infantry crossbowmen 3-4 bezants (one-sixth to one-quarter of a knight's salary); infantrymen 2-3 bezants (one-eighth to one-sixth of a knight's salary).

However, although I have included knights in this list they were frequently paid instead with the money-fiefs mentioned earlier, in which case their average monthly income was 25-50 bezants, or on rare occasions even more.

Mercenaries (the term 'hired soldiers' is probably more technically accurate) were fairly inevitably of great importance in Outremer from the very beginning of its existence, at least partially compensating for the critical shortage of feudal manpower that we have already noted. The need for them increased in the 13th century as feudal contingents were reduced by territorial losses to the Moslems, by which time the real problem was how to pay for their services, something to which we shall return anon.

All mercenaries were contracted on a monthly basis, contracts being renewed on the first of the month. Breach of contract was a very serious offence, punishable in a knight's case by confiscation of his money-fief if he had one or of his armour and equipment, probably including his horse, if he did not. The punishment of non-knightly mercenaries was considerably more severe, for they might have their hands mutilated with hot irons. The employer could normally only be at fault if he failed to pay his men on the set date, but this was quite commonplace and mercenaries whose pay was in arrears were entitled to sell off their equipment and live off the proceeds while still under contract, owing no military service until the outstanding debt had been paid (when, presumably, they had to redeem their gear from the pawnbrokers!). Knights and sergeants holding money-fiefs were somewhat better off from this point of view, because their contracts usually had a clause assuring them that if the specific revenues from which they were paid should be unobtainable, for whatever reason, then they were to be paid instead from some alternative source of income. Even then, however, it was specifically stated that if the king's own revenues should be cut off by enemy action or acts of God (eg, pestilence or a poor harvest) then he would not be obliged to honour his mercenaries' back pay. Although they were commanded in the field by his lieutenant, the Marshal, the Constable was responsible for the employment and fair payment of mercenaries, not only the king's but those hired independently by the feudal lords, from whom he collected and distributed the appropriate payments.

The size of the mercenary element, of course, depended on the Franks' ability to pay for it. The large numbers of *soudoyers* (paid soldiers, the name deriving from their pay, or *solde*, the origin of our word 'soldier') that there were to be found in the East is a sure sign of willingness to buy their services, and although, as I have already mentioned, the Frankish crown was often if not permanently in financial straits, the money was nevertheless somehow found to hire them. But how? Well, other than the money-fief already discussed there were a variety of methods by which mercenaries could be, and were, employed. Some were actually provided on a feudal basis by vassals who owed *service de compaignons*, which required that the vassal should raise and pay a specified number of mercenary soldiers himself. Others were paid for by affluent crusaders on their return to Europe, such as the 40 knights left with a year's pay by Walter d'Avesnes when he left for home in 1218; the French Regiment of 100 knights and 100 sergeants established at Acre by Louis IX on his departure in 1254 also falls into this category. Obviously the state could afford to pay for some out of its various sources of income, which included special military taxes such as those levied in 1166 (ten per cent on the value of movables) and 1183 (one per cent on property and debts, two per cent on baronial and ecclesiastical income), plus import and export duties, market dues, tolls on caravans and pilgrims, various royal business monopolies (for instance dyeing, tanning and brewing), and duties on products such as pepper, cloves, lemons, sugar and so on.

However, these were insufficient for the maintenance of particularly large numbers of mercenaries, and the majority by far would appear to have been financed instead by pecuniary aid from the West, notably from the Pope and the King of France. Very occasionally this assistance took the form of a self-contained contingent of troops, the continued existence of Louis IX's French Regiment at Acre, the nucleus of the kingdom's lay armies in the 1260s and 1270s and of vital importance right down to 1291, being effectively maintained by this means. A papal council of 1274 even envisaged that all European kings should similarly maintain fixed quotas of knights in Outremer, although it seems unlikely that this ever came about. More often financial aid came as lump sums of money, such as that provided throughout most of the 13th century by the Pope, or the 150,000 silver marks left to the King of Jerusalem and the Orders of Hospital and Temple in Philip II's will in 1222 for the maintenance of 100 mercenary knights each for a period of three years (marks being a money of account worth two-thirds of a *livre* each, or 160 deniers).

A more famous and much-quoted example is provided by the considerable sum sent to Jerusalem by King Henry II of England in atonement for the murder of Thomas à Becket, amounting to 42,000 marks of silver and 500 of gold. That part which was lodged with the Templars was employed in 1187 to hire mercenaries for the Hattin campaign, allegedly (but improbably) paying for as many as 1,200 knights and 7,000 foot-soldiers who fought under the English standard and bore lions on their shields.

Finally, other than the Military Orders there remain two further sources of troops from which Frankish armies could occasionally anticipate assistance, these being Moslem allies and, in the second half of the 13th century, the Ilkhanid Mongols. Bedouin were often to be found in Frankish armies, particularly in the role of scouts or spies, and sometimes there were Assassins too, but more usually Moslem assistance resulted from alliances with rival Moslem amirs, kings and princes, one (or occasionally both) of the contending parties usually enlisting Frankish support. The classic example of this policy dates to 1108 when Baldwin II of Edessa was allied with Jawali, the Amir of Mosul, while Tancred of Antioch was allied with Jawali's rival, Ridwan of Aleppo! An example of the terms by which such an alliance might be concluded are provided by a treaty drawn up between Raymond III of Tripoli and Saladin in 1186; Raymond received horsemen, infantry, crossbowmen and armaments from Saladin, plus the promise of immediate military assistance on request, in exchange for his guarantee of neutrality in any conflict between Saladin and the King of Jerusalem. Money might also change hands.

Assistance from the Mongols of Ilkhanid Persia, on the other hand, resulted more from their intense hatred of the Mamluks than any special liking of the Franks, an enmity which persisted unabated even after the Ilkhanids had themselves become Moslems in 1295. Their aid to the Frankish cause usually took the form of independent expeditions launched from occupied Rum (Seljuk Anatolia) against the Mamluks of Northern Syria, such as in 1259-1260, 1271 and 1281. Some Frankish leaders occasionally lent timid support to these invasions, the Prince of Antioch accompanying the Mongol army in 1259, for instance (Antioch itself being tributary to the Mongols from 1246). One of the most remarkable armies of the Crusade era appears in this context, in fact, when in 1281 an army of pagans, Moslems and Christians, comprised of Ilkhanids, Seljuk Turks, Cilician Armenians, Georgians and Knights Hospitaller, fought side by side against the Mamluks under the command of a Mongol general. It would be interesting to see how such a combination would make out on the wargames table.

A couple of figures from campaigns of the late 12th century supply us with details of more typical Frankish armies. The army of 1183 which I have mentioned on several occasions over the last few pages is one. It consisted of 15-20,000 infantry, 1,300 or 1,500 knights and 1,500 Turcopoles. The Hattin campaign of 1187, however, provides an even more comprehensive breakdown, the army of this occasion allegedly comprising 1,000 knights, 1,200 mercenary knights, 4,000 Turcopoles, 25,000 infantry and 7,000 mercenary infantry. This was the largest army the Franks of Outremer ever mustered, but these particular figures are nevertheless rather high; having said that one can only guess at what they should be, although most of the other sources for this battle give 18-25,000 infantry, 1,000 or 1,200 knights and 'innumerable' Turcopoles. None, incidentally, mention mounted sergeants although it seems likely that they are intended by the 'mounted poulains' mentioned in one source, or are possibly included with the Turcopoles. Nor do any of the sources specifically mention how many of these troops were provided by the Military Orders, although Moslem reports tell us that 200-260 Hospitallers and Templars were executed after the battle. However, the importance of the Military Orders is a subject to which we shall have to return in Chapter 5, for after the mid-12th century it was realistically they, not the feudal contingents that we have discussed in this chapter, who were the mainstay of the Frankish host.

Chapter 4

Raising, financing and organising armies: the Moslems

Unlike Frankish armies, the composition of which was basically consistent from one end of Outremer to the other, those of the Moslems were relatively diverse. In 12th century Fatimid Egypt the army was comprised largely of Arabs, Berbers and Sudanese. Those of the Syrian city-states, on the other hand, were mainly of Turks and Turcomans, while Nur ed-Din and Saladin employed many Kurdish soldiers in their regiments, and the majority of Moslem armies included at least some Bedouin tribesmen. Yet despite this apparent diversity there were nevertheless two things that were common to the organisation of nearly all Moslem forces. These were the *iqta* and the *mamluk*.

The iqta was a grant of land comparable to, but distinct from, the Frankish fief. It was a Buyid institution in origin, the Buyids being a 10th century dynasty that ruled much of what is today Iran. Under them it was simply a grant of confiscated or uncultivated land, and rare at that, but when the Seljuks took over the ex-Buyid realm *iqtaat* were adopted as a means of paying their soldiers and consequently became more widespread and of a more obviously military character. The Seljuk conquests of the 11th century were responsible for the iqta's widespread introduction throughout the Middle East, and the basic concept of the military iqta was standardised at the end of the 11th century by Nizam al-Mulk, the celebrated vizier of both Alp Arslan, the victor of Manzikert, and his son Malik Shah. As established by Nizam the iqta combined the administration of an area with the assignment of its revenues to the holder, who was called an *iqtadar* or *muqta*. It was not hereditable, was generally granted in the form of scattered estates to prevent the holder from winning a following in a particular area, and unlike its Frankish equivalent was still subject to administrative supervision by the government. In addition Nizam stressed that iqtaat should be reassigned every two to three years 'lest their holders become too firmly entrenched and begin to cause disquiet'.

The fact that the iqta could be reassigned at all is important. Unlike the fief, it represented not a personal estate but payment in land revenue for military service. The iqta was quite simply no more than a right to income, and since the iqtadar was a soldier (or an official) who might need to be posted off to some far corner of the Sultanate it was essential that the iqta, as his means of income, could be transferred with him. From this point of view the iqta is comparable to the Frankish money-fief, a similarity which is strengthened by the fact that in the 11th century at least some iqtaat were actually granted in money rather than land. The iqtadar was entitled to only a specific sum in cash and/or kind from the villages of his iqta, this being his actual pay. The fact that he may have had to levy this himself on the due date, and in addition usually preferred to personally supervise his harvests between April and July (which was therefore a good time for the Franks to invade), were key factors in the inability of Moslem armies to remain in the field for prolonged periods.

The value of such income is not fully known, but Saladin's vizier indicates that in 1181 the average income of an amir (nobleman) was 429 dinars per annum. Regular soldiers were paid about a third or a quarter of the value of their iqtaat in cash plus an allowance in barley and wheat, this being called the 'full rate' of pay. Banu Kinana Bedouin and ex-Fatimid soldiers received pay at half rate, naval personnel at quarter rate (given elsewhere as five-eighths to three-quarters rate), and Arab auxiliaries, with some exceptions, were paid at one-eighth rate. In addition it was customary for Moslem soldiers to receive a special additional grant at the commencement of a campaign to cover their expenses—Shirkuh's expeditionary force in Egypt in 1168, for example, receiving 20 dinars per man. Another Ayyubid author writing in the early 13th century records that by then the iqta of an amir produced an income of 600-1,000 dinars per annum, which is comparable to the income of a Frankish knight—especially since the source is referring to what were called 'ghost' dinars *(dinar djaishi),* units of account worth only four-fifths of a dinar each in real terms. At the beginning of the Mamluk era (mid-13th century) the iqta of a Royal Mamluk or a member of the *al-Halqa,* for which see page 47, produced the much higher incomes of 83-125 dinars per month, that of an amir of ten (an officer commanding ten men) producing as much as 90-260 dinars, each of his ten men having their own iqtaat producing 20-60 dinars a month; this was five or ten times the pay of a minor governmental official at a time when 24 dinars a year was a working man's basic living wage.

It is, however, hard to reconcile these figures with those of Saladin's period, or with a reference in one 12th century source to Frankish soldiers earning a hundred times as much as Moslems which, although an obvious exaggeration, nevertheless indicates that Franks received higher pay (in reality between two and five times as much). But it should be borne in mind that inflation was running incredibly high in the Moslem states by the mid-13th century, so high that whereas in Ayyubid times a silver dinar was worth six dirhams, in Baibars' time it was worth $28\frac{1}{2}$! Either way, the strain that the granting of iqtaat placed on the state treasury was immense, and the greatest part of any Moslem state's gross revenue was allocated in one form or another to the army. We know that in 1189 the Egyptian treasury allocated as much as 4,653,019 dinars to paying the army, either in iqtaat, stipends or special bounties. Hardly surprising, then, that Moslem rulers often resorted to devaluation of the dinar or reductions in army pay in an attempt to overcome their deficiency of cash.

Fairly inevitably in various areas at various times iqtaat became hereditable, particularly those of the more powerful landholders. Nur ed-Din, King of Aleppo 1146-1174, was perhaps the first to make iqtaat hereditable. He saw to it that even an infant son could inherit an iqta, and that this policy paid dividends is witnessed by contemporary historians, who relate how his iqtadars always fought valiantly because they knew they were protecting their own property. Saladin too made iqtaat hereditable when he became master of Egypt, also abandoning the old Fatimid policy by which they had been granted to the iqtadar partially in return for a fee.

The granting of an iqta involved in return the military service of the iqtadar, who was usually an amir, with as many men as he could muster, these comprising his *idda* or retinue. Later, under the Ayyubids and Mamluks, specific numbers of soldiers had to be supplied according to the size of the iqta, references to 'iqtaat of ten', 'iqtaat of 25', 'iqtaat of 100' and so on reflecting this practice, organisation quite clearly being on a decimal basis. Parts of the amir's iqta were usually parcelled out to his *mamluks* for their own pay by a system comparable to subinfeudation, Ayyubid amirs at least receiving two estates, the *khassa* and the *khubz,* of which the latter was specifically for the maintenance of his troops. Under the Mamluks this comprised as much as two-thirds of his total iqta. The Mamluks also stratified the size of the amirs' contingents, calling them 'amirs of five', 'amirs of ten', 'amirs of 40' (also called 'amirs with bands') and 'amirs of 100', referring to the sizes of their retinues. Even these titles are misleading since contemporary sources state that an amir of ten could command up to 20 soldiers, an amir of 40 up to 70-80 and an amir of 100 up to 110-120, and in fact single amirs employing as many as 500-700 soldiers or even more are also to be found, and the official quotas were often exceeded. In battle the command of an amir was probably greater still since the contingents of lower-ranking amirs might be added to his own.

Organisation was probably based on units of 100 or possibly 200 men and regiments of 1,000, these figures all excluding the officers. Under both the Ayyubids (Saladin's dynasty) and the Mamluks the standard unit was called a *tulb,* apparently either a Kurdish or a Ghuzz institution but probably the former. In 1171 Saladin's 194 Egyptian tulbs were each 70, 100 or 200 strong, but in reality the tulb varied greatly and basically *any* company led by an amir in wartime constituted a tulb. It was therefore similar in many ways to the Frankish constabularia. A much later source states that the Royal Mamluks at least were not organised into formal units at all until they set out on campaign, and that it was the Sultan himself who decided their size.

Although they included freemen, the soldiers who went to make up the amirs' contingents were, for the most part, slave-soldiers called *ghulams,* of whom the white slaves—principally Turks but also Byzantines, Georgians and Armenians—were properly called mamluks, a name deriving appropriately enough from the Arabic word for 'owned'. William of Tyre describes them in these terms: 'It is the custom of Turkish satraps and great chiefs, who in Arabic are called amirs, to raise certain young men with great care, of whom some are slaves captured in battle, others being bought or perhaps born of slave mothers. These youths are instructed in the art of war and, when they have attained manhood, are given wages or even extensive possessions according to their individual merits. In their own language these men are called mamluks. They are entrusted with the protection of their lord in battle, and it is upon them—to no small extent—that the hope of victory depends.' On completion of their training, when they had become competent soldiers, they were legally freed and each given part of their master's estate for their own iqta, several usually sharing a village between them (the 'wages' to which William refers). The fact that they were therefore both trained and subsequently kept at their master's personal expense ensured, theoretically at least, their loyalty to him, a point on which William romanticises at some length.

Moslem sources, however, do not altogether support William's somewhat rose-tinted view of mamluks. Although one says that an obedient mamluk is better than a hundred children ('the latter desire their father's demise, the former his long life'), another accuses the mamluk of haughtiness and ingratitude, relating how he would not let himself be treated as less than his master's equal, and would not be satisfied with anything less than the leadership of an army or the command of a regiment once he had been freed. The most senior mamluks did become amirs in time, although to rank as an amir at all a mamluk had first to command at least five soldiers of his own, and it was generally only Royal Mamluks that made the grade. As mentioned above, not all the amirs' soldiers were mamluks anyway, and large numbers of freemen could sometimes be found in both the *askars* (the provincial regiments) and the amirs' personal retinues, notably Kurds under both Nur ed-Din and Saladin. The 12th century Banu Munqidh prince Usamah, whose name will recur frequently throughout this book, himself at various times served as a paid freeman in the askars of Mosul, Damascus, Egypt and Aleppo.

The provincial askars numbered from a few hundred men to several thousand depending on the size of the district or city. They were usually personal regiments under the command of autonomous local governors or princes who went under a bewildering array of titles including most commonly *atabeg* (guardian, or regent), *malik* (king) and amir. The askars of the principal districts and city-states of Syria can be taken as follows, the figures on the right probably including volunteers and the smaller contingents of local amirs:

Antioch (1098)	2,000 men		
Aleppo	1-2,000 men	⎫	
Damascus	1,000 men	⎬	(1149) 6,000 men
Albara (1170)	200 men	⎭	
Hamah (1179)	1,000 men		
Homs (1167)	500 men		
Shaizar			(1111) 5,000 men
Diyar Bekr	1,000 men	⎫	
Mardin	1,000 men	⎬	Jazira (1176) 6,500 men
Harran (1242)	1,000 men		
Mosul	2,000 men	⎭	

Nur ed-Din actually succeeded in uniting all of these, and Asad ad-Din Shirkuh, acting as his deputy, added Egypt to the fold in 1168. The Egyptian askar as reorganised in 1181 by Nur ed-Din's self-appointed successor, Saladin, consisted of 8,640 men made up of 111 amirs, 6,976 *toassin* (elite mamluks) and 1,553 *qaraghulams* (literally 'black slaves', denoting non-white cavalry, probably Berbers, Arabs and Negroes). Al-Maqrizi, a later Mamluk author, defines toassin, or *tawashi,* as meaning 'a trooper whose pay ranges from 700 to 1,000 or 1,200 dinars and who has a baggage train of ten or less animals, horses, hacks, mules and camels, plus a servant to carry his armour.'

Egypt was one of the richest countries in the world at the commencement of the Crusades, with a dense if unwarlike population. Its ruling dynasty, the Fatimids, had come to power as far back as 909 but by the late 11th century was on the decline. Nevertheless, under Caliph al-Mustansir (d 1094), the still-substantial army comprised the following contingents:

Cavalry 20,000 Qayrawan, Berbers from North Africa; 15,000 Batilis, Berbers from North-West Africa; 30,000 mixed mercenaries, Negroes and others; and 50,000 spear-armed Bedouin from the Hijaz.

Infantry 20,000 Black Masmudis, 'men of good stature but hideous appearance, fighting with sword and spear'; 10,000 Easterners, Egyptians born of Persian or Turkish parents; 30,000 *Abid al-Shira* or 'Purchased Slaves', Sudanese Negroes; 30,000 sword-armed Zanj, Bantu-speaking East Africans from southern Ethiopia; and 10,000 Bodyguards.

In addition there was the central corps of Royal Mamluks which, under the last Fatimids, numbered about 5,000 men; the Sibyan al-Khass, an elite 'Young Guard' of 500 Daylamis; and the personal mamluk regiments of the amirs. The Sudanese units were the most important, of which the four leading regiments by the mid-12th century were the Rayhaniyah, Juyushiyah, Farahiyah and Alexandriyah, the Juyushiyah apparently being the biggest at some 10,000 men. Although black cavalry are occasionally encountered in the sources, Negroes fought mainly as infantry, both spearmen and archers but principally the latter. Their employment in such large numbers is most easily explained by the observations of an Englishman present at the training of Khedivial troops in Egypt in 1825: 'When the negro troops were first brought down to Alexandria,' he reported, 'nothing could exceed their insubordination and wild misdemeanour; but they learned the military evolutions in half the time of the Arabs; and I always observed they went through the manoeuvres with ten times the adroitness of the others.'

When Saladin came to power in 1169 the Fatimid army had seemingly shrunk, but it nevertheless still included 30-50,000 Sudanese infantry and some 40,000 cavalry, the latter probably including qaraghulams and auxiliaries as well as mamluks. Although the white troops accepted their change of masters, the Sudanese revolted the same year, slighted by the promotion of Saladin's officers at the expense of their own. Saladin crushed them in the 'Battle of the Blacks' in the streets of Cairo and drove the disbanded survivors into Upper Egypt, where their resistance was broken over the next five years. The Sudanese present in Saladin's own army at Arsuf in 1191 were undoubtedly from new regiments raised after 1169, and Sudanese infantry are again recorded in an important role in 1221, when 1,000 were killed during King John de Brienne's withdrawal from Damietta. However, their numbers were much smaller than before and continued to dwindle so that by the time the Mamluks came to power in 1250 they had apparently disappeared altogether.

The names given to the Fatimid Negro regiments mentioned in the paragraph before last are characteristic of the pattern that all ghulam regimental titles followed. Some were named according to their country of origin (eg, the Sudaniyah, from the Sudan), others according to the place where they were posted, as with the Alexandriyah and Asaqila regiments based at Alexandria and Ascalon respectively. From the 10th century onwards, however, most were named after their master, further emphasising the personal tie between owner and purchased slave that was the keystone of the mamluk system. Saladin's personal regiment was called the Salahiyah (his name actually being Salah ad-Din), Nur ed-Din's was the Nuriyah, and Sultan al-Kamil's the Kamiliyah; similarly the Hafiziyah were named after Caliph al-Hafiz and the Juyushiyah after the vizier Amir al-Juyush (the Fatimid viziers, who usually commanded the army, having their own substantial bodyguards, usually comprised principally of Armenians and Sudanese).

Inevitably, when their master died or was killed the ghulams of such a regiment usually had to find similar employment elsewhere, in the askar of his successor, in the al-Halqa, or in the Saifiyah element of the sultan's Royal

Mamluks (see below). Strangely enough, though, they were not automatically disbanded or reorganised under such circumstances, instead retaining their master's name and continuing to exist as an individual unit until all their members had died out, retired or joined other regiments. For example the Asadiyah, the personal regiment of Saladin's uncle Asad ad-Din Shirkuh, was still serving as an element of the Egyptian army as late as 1192, despite the fact that Shirkuh himself had died 23 years earlier in 1169.

The nucleus of Fatimid, Ayyubid and Mamluk armies alike was provided by the Royal Mamluks. As we have already observed, according to one source these numbered some 5,000 under the late Fatimids, and of these about a thousand formed the Caliph's personal guard, the al-Ghilman al-Khassa. Saladin's own Royal Mamluks probably also numbered 1,000, although his son and successor al-Aziz (1193-1198) had in all 8,000 Royal Mamluks, while al-Kamil (1218-1238) and as-Salih (1240-1249) had 10,000. However, the latter figures refer to Royal Mamluks in a less specific sense, these including, in addition to the reigning sultan's own guards (the *al-Khassa* or *Khassakiyah*), the mamluk units of former sultans (the *Sultaniyah*) as well as the units of deceased senior amirs (the *Saifiyah*). This also explains the even higher numbers of Royal Mamluks employed under the Mamluk sultans themselves, as many as 12-16,000 under Baibars (1260-1277), of which al-Maqrizi, who gives the figure of 12,000, says 4,000 each were posted in Damascus, Cairo and Aleppo. On the whole, however, the Royal Mamluks were all stationed in Cairo, holding iqtaat of up to half a village each in the surrounding countryside.

Under Saladin an additional elite bodyguard unit was the *al-Halqa al-Khassa,* which played a prominent role in most of his later campaigns. First recorded in 1174, the al-Halqa was made up of non-mamluk cavalry holding small iqtaat of their own. They were therefore largely Arabs and native Egyptians (neither of whom were permitted to become mamluks) and the sons and descendants of mamluks, the *awlad al-nas* or 'sons of the people', who were regarded as second-class by the military elite because they had not been born on the steppes as true Turks; few of these attained any rank higher than amir of ten during the Crusade era. Under the Ayyubids the al-Halqa continued to perform bodyguard duties, and at the time of the Seventh Crusade the chronicler Joinville describes them as the sultan's bodyguard, although he mistakenly calls them mamluks. Under the Mamluks themselves the al-Halqa often, if not always, outnumbered the Royal Mamluks and continued to play a leading role in battle until at least the end of the Crusade era; at the Battle of Homs in 1281, for example, the al-Halqa formed the centre of the battle-line alongside the Royal Mamluks, comprising 4,000 men compared to the latter's 800.

The al-Halqa were normally posted in the provinces under the Mamluks. A later source records as many as 24,000 in Egypt, 12,000 in Damascus, 6,000 in Aleppo, and a total of 9-11,000 in the remaining provinces of Homs, Hamah, Gaza, Safed and Tarablus (Tripoli), but these figures are highly improbable, especially since we know from other sources that by the early to mid-14th century the al-Halqa had undergone a considerable decline and become basically an obsolescent formation. One source gives a grand total of 12,000 al-Halqa for the end of this era, which seems far more realistic. As for internal organisation, we know that every 40 al-Halqa were led by a muqaddam al-Halqa ('commander of al-Halqa', equivalent to an amir of ten), every hundred by a *bash,* assisted by a *naqib,* and every 1,000 by an *amir mia muqaddam alf,*

1 *Sudanese archer; others were spearmen with large, round shields, and some probably wore armour.* **2** *12th century Egyptian cavalryman wearing a quilted corselet called an* al-qutun *('cotton').* **3** *11th-13th century Seljuk Turk.* **4** *Mamluk warrior of the late 13th century; they often wore uniform colours, notably red and yellow.*

all these officers only holding their rank during wartime. In addition the mamluk amirs of 100 theoretically commanded regiments of 1,000 al-Halqa in times of war (presumably as the amir mia muqaddam alf's superior) and were consequently known as 'amirs of 1,000'. However, in practice this may never have actually been the case, especially since in early Mamluk times there were only 9,000 al-Halqa in Egypt compared with *24* amirs of 100.

With the exception of the Negroes, and the Armenians employed in the role of archers by the Fatimids, all the troops so far mentioned fought as cavalry. As we shall see in Chapter 10, Turkish horsemen sometimes dismounted in battle, but on the whole mamluks would not deign to fight on foot. The *Itinerarium* records how, before the battle of Jaffa in 1192, Saladin's Kurdish soldiers had suggested that the mamluks should dismount and creep into the Frankish camp to seize King Richard while the Kurds themselves kept watch on horseback, to which the mamluks haughtily replied, 'It is rather *your* business to go on foot, for we are nobler than you. We are content with that kind of warfare which rightly belongs to us. This foot service is your concern.' It was fairly inevitable, then, that in Syria, Iraq and the Jazira infantry should play a very secondary role. They were generally supplied by volunteers or town militias and appear most frequently either in battles in the immmediate vicinity of their home towns or in sieges.

Many of the town militias were probably provided by the *Ahdath,* one of the many paramilitary organisations which existed in the Middle East in mediaeval times, other similar organisations being the *Ayyarun* and the *Fityan.* These were occasionally little more than bands of organised ruffians, although at other times they comprised almost chivalric associations made up of ex-military men.

The Ahdath were particularly important in Aleppo and Damascus, where their role was officially one of maintaining public order, although they not infrequently usurped the municipal authority. One observer described the Aleppene Ahdath in 1057 as 'a group of people . . . who possess the city more than its possessors and hold sovereignty more than its sovereign'. Such part-time troops received an annual payment the value of which is unknown, often demanding an increase on occasions of disorder.

In the Moslem world of the 12th century foot-soldiers were basically an Egyptian phenomenon, so it is hardly surprising to find that when Saladin took over from the Fatimids he similarly raised some regular infantry units of his own, although we have no idea of their numbers. Under the cavalry-oriented Mamluks too there appear to have been some regulars, such as the axe-armed Tabardariyah or the 1,000-strong Aqjiyah regiment installed as part of al-Marqab's garrison on its capture in 1285. But on the whole they, like the Ayyubids, relied on volunteers and irregulars for infantry, many of whom were supplied by the al-Ashair, semi-nomadic or sedentary Syro-Palestinian and Lebanese Bedouin who fought principally with bow and sling. By these various means the Mamluks apparently raised up to and even in excess of 100,000 infantry for their sieges of Tripoli in 1289 and Acre in 1291, and it seems likely that such potential was also available to the Ayyubids. The volunteers, incidentally, were usually a mixture of *ghazis* (warriors of the faith), to whom, like the crusaders themselves, fighting the infidel was part of their religious duty, and *muttawwia*, irregulars raised for the duration of a campaign. Both were remunerated with loot at the close of the campaign, although the latter at least also appear to have been paid, probably at about one-eighth of the rate of mamluk troops. Such volunteers could come from as far afield as Baghdad, Anatolia and the Maghreb.

Other irregular troops were provided by Bedouin, Kurdish and Turcoman tribesmen, of whom the Bedouin were by far the most numerous. The term Bedouin itself (a collective form of *Bedu,* a single nomad, the real plural of which is *Bedawi*) derives from *Badia,* their name for the desert, meaning 'Waste' or 'Wilderness'. They were then and still are the ultimate desert-dwellers, leading hard lives which basically consist of a perpetual struggle for survival against the elements and each other. Their organisation was tribal, each tribe consisting of a number of clans of about 2,000 members (therefore probably about 400 able-bodied men), the basic raiding unit. A slightly later Mamluk source has a list of tribal contingents that range from 100 combatants each for a number of small unnamed tribes and 1,000 or 2,000 for the larger tribes, to 24,000 for the very largest, the Banu Fadl. Within the clan smaller groupings comprised *hamoula* or *fakhd,* broadly speaking meaning 'lineages' with the same paternal great-great-grandfather. The chief of one of the most powerful clans was normally proclaimed *sheikh,* or *saiyid,* usually on the basis of his wisdom, abilities as a leader and warrior, and his personal good luck. Theoretically leadership was not hereditary but it usually tended to be and one family might hold this position for many generations.

Bedouin auxiliaries fought in Seljuk, Fatimid, Ayyubid and Mamluk armies alike, their pay—inevitably enough for a people to whom banditry was second, if not first, nature—taking the form of booty, often looted from the corpses of both sides after the battle. In a review of Saladin's army in 1171, 7,000 Bedouin are recorded, and of these 1,300 were apparently regulars fighting for pay like other freemen. However, the Bedouin were under no formal obligation whatsoever to supply troops to anyone, and such contingents as served did so at their sheikh's discretion and as a result were not consistently reliable. For this reason the Mamluks counted only their most powerful sheikhs as amirs, less important chieftains being regarded as equal in rank only to al-Halqa officers.

The chiefs of Turcoman tribes, on the other hand, were graded as amirs of ten, 20 or 40 by the Mamluks, largely because they often received their grazing lands from the sultan as military fiefs. Like the Bedouin, the Turcomans were nomadic herdsmen, although they herded sheep rather than the camels most commonly reared by the former. They had originally come from Central Asia and had formed part of the Ghuzz, the name 'Turcoman' only first appearing in the late 10th century. The Seljuks who conquered most of Persia, Iraq and Anatolia in the course of the 11th century were themselves a Ghuzz horde, and fairly inevitably most of the Turkish principalities of Syria therefore relied heavily on Turcoman tribesmen, and they provided the backbone of Rumi (Anatolian Seljuk) armies throughout this era. They were fierce if indisciplined soldiers, with no respect for authority, and fought mainly in the hope of obtaining plunder, the absence of this particular stimulant generally resulting in their swift abandonment of the army. Their numbers were considerable and in the early 12th century it was possible to raise 20-50,000 Turcomans from the Jazira alone, while the Mamluks claimed they could raise as many as 180,000 between Gaza and Diyar Bekr. After 1072 Turcoman tribesmen could even be found in Fatimid armies, some being present at the Battle of Ascalon in 1099. Nur ed-Din and Saladin made considerable use of them, the former's lieutenant Shirkuh hiring 6,000 for his third invasion of Egypt, apparently paying as much as 200,000 dinars for their services.

The third source of auxiliary Moslem troops was the Kurds, a hill-people from the mountainous district of north-west Iran whom Marco Polo describes as 'lusty fighters and lawless men very fond of robbing merchants.' They were armed like the Bedouin except that some used bows, and like both the Bedouin and the Turcomans they fought principally for loot so were disheartened by long or unsuccessful campaigns. They were particularly prominent in the armies of Zengid, Ortoqid and Ayyubid princes, both as auxiliaries and paid *askaris,* but never more so than under Saladin, himself a Kurd. He disbanded many of his Kurdish units after the Battle of Montgisard, for which disaster he held them responsible. Nevertheless Kurds remained an important element of Ayyubid armies until the dynasty came to an end in 1250, and the Mamluks too could raise large numbers of Kurdish auxiliaries, apparently as many as 20,000.

In addition to the usual auxiliaries there were also the *Wafidiya* or 'Immigrants', sometimes called the *Mustamina* ('those who seek asylum'). These were large foreign contingents serving under their own leaders in the late Ayyubid and Mamluk armies, comprised of Shahrazuriyah Kurds and Khwarizmians under the former and Mongols under the latter. The Khwarizmians, themselves refugees from the Mongol onslaught, took service under Sultan as-Salih in 1244. There were 10-12,000 of them under four chieftains of whom the senior was called Barbeh or Berke Khan (the Mamluks made his name more grandiose, calling him Husam ad-Din Berke Khan al-Khwarizmi). These Khwarizmians recaptured Jerusalem from the Franks in 1244 and were largely responsible for the Moslem victory at La Forbie the same year, but they subsequently dabbled once too often in Syria's complex politics and were crushed in battle by as-Salih only two years later. Nevertheless, some are still to be found in both royal and provincial askars as late as 1260.

The immigration of Mongols began soon after, 200 entering Mamluk service in 1262, more than 1,300 in 1263, and another 662 plus several smaller bands in 1264, in all some 3,000 Mongols entering the Mamluk state during Baibars' reign. Like the Turcomans, Kurds and Bedouin, the Wafidiya retained their status as freemen but, unlike the other auxiliaries, many actually served in regular mamluk units, usually those of the amirs but sometimes even in the Royal Mamluks; most of the first band of 200 Mongols, for instance, entered as-Salih's old elite regiment the Bahriyah as-Saliyah (often called mistakenly the 'River' regiment by modern authorities), the unit responsible for the overthrow of the Ayyubids and the setting up of the Bahriyah Mamluk dynasty. Some Wafidiya even served in the sultan's personal bodyguard, the Khassakiyah, but most were enrolled in the al-Halqa and largely graded lower than mamluk troopers. Even their chieftains were deliberately given only very low ranks, usually muqaddam al-Halqa, which occasionally resulted in some bizarre situations, such as in 1297 when the Ilkhan Hulagu's son-in-law Turghay was given the rank amir of 40 despite the fact that he had entered Mamluk service with a vast number of Kalmuk horsemen estimated by one contemporary at *18,000*! Like mamluks, the Wafidiya received iqtaat.

One last, and unexpected, source of troops were Frankish mercenaries. As early as 1111 the Fatimid governor of Ascalon had 300 Franks forming his bodyguard, although this was 'by arrangement' with King Baldwin I in preparation for the proposed surrender of the city. In 1148 we hear of 3,000 Franks captured at Attaleia during the Second Crusade taking service with the Sultan of Rum, and the Rumi Seljuks seem to have remained enthusiastic employers of Franks throughout the 13th century, largely Cypriots but also Frenchmen, Germans and Italians. The Moslems of Egypt and Syria also thought highly of Frankish soldiers, and during negotiations in 1191 Saladin himself is alleged to have proposed that in exchange for considerable territorial concessions he should receive for one year the services of 2,000 knights and 5,000 infantry for use against his rival the Zengid prince of Mosul. However, concrete references to Franks in Levantine Moslem employ are rare, although it is apparent from one source that one of the knights who gave advice to King Guy before the Battle of Hattin had served in a Moslem army at some time, and in 1227 the presence of several knights is recorded in Damascus. Later still the historian al-Maqrizi records Sultan Baibars to have employed Frankish knights after the fall of Caesarea and Haifa in 1265, some actually being granted iqtaat in place of their old fiefs!

It is self-evident that, all in all, the Moslems could, and usually did, outnumber the Franks, and the fact that the Frankish kingdom survived for as long as 200 years in the face of such odds resulted mainly from the Moslems' own internal dissension rather than Frankish martial supremacy. If the Moslems could have ever launched a concerted attack on all fronts simultaneously then the Frankish states would not have stood a chance; 1187 proved that, and the parallel with the present-day Arab-Israeli situation is obvious. Fatimid field armies alone could comprise many thousands of troops, their armies at Ascalon (20,000 men), First Ramla (11,000 cavalry, 21,000 Sudanese infantry) and Second Ramla (20,000 cavalry, 10,000 Sudanese infantry) being in excess of the largest muster of which the Kingdom of Jerusalem was capable. As we have seen, the Syrian amirs too could individually raise up to 2,000 horsemen each from their own askars, and by utilising Turcoman and Bedouin auxiliaries, of whom tens of thousands were potentially available (subject to one's ability to pay them), their armies could be increased to 10,000 or more. Nur ed-Din, after taking Damascus, could have probably raised as many as 10-15,000 mamluks without recourse to auxiliaries, while Saladin in 1187 had a field army that comprised some 12,000 askaris and perhaps as many auxiliaries and ghazis, and ten years earlier he allegedly raised 18,000 qaraghulams, 8,000 toassin and an unknown number of infantry for a campaign against Ascalon and Gaza.

It was, however, the Mamluks who raised the biggest armies of all; 40,000 mamluks are recorded in a campaign against the Sudan in 1289, 10-19,000 were present at the siege of Tripoli the same year, and 60,000 horsemen—mamluks and auxiliaries—attended the final siege of Acre, this being in addition to perhaps 100,000 or more infantry on both the latter occasions. Against such overwhelming odds the extinction of Outremer was, from the outset, simply a question of time.

Chapter 5

The Military Orders

The Military Orders were one of the few crusader institutions which could lay any claim to originality, combining as they did the concepts of knighthood and monasticism. With greater financial resources and manpower potential than any individual baron of Outremer, or even the whole lot lumped together, they were without doubt the most important source of troops in the crusader states. Unlike the transitory bands of crusading knights who came and went with every spring and autumn, they provided a permanent, ready source of trained fighting men in a state of permanent mobilisation, the Orders' very existence being based on the premise of war. 'In addition,' Joshua Prawer has observed, 'training formed part of their daily schedule and the continuity of their existence turned them into a repository of military tradition and experience. No European host on a Crusade could dispense with the advice of the Orders. They knew the East and the Moslem foe, with all his strengths and weaknesses.'*

Contingents of Templars and/or Hospitallers appeared in every army mustered by the King of Jerusalem from the mid-12th century onwards. Their military services, however, were not obligatory, the great Orders of Temple, Hospital and Teutonic Knights being answerable directly—and only—to the Pope. Although they were always prepared to fight the Moslems they would not necessarily fight exactly where and when the king wanted them to, and it was often deemed necessary to encourage their military assistance by promising extra-large shares of the spoils or other allurements; in 1220, for example, King John de Brienne promised the Teutonic Knights as much as *half* of all the plunder of Damietta.

The Orders even drew up their own treaties and alliances independently of the crown, the interests of the Order always being placed first and foremost even at the risk of endangering the peace of the kingdom. Immune even to sentences of excommunication issued by clergymen outside of the Order, and with the Pope their only suzerain, there was no real limit to their power, and as they grew ever stronger they became a law unto themselves. Their very presence on the battle-field cost the king full command of his army, and despite all their monastic vows it was, on a number of occasions, their own sinful pride and arrogance that lost the day. A bitter rivalry between Temple and Hospital that could, and even did, lead to bloodshed was yet another effect of their ambition, but, having said that, it is worth noting that the two Orders did nevertheless co-

---

* *The Latin Kingdom of Jerusalem*, Weidenfeld and Nicolson, 1972.

operate with each other on occasion, notably—but not solely—on raids into Moslem territory. In 1266, for instance, we hear of 50 Templar crossbowmen from Safita being killed on their way to reinforce the Hospitaller fortress of Krak des Chevaliers, and the garrison of the Templar fortress of Safed apparently included Hospitaller knights at its fall the same year.

The resources at the disposal of the Military Orders, coupled with the immeasurable importance of castles in Outremer, meant fairly inevitably that before long their principal role had become one of holding and garrisoning fortified places, not only in the Kingdom of Jerusalem but in Tripoli, Antioch and even Cyprus. The granting of fortresses to the Orders started with Bethgibelin, near Ascalon, which was assigned to the Hospitallers by King Fulk in 1136, and this practice became more and more frequent, with ever-increasing alacrity during the 13th century. At first the grants were exclusively royal castles, but before long they also included seigniorial castles (as well as their accompanying fiefs) which the owners could no longer afford to defend, a situation which steadily worsened throughout the 13th century as the resources of the native nobility dwindled.

The Order of the Hospital had 20 castles by circa 1160, 25 by 1180 and 29 by 1244, a huge increase when one considers that by then less than a quarter of Outremer was still in Frankish hands compared with what they had held in 1160. The Templars held somewhat fewer, a maximum of some 18 being in their hands in the late 12th century, and both of these figures refer only to major fortifications. In all, the Orders owned or garrisoned between them many, many more castles than did any single Frankish ruler, even including the king himself, and the chronicler Ernoul describes how Thoros II of Cilicia, visiting Jerusalem in the mid-12th century, said to King Amalric I: 'I could not find any castles, cities or towns which belonged to you except for three. All the rest belong to the religious orders.' The castellans of both Hospital and Temple were apparently required to swear oaths on holy relics never to surrender their castles except, it would seem, on their Grand Master's express orders, although this stipulation was not always observed; King Amalric, for instance, regardless of their immunity from any authority but the Pope's, actually seized and hanged 12 Templar brethren on one occasion for surrendering a castle without his permission.

In addition to their territorial possessions in the East the Orders also received estates throughout Europe from large numbers of benefactors, holding property in England, Ireland, Scotland, France, Spain, Portugal, Italy, Sicily, Germany, Scandinavia, Hungary and later Cyprus and, after the Fourth Crusade, Greece and Romania. Matthew Paris, a 13th century English chronicler, estimated the property of the Hospital in the mid-13th century at 19,000 manors, and of the Temple at 9,000 manors and, although improbable, such figures are representative of the way contemporaries saw the wealth of the Orders.

It was from their European commanderies that the Convents of Outremer drew their supplies, shipped out to the East regularly in their own vessels, as well as reinforcements in times of great need, such as after the disaster of Hattin in 1187 and the fall of the key Hospitaller fortress of Arsuf in 1265. The commandery itself was common to the organisation of all the Orders, comprising a unit of brother knights and brother sergeants (usually 12 or more brethren, the knights apparently outnumbering the sergeants) under an officer called a commander, a *Pfleger* or *Hauskomtur* in the case of the Teutonic

Knights and a *comendadore* in the case of the Spanish order of Montjoie. The headquarters of each Order was the Convent of Jerusalem under the Grand Master himself, with lesser Convents in Antioch and Tripoli under provincial Commanders. The Temple and Hospital had 14 and 12 commanderies respectively in Syria, plus others in Cilicia and Cyprus, in addition to fortress garrisons which, although they had a nucleus of brethren, were by necessity largely mercenary, the Orders being the most important employers of mercenaries in Outremer.

There were three main Orders active in Outremer—the Hospitallers, the Templars and, to a lesser extent, the Teutonic Knights—plus several of lesser importance. These we shall now consider individually.

The Hospitallers

The Hospitallers were so named because of their original foundation *circa* 1070 as a nursing brethren for pilgrims in the monastery hospital of St Mary of the Latin in Jerusalem. They were granted papal protection in 1113 as the Order of the Hospital of St John, the nursing role of the Order predominating at first and remaining important throughout this era. Membership was largely French but included many Englishmen and Italians. Military brethren may have been present in the Order as early as 1126, when a constable is recorded, or 1130, when a papal bull refers to the Hospitallers as a fighting body, or at the very latest by 1137 when the Order was granted the fortress of Bethgibelin. However a brother knight does not occur in any Hospitaller document until 1148, and prior to the mid-12th century it is probable that the majority of whatever armed forces it maintained were supplied by mercenaries—possibly even including Templars. Thereafter their military responsibilities steadily increased, and statutes of 1204-1206 indicate that the Order's organisation was by then based on its military brethren, both knights and sergeants.

Their military hierarchy, modelled on that of the Templars, was headed by the Marshal, though inevitably the Master himself had supreme command. The Marshal only first appears in the 1160s, although as already mentioned a Constable is recorded as early as 1126 and lasted until at least 1169, probably as the Marshal's lieutenant. Immediately beneath the Marshal came the *Gonfanonier* (the Order's standard-bearer), the Commander of the Knights, and the Master Esquire of the Convent. Of these the Commander, first recorded in 1220, was an officer appointed by the Marshal to lead a force in his absence, while the Master Esquire was a brother sergeant responsible for all the esquires and grooms. Three other officers known to have existed were mercenaries, these being the Master Crossbowman, the Master Sergeant, and the Turcopolier. The Turcopolier was commander of the Turcopole light cavalry employed by the Order and regularly referred to in their service, such as in the invasion of Egypt in 1168, at the Battle of Arsuf in 1191, and at La Forbie in 1244.

The brethren-at-arms of the Order consisted of knights and sergeants (the latter invariably outnumbered by the former), although this distinction is only first made in 1206, at which date each brother knight was accompanied on campaign by four horses and probably two esquires, each brother sergeant having only two horses and a single esquire, the esquires being drawn from amongst the serving brethren as was the custom in all the Military Orders. At the end of the 13th century the knight's complement of horses was reduced to three. Incidentally, brother sergeants of both Hospital and Temple included converted Moslems.

As well as the brethren-at-arms themselves and the Turcopoles mentioned above additional troops were supplied by *confratre* or *confrère* knights and *donats,* these being non-brethren affiliated to or permitted to join the Order for a limited period of time under special conditions, such as a donation of property. There were also feudal vassals from the Order's estates, allied contingents (sometimes including Moslems), and the inevitable mercenary knights, sergeants and infantry. Unfortunately contemporary chroniclers usually fail to distinguish between the actual brethren-at-arms and these various types of auxiliary, so it is hard to judge with any accuracy exactly what the full strength of the Order in Outremer might have been at any one time. However, figures can be found scattered in the various sources which at least give us an idea of its potential.

The earliest large force recorded, in 1168, consisted of 500 knights and 500 Turcopoles promised to King Amalric I for his invasion of Egypt. It was probably comprised chiefly of mercenaries (or so we can assume from the fact that the Master, Gilbert d'Assailly, raised huge loans to finance this force), although four years earlier a visitor to Jerusalem wrote that the Hospital was capable of housing 400 knights in addition to pilgrims and the sick. During the Fifth Crusade the Order appears to have provided 700 knights (or, more probably, horsemen, therefore including Turcopoles and sergeants) and 2,000 'persons', presumably foot-soldiers, while for an attack on Hamah in 1233 a force of 100 knights, 300 mounted sergeants and 500 or 1,500 infantry was mustered, and this appears to have represented almost the full strength of the Convent of Antioch at that date. In 1244 some 200-325 Hospitaller brethren were killed at La Forbie, while five, 15 or 26 escaped and others were taken captive, which suggests an overall total well in excess of 350; 200 Hospitaller Turcopoles were also killed. Most of the Convent of Jerusalem's brethren-at-arms appear to have been lost when Arsuf fell in 1265, 80-90 being killed and 180 captured, a further 45 brethren being killed in an engagement at Caroublier the following year. At the fall of Tripoli in 1289 40 brethren and 100 horses were lost, this being considered so grave a loss that steps were taken to bring in reinforcements from Europe.

Garrison strengths where recorded are often considerable, although these were certainly largely mercenary and the proportion of brethren-at-arms must have always been small, probably comprising a complement of no more than 50 or 60 men. In 1203 the Hospitaller garrisons of Krak des Chevaliers and al-Marqab together mustered an army of as many as 4-500 cavalry and 1,000-1,400 infantry, plus Turcopoles, while in 1212 the same two fortresses are recorded to have been garrisoned by 2,000 and 1,000 men respectively even in peacetime. By 1271 Krak's garrison included 200 brother knights and brother sergeants under the Marshal, and al-Marqab in 1280 was held by 600 horsemen (obviously not all brethren), presumably supplemented by infantry in both instances.

Perhaps the most reliable piece of evidence of all for the total strength of the Hospitallers in Outremer is a letter written by the Order's Master, Hugh Revel, in 1268, in which it is specifically stated that by that date the Order could muster only 300 brother knights in the whole of Syria (ie, including the Convents of Antioch and Tripoli). Even more revealing is another statement in the same letter where it is claimed that in the past the Order had been able to muster

1 *No contemporary illustrations of Turcopoles are known to exist, but this gives an idea of their probable appearance; armour was light where worn, and arms included bow, light lance and sword.* 2 *Knight Templar wearing the white surcoat and red cross of his Order.* 3 *Knight Hospitaller wearing the heavy, hooded black* cappa clausa *that was the Hospital's uniform until the mid-13th century, when a surcoat was substituted, this changing from black to red in 1259; the cross was white.* 4 *Bedouin tribesman; Bedouin wore no armour and fought only with sword and cane lance.*

10,000 men. Allowing for vassals, Turcopoles, mercenaries, serving brethren and so on the claim is not altogether an impossible one.

The Templars

Unlike the Hospitallers, or for that matter the Teutonic Knights, the Templars were from the outset a purely military Order, and in fact the Hospitallers' military organisation was to a great extent based upon the military institutions of the Temple. The belligerence and military importance of the Templars is well documented by contemporaries such as Jacques de Vitry, who wrote circa 1225 that 'when the Templars were called to arms they did not ask how many the enemy were, only *where* they were'. King Amalric II, writing to the King of France, said of the Templars that 'in them indeed, after God, is placed the entire reliance of all in the East', and even the 12th century Byzantine chronicler Cinnamus believed that 'the man in command of [all] the knights in Palestine' was he 'whom the Latins call the Master of the Temple'.

The Order's origins, however, were humble. It was initially founded in Palestine in about 1118 by two French knights, Hugh de Payens and Godfrey de St Omer, for the protection of pilgrims on the road from Jaffa to Jerusalem. At first its handful of knights, only nine of them in all, relied on gifts and cast-offs for their clothes and keep, and as a result they were called the Poor Knights of Christ, but before long King Baldwin II granted them lodging in a section of the royal palace of Jerusalem which was supposed to have been the site of the Temple of Solomon; hence the Order's full title, the Poor Knights of Christ and the Temple of Solomon. They were granted papal protection as a Military Order in 1128.

Military command was basically as per that described above for the Hospitallers, officers including the Marshal, Commander of the Knights, Gonfanonier, Master Esquire, Turcopolier and others. Likewise, in addition to brethren their forces included vassals, mercenaries, allies (sometimes Saracens) and the inevitable Turcopoles, there apparently being a Turcopolier present in each commandery. Some indication of proportions is provided by the Templar garrison of Safed, recorded circa 1243 to have consisted of 50 brother knights, 30 brother sergeants, 50 Turcopoles, 300 crossbowmen, 820 esquires, workmen and others (largely natives) and 400 slaves. The proportion of Turcopoles to brethren (or possibly to brother knights only) would appear to have been basically on a 1:1 ratio, as with the Hospitallers. For example, at La Forbie in 1244, where the Templars may have lost as many as 312 brethren, they also lost 324 Turcopoles. Foot-soldiers in the Order's employ were organised in companies of 50 men, Moslem sources recording 15 such infantry companies in the garrison of Le Chastellet.

Military brethren again consisted of knights and sergeants, with the latter in existence at least as early as 1147. The distinction between them was almost inevitably more noticeable than amongst the less militaristic Hospitallers, and by 1250 an initiate seeking entry into the Order as a brother knight had first to prove that he was the son or descendant of a knight, a qualification which was likewise demanded by the Hospitallers and the Spanish Orders too within the next two decades.

Again the full strength of the Order in Outremer is unknown and can only be surmised from the various references to be found amongst contemporary records. In 1152 a letter records that the Order could 'only gather 120 knights and 1,000 serving brethren and hired soldiers' to fight in Antioch, while in the Kingdom of Jerusalem as early as 1157 85 or 88 Templars were captured and allegedly 300 killed in an engagement with Nur ed-Din. Conversely at Montgisard in 1177 there were as few as 80 brethren present, despite the kingdom's Convent having summoned all its available knights for the action; the figure would seem to indicate that the Templars' full strength had not yet assembled when the army marched, particularly since at about the same date William of Tyre records that 'there are in the Order about 300 knights . . . and an almost countless number of lesser brethren'. In the disastrous year of 1187 we hear of 90 Templars being killed in the skirmish at Cresson and of a further 260 (a figure which probably includes Hospitallers) being executed after Hattin, from which battle a number of others escaped, which would imply that their total strength on the latter occasion was in the region of 300, the usual estimate for the number of Hospitallers at the same battle being about 250.

In the early 13th century Jacques de Vitry records that the Convent of Jerusalem still comprised about 300 brother knights (supplemented by the usual auxiliaries). Another source of similar date records their stables in Jerusalem holding up to 2,000 horses which, allowing for those of mercenaries and sergeants as well as spare mounts (Templar knights being accompanied by two horses, as well as two esquires) seems to support de Vitry's figure. The garrisons of frontier fortresses were as large or even larger. When La Chastellet fell in

1179 its Templar garrison appears to have comprised 80 knights (and sergeants?) and 750 infantry plus servants and craftsmen, while an anonymous 13th century source records the garrison of Safed as 1,700 men in peacetime rising to a wartime strength of 2,200.

The Temple, like the Hospital, appears to have supplied 700 'knights' and 2,000 others during the Fifth Crusade, probably chiefly comprised of mercenaries, while at Darbsaq in 1237 100 brethren and 300 crossbowmen in the employ of the Order are reported to have been killed, there possibly being in all about 200 brethren in the Principality of Antioch's Convent at this time. As already mentioned, 312 brethren were killed at La Forbie in 1244 and between four and 36 more escaped, although Matthew Paris records that the whole Convent (the figure of 300 brother knights again appears) was lost. Six years later 285 Templars were killed in the main battle at El Mansurah, others being killed or captured in earlier and subsequent engagements. There were perhaps 240 at the fall of Acre in 1291, compared to possibly 140 Hospitallers, only 15 Teutonic Knights and 25 and nine brethren respectively from the Orders of the Hospitals of St Lazarus and St Thomas Acon (for which see below). Finally, the waterless island of Ruad off Tortosa was garrisoned by as many as 120 Templar knights and 500 Syrian archers at the time of its capture by the Mamluks in 1303.

After the fall of the Kingdom of Jerusalem the Templars withdrew their headquarters first to Cyprus, then to France. Within a few years of this the Order came to an ignominious end. Its great wealth had aroused the jealousy of the avaricious King Philip the Fair of France who, with papal support and trumped-up charges of heresy and worse, instigated the arrest of the Order's members on an international scale in 1307-1308. Following a series of prejudiced trials backed up by 'confessions' extracted under torture the Order was officially suppressed in 1312, the last Grand Master, Jacques de Molay, being burnt at the stake as a heretic in 1314. Full accounts of the whole affair make disturbing reading.

The Teutonic Knights

The sinister reputation of the Teutonic Knights, with which anyone who has read Henryk Sienkiewicz's *The Teutonic Knights* will be uncomfortably familiar, resulted not from their brief Levantine career but rather from their infamous activities in Prussia, Lithuania and Poland, with which we are fortunately not concerned here. The Order was nevertheless actually founded in Outremer in 1190 when, during the Third Crusade, merchants of Bremen and Lübeck established a hospital for the care of German pilgrims at the siege of Acre. It turned military in 1198 when many German knights joined following the abortive German crusade of 1197. The Order went under a variety of names until 1220, when it adopted its full title of the Hospital of St Mary of the House of the Teutons of Jerusalem. It was always exclusively German and, except for Romania, the Baltic lands and (briefly) Hungary, outside of Outremer it held estates only in Germany itself.

Officially the Order's headquarters was always at Acre, despite the fact that the Templars drove them out of the city on one occasion, but their chief stronghold from 1229 until 1271 was actually Montfort, which they renamed Starkenberg. However, in Syria the Order was always very much overshadowed by the Temple and the Hospital, and it instead concentrated most of its attentions in the Levant on enterprises in Cilicia, where the main fortresses amongst its many possessions were Adamodana and Harunia. Even so, Teutonic contingents were present at most major engagements of the 13th century including Bahr Ashmun (1221), La Forbie (1244) and El Mansurah (1250). Fifteen brethren were present at the fall of Acre in 1291, of whom only the Order's *Hochmeister* or Grand Master escaped alive. The Order thereafter transferred its headquarters to Venice before moving on to Marienburg in Prussia in 1308.

Like the Templars and Hospitallers, the Teutonic Knights employed large numbers of Turcopoles, these probably supplying the bulk of the allegedly 300-strong Teutonic contingent at La Forbie and certainly comprising the greatest part of Starkenberg's garrison at its fall in 1271. They also had brother sergeants, confrère brethren (called *halbbruders*), mercenaries and the vassals of the Order's estates.

The Hospitallers of St Lazarus

After the Temple and the Hospital the Order of St Lazarus or St Ladre was the third Military Order to be established in Outremer. Like the two main Orders it had commanderies in Europe (eg, Burton Lazars in Leicestershire) as well as Syria, where it had houses in Jerusalem, Acre, Ascalon, Tiberias, Caesarea and Beirut. This was essentially a Hospital Order concentrating on the treatment of leprosy and was probably established as an offshoot by the Hospitallers themselves during the second decade of the 12th century, turning military by mid-century (one authority says circa 1123). Templar brethren who contracted leprosy were transferred to the Lazars, as probably were Hospitallers, and even lay knights who contracted this disease had to join the Order (although they had first to provide substitutes to render service for their fiefs).

The Master of the Order was said to have been a leper himself, as were the brethren-at-arms, but as well as these unclean brethren there were also non-lepers, although the number of military brethren was never particularly high and Jean Sire de Joinville's statement about the Master of St Lazarus 'who held no rank in the army' best sums up their military importance. Nevertheless a Lazar contingent was present, and wiped out, at La Forbie, while in 1253 they formed part of the army under St Louis which encamped before Jaffa, an impetuous attack led by their Master seeing all but four of the brethren killed. In 1291 25 brethren were present at Acre, all of whom were killed. The Order ceased to involve itself in military activities from the early 14th century.

The Hospitallers of St Thomas Acon

The Hospitallers of St Thomas of Canterbury at Acre, usually called the Knights of St Thomas Acon, were established in Acre as a nursing Order after the recapture of the city by King Richard I of England and King Philip II of France in 1191. Membership was restricted to Englishmen and it was always a small Order, probably not turning military until the Fifth Crusade of 1217-1221 or possibly even as late as Prince Edward's Crusade of 1271, the nine brethren present and killed at Acre in 1291 being adequate testimony of its military potential. After the fall of Acre they established a preceptory in Cyprus and with the Hospitallers and Templars held some fortresses there, but thereafter the Order underwent a gradual military decline.

The Knights of Our Lady of Montjoie

Named after a hill outside Jerusalem, this Order was established in Spain in 1175 by Count Rodrigo Alvarez of Sarria in Leon, an ex-Santiagan knight, and received its first grants in Outremer (from Baldwin IV) the next year on condition that he and his followers would commit themselves to the fight against the Moslems in the East. The Order held property in Spain and Italy but was not of considerable consequence in Outremer, although Sibylla (later Queen Sibylla) assigned them four towers in Ascalon in 1177, and in 1180 the Prince of Antioch was prepared to grant them castles in his principality, although he apparently never did. After 1180 the eastern sources make no further mention of the Order, although one authority says a small contingent of its brethren was present at Hattin.

Whichever is the case, the Order did not prosper in the East, withdrawing to its commanderies in Aragon soon after the Frankish defeat of 1187. Amalgamation with the Temple was proposed in 1186 but did not take place until 1196, the Order joining itself to the Hospital of the Holy Redeemer, another Spanish order, in the meantime (1188). In Spain they became known as the Order of Trufac.

Other Orders

A few other lesser Orders are known either from contemporary crusader maps or references to the final siege of Acre in 1291. These include the Order of the Trinity, Order of the Sword, Order of the Holy Spirit and Order of St Lawrence of the Knights, about all of which little or nothing is known.

Chapter 6

The Assassins

Although most people have probably heard of the Assassins, most of what they have seen in films or read in novels is fiction, or at best a subtle distortion of fact. Their true nature and origin requires a little more explanation, which we must begin by backtracking a few centuries to the year of the Prophet Mohammed's death, 632, when one of his earliest disciples, Abu Bekr, was appointed as his successor. Agreement on Abu Bekr's election, however, had not been unanimous, many Moslems maintaining that the claim of Mohammed's cousin and son-in-law Ali was stronger; this faction was consequently called the 'the party of Ali', the *Shiatu Ali*, a name soon shortened to *Shia*. Without entering into the complexities of the politico-religious discord they represented it should be understood that these *Shiites* came in time to differ fundamentally in beliefs and doctrine from the orthodox or *Sunni* Moslems, and their political party very soon evolved into a religious sect. Later, after 765, the Shiites themselves split into two factions which can be described most simply as moderates and extremists, and although the latter were the minority it is with them that we are here concerned. They were called *Ismailis* after their leader Ismail, and their sect, operating often—by necessity—in secret, soon achieved a high degree of internal organisation; and after the 11th century the Ismailis in Syria were to become known as—you've guessed it—Assassins.

It was in the second half of the 11th century that the Ismaili movement gained fresh momentum under the leadership of a Persian convert named Hasan-i Sabbah, who promulgated a new doctrine, the *dawa jadida* or 'new preaching', which advocated rejection of the world as it stood, in so doing promoting revolution and violent change within the Moslem world. By 1090 he had established himself in the inaccessible fortress of Alamut ('Eagle's Teaching', so-named because an eagle is alleged to have revealed its strategic value to an ancient king) in the mountains of Daylam in modern Iran, and a phase of Ismaili fortress-seizing and building ensued in the surrounding Rudbar region, culminating in the possession of some 35-40 forts, followed by similar conquests in Quhistan (70 forts) and Syria (ten forts by circa 1150), with a single isolated fortress at Gird Kuh in Qumis. The reign of the Assassins had begun.

Not that the Persian Ismailis were ever known as Assassins—as already mentioned, this name was localised to Syria—but they might just as well have been, because assassination, well-suited to their revolutionary values, was from the outset a major weapon in the resurgent Ismaili political armoury. Their first murder took place late in 1091, and the first of their truly *political* assassinations in October the next year, the execution of no less a personage than the famous Seljuk vizier Nizam al-Mulk. Thereby began a 'war of terror'. Indeed the Ismailis or Assassins may be fairly considered as the world's first terrorists in the modern sense of the word, the ancestors of today's Red Brigade, Black September and Baader-Meinhof gangs in their planned and systematic use of terror as the ultimate political weapon.

Understandably, then, the word 'assassin' and its meaning found their way into our own and most other European languages as a result of the Ismailis' activities. The word itself actually derived, via Ashishini, Assassini, Heyssisini and other variants, from the Arabic *hashishi* and its plural *hashishiyyun*, referring to the narcotic drug hashish. Probably the frequent reference to Syrian Ismailis as hashishi by Moslem contemporaries* was intended as a form of abuse, a comment on their unorthodox beliefs and activities, much like we might refer to a pipe-dreamer without intending that the individual should be understood as a 'pot-head'. It was fairly certainly *not* intended to imply that Assassins about to make a 'hit' were stoned up to their eyeballs on hashish! By the 13th century, then, 'assassin' had passed into common European usage and, although a 14th century editor defined its meaning as 'one who kills others for money', its modern-day meaning remains largely true to the activities and tenets of the mediaeval Ismailis— a murderer motivated by fanaticism and radical beliefs who kills public figures by stealth and treachery.

The Ismailis' main targets were rulers, military officers, state officials and anti-Ismailian theologians, and their assassinations were often dramatic, taking place under the noses of friends, guards and families in mosque or court or other public places. One of their main ideals in committing these murders was tyrannicide, the removal of unworthy or unrighteous leaders, a motive still claimed by their terrorist descendants today. In execution their assassinations were almost ritualistic; only the knife was ever used and a new knife was issued for each murder, sometimes, apparently, with the name of the victim engraved on the blade, but not—despite what several sources imply—poisoned. The murder itself was regarded as a pious deed which the perpetrator made no attempt to shirk, even though he knew he would almost certainly die in its execution—'without considering the consequences of the deed nor the possibility of escape' as William of Tyre puts it. 'The most blessed,' so their leader claimed, 'are those who shed the blood of men and, in revenge for such deeds, themselves suffer death.'

Western writers sought to explain this by stories of a promised paradise, with the Assassin initiates being drugged (with hashish) and carried into a secret beautiful garden, which they were told was heaven; and the only way to attain it again thereafter was by being killed in the service of their Grand Master. It is certainly likely that by being killed thus they believed they would, like all good martyrs, go to paradise, but it is perhaps more relevant to take this fatalism as an indication of the extent of their obedience, loyalty and devotion. Another story repeated in various forms in a number of western sources provides further evidence of their unquestioning obedience, relating how on their Master's word of command a number of Assassins calmly leapt to their deaths from the battle-

---

* Most Moslem sources actually refer to the Assassins by their alternative names of *Nizaris* or *Batinis*, or occasionally *Malahida* ('heretics'). The term Assassin itself is to be found chiefly in the Christian and Jewish sources.

ments of his fortress, merely for the edification of his guests.

Those Ismailis who actually carried out the assassinations were called *fidais* (devotees) or *fidawis* (those ready to offer their lives for a cause), apparently trained from early youth until they attained manhood—Marco Polo says from the age of 12 until they were 20; in Persia these possibly came to represent a distinct group within the Ismaili movement, but not so in Syria where any Ismaili was considered capable of such tasks. Among themselves the bulk of Assassins referred to each other as *rufaqa* or 'comrades'. The only other grade of Ismaili that we encounter regularly in the sources is the *dai* or 'propagandist', who is usually out and about trying to drum up converts to the Ismaili faith. The total number of Ismailis during this era is unknown, but those of Syria appear to have numbered 40-60,000 souls, men, women and children. A source which claims they raised 10,000 men against the Franks in 1128 is probably over-optimistic, this more probably representing the total number of able-bodied men available for military service; for unlike all their Moslem neighbours the Ismailis did not employ mamluk slave-soldiers but relied entirely on the service of their own followers for both cavalry and infantry, the former being supplied by the wealthier among them. Pay appears to have been largely in the form of booty. They were clearly fierce fighters much feared by their adversaries, and we hear more than once of Sunni Moslem troops fleeing before them ere a blow had been struck.

They do not seem to have worn any form of distinctive dress, although one description mentions Syrian Assassins dressed in white clothes. Fidais on a job more often than not wore disguises anyway, suited to their particular assignment, and in various anecdotes they are to be found dressed as Frankish and Turkish soldiers, Syrian Christians, courtiers, merchants, monks, sufis and religious ascetics. They apparently even learnt to speak the appropriate languages, including Latin, Greek, Italian, French, dialects of Arabic and many others. That the man standing beside him might turn out to be a fidai must have therefore been the recurrent nightmare of each and every man who crossed the Assassins.

The Assassins of Syria, with whom we are primarily concerned here, at first operated from Aleppo, until 1113, and then Damascus until 1130, but both phases of their operations ended in suppression and considerable bloodshed, as many as 6,000 to 20,000 Ismailis allegedly being massacred in Damascus. Their final establishment in Syria dates to 1132, when the amir of al-Kahf in the mountain area called Jabal Bahra (today's Jabal Ansariyya) sold them the fortress of al-Qadmus, al-Kahf itself being ceded to them by his son a few years later. Kharibah was captured from the Franks in 1136 or 1137, and Masyaf—the most important of the Assassins' Syrian strongholds—was captured from the Banu Munqidh (Usamah's family) in 1141. Other fortresses captured in the same area at about this time included al-Khawabi (Coible), ar-Rusafa, Qulaia (Coliath) and al-Maniqah. Ollaiqa was added later under their most famous leader Sinan ibn Salman ibn Mohammed, known as Raschid al-Din but referred to in Frankish sources as Le Vieux de la Montagne, 'the Old Man of the Mountain'; in Moslem sources he is described simply as the Sheikh, meaning 'old man' or 'elder'. He was educated at Alamut with the future Grand Master Hasan, who sent him to Syria in about 1155. On Hasan's succession to the Ismaili leadership at Alamut (1162) Sinan revealed himself as his deputy in Syria, although after Hasan's death in 1166 Sinan threw off the overlordship of

Alamut and pursued an independent policy and doctrine, killing various Ismaili emissaries who were sent from Persia to assassinate *him*!

Although some fighting took place between the Assassins and the Franks (for example at Marj es-Safar in 1126, al-Maniqah in 1151 and Shaizar in 1157), it should be pointed out that until the 13th century the Assassins were invariably more interested in knocking off Sunni Moslems than they were Franks. At first Sinan's principal foe was Nur ed-Din, the Moslem King of Aleppo who, although warned off by having an Assassin dagger left on his pillow while he slept, was actually planning an attack on the Ismailis' Syrian strongholds when he died in 1174. The vacancy he left behind as the Assassins' chief enemy was easily filled by Saladin, a devout and orthodox champion of Islam. His determination to unite Islam and stamp out heresy forced the Ismailis into a much closer relationship with the anti-Ayyubid Zengids of Mosul and Aleppo than they would have previously entertained and in 1175, as Saladin laid siege to Aleppo, Assassins entered his camp to murder him at the instigation of the city's atabeg. Unfortunately (or fortunately according to your convictions) a local amir recognised and intercepted them, was promptly knifed, and in the ensuing mêlée all of the Assassins were killed, the last being cut down in the very act of entering Saladin's tent.

There was a second attempt on his life the next year during the siege of Azaz. This time he was resting in the tent of one of his senior amirs when an Assassin, disguised as one of his own soldiers, dashed in and struck him on the head with a knife, which would have been a fatal blow but for the fact that the sultan was wearing a mail cap beneath his turban. A second blow, this time to the neck, was frustrated by the mail collar of his *kuzaghand* (a type of armour), and before a third blow could be struck one of Saladin's attendants grabbed the knife by its blade, cutting his fingers to the bone in the process, and despatched the Assassin. Two more Assassins followed the first into the tent, but by now Saladin's amirs had recovered from their initial surprise and the attackers were killed, as too were some of the sultan's officers.

The contemporary Moslem historian Kemal ad-Din reported that kings took care not to attack Sinan's territory 'for fear of the murderous attacks of his henchmen'. Both these attempts on Saladin's life were therefore probably in revenge for his attacks on Ismailis at Sarmin, Maarrat Nasrin and elsewhere in 1174-1175, and it was coincidental that the first also suited the atabeg of Aleppo's plans. The Assassins of this era were not, after all, 'daggers for hire', although where their aims coincided with those of third parties they were often prepared to accept payment for murders which they had already planned. Third parties, such as the Zengids of Mosul and Aleppo already mentioned, were frequently prepared to enlist Assassin aid to their own ends, irrespective of religious convictions, complying with their aims for as long as it proved expedient (and safe—which it was not always). Some stories of such complicity by third parties, such as were extracted from Assassin prisoners under torture, were probably, in fact almost certainly, untrue, and it is equally likely that the Assassins were accused of (and claimed, in order to further their reputation) murders with which they did not have the slightest connection.

It is interesting to surmise what would have happened if the Assassins *had* been successful in their attacks on Saladin. Certainly there was no other Moslem leader with the personality or strength to replace him at that time, and it seems likely that the Moslem unity for which he strove would have taken decades longer to achieve, with the power of the Franks undiminished by the major defeat which only Saladin could inflict upon them; Hattin would never have happened, and in fact the tables could have been reversed to the point where, conceivably, a Frankish invasion of leaderless Egypt would have resulted, in time, in a total Frankish victory. But Saladin's armour had saved him. Probably he had been wearing it since the first attempt on his life in 1175, in the same way that most Seljuk princes and officers in the East were wearing armour under their clothes for fear of Assassins as early as 1100. However, what must have been most unnerving of all was that the three Assassins cut down at Azaz were not only *dressed* like Saladin's own soldiers, *but had actually been recruited into his personal bodyguard*!

As a further precaution he now took to sleeping in a specially-constructed wooden bunk built like a tower, and in addition would allow nobody to approach him who he did not know. He also marched on the Assassin stronghold of Masyaf itself, encamping before its walls in August 1176 while the Old Man was away. Sinan now seems to have adopted a new policy, toying with the sultan but apparently no longer intent on killing him. It is probably to this stage in the proceedings that a story recorded by Kemal ad-Din belongs. He records how Sinan sent an envoy to Saladin with a message that was to be delivered only in private. Saladin, understandably cautious, had the messenger searched then dismissed most of his courtiers, retaining only his guards. The messenger, however, reminded him that the message was for his ears alone, so Saladin dismissed all but two of his mamluks and demanded that the Assassin should now give his message. Again the messenger repeated that he was to speak alone with Saladin. 'These two are not leaving,' said the sultan. 'Deliver your message if you so wish, otherwise begone.' 'Why don't you send these two away like you did the others?' asked the messenger. 'I look upon these men as if they were my own sons,' replied Saladin, 'and they and I are like one.' Then the messenger turned to the mamluks and said, 'If I were to order you in the name of my master to kill this sultan, would you?' Saladin could not have expected their answer: 'Yes,' they said, drawing their swords, 'command us as you wish.' And the messenger, presumably having thus delivered his message, turned and left, taking the two mamluks with him.

Saladin must have mistrusted his guards for some time to come after these two episodes, for the two mamluks in the latter instance were undoubtedly what in modern espionage parlance would be called 'sleepers,' planted in Saladin's court Heaven alone knows how long before. We hear of such Assassin sleepers on numerous other occasions too, sprinkled throughout the enemy's camps and courts for prolonged periods of time, years even, gaining their victims' confidence and trust, harmless until, at the chosen moment, they received their final instructions to kill. Patience apparently came easy to them and was undoubtedly part of their strict training. So bodyguards were not always the answer, and Saladin was not the first to discover it; Toghtekin's successor Buri was mortally wounded in 1131 by two Assassins dressed as Turkish soldiers who were enrolled in the special heavily armed guard which he had recruited to protect himself *from Assassins*. Some people were born losers. The only solution to this sort of problem was, as the author of a French crusading treatise realised in 1332, that you should employ no-one in your household 'save those whose country, place, lineage, condition and person are certainly, thoroughly and clearly known.' Even then, it seems likely that an Assassin could infiltrate their ranks or bribe another to do the job.

Although shaken, Saladin was not yet beaten. Hearing that Sinan was over-looking his camp from a nearby hill, accompanied by only two attendants, the sultan ordered his guards to kill or capture him. But they returned empty-handed, claiming that the Old Man had used powerful magic that stopped them in their tracks and rendered their weapons useless (shades of fantasy wargaming!). This seems to have disturbed Saladin even more, and that evening he surrounded his tent with a carpet of chalk dust and ashes to record whether or not anyone was creeping around it at night. The next few nights passed without incident, but then late one night he awoke suddenly just in time to see someone glide out of the tent. On the pillow beside his head lay some hot scones characteristic of those baked by Ismailis, together with an Assassin dagger and a note bearing threatening verse—probably something on the lines of that left on Sultan Sanjar's pillow nearly 60 years before: 'If I did not wish the sultan well the dagger which was stuck into the hard ground would have been thrust into his soft breast.'

Rushing outside Saladin found that the intruder's feet had left no marks in the ashes and chalk dust (probably because, as seems likely from other similar instances, one of Saladin's attendants quartered elsewhere in his pavilion had been bribed to heat the scones and been given the dagger to leave on his master's pillow). But Saladin was convinced that Sinan himself had visited him that night; for the Old Man was, after all, acredited with other magical skills such as stopping falling rocks and casting no reflection on the surface of water. He was also supposed to be telepathic and clairvoyant, knowing immediately whatever befell his fidais and being able to answer by a simple 'yes' or 'no' questions which were thought but unasked. For Saladin it was the last straw; he appears to have thereafter come to some tacit understanding with Sinan in exchange for raising his siege of Masyaf, and was never again bothered by nocturnal visitations.

The last major success of Sinan's career, and that about which there is the most conjecture, was the murder of Conrad of Montferrat in the streets of Tyre in 1192. As already stated, the Ismailis were not particularly interested in the assassination of Franks (their first murder of a Frank, Raymond II of Tripoli, dates only to 1152), and such contracts as they did fulfil on Frankish leaders were probably at the instigation of third parties. Who the third party was on this occasion is where the conjecture enters into it. Of his two murderers, disguised as monks, one was taken alive and when 'questioned' confessed that Conrad's political opponent King Richard of England had instigated the attack. However, a pro-Zengid source states quite categorically that Saladin was the instigator and that the stories of Richard's involvement resulted quite simply from the current (and mistaken) opinion that was widespread amongst the Franks, adding that Richard too was to have been killed. A much later Ismaili source claims that the idea was Sinan's but received Saladin's blessing.

All in all it is undeniable that Richard had the most to gain from his rival's death since Conrad, as well as being his political enemy, was in communication with Saladin at the time of his death; and interestingly Philip II of France, prior to his own departure for home the previous year, had been in fear for his own life at Richard's hands, actually sending an envoy to Sinan for assurance that the Assassins were not plotting his death on Richard's behalf. Besides, it is also hard to see what advantage Saladin stood to gain by removing such a thorn from Richard's side. Certainly English chroniclers of the event were overcome with a sudden compulsion to forge letters, ostensibly written by Sinan, claiming responsibility for Conrad's death. And King Richard, continuously accused of training his own assassins on the model of Sinan's, actually found it necessary on his return to England to hire 15 villains to plead guilty to partaking in such operations against himself. Methinks he doth protest too much . . .

Sinan died a year later in 1193, to be succeeded by a Persian named Nasr who restored the Syrian Ismailis to the fold of Alamut. Thereafter no further assassinations of Moslems are recorded in Syria, only Franks. Instead the Assassins finally began to cash in on their reputation, exacting payments from both Frankish and Sunni Moslem leaders under threat of assassination. Frederick II's emissaries allegedly paid as much as 80,000 dinars in 1227 in exchange for a promise of safe conduct for the Emperor during his Crusade, and the Sultan of Rum paid an annual 'protection' tribute of 2,000 dinars. Joinville records that the Assassin emissaries sent to Louis IX at Acre similarly demanded tribute for their master, stating that the Holy Roman Emperor, the King of Hungary, the Sultan of Egypt and others (King Alfonso of Castile and the kings of Yemen are mentioned in other sources) did so each year 'because they know that they can only live as long as it pleases him.'

Strangely, the Assassins in turn paid tribute to the Military Orders of Hospital and Temple even while this was going on. The Orders had exacted their pound of flesh annually from many Ismaili villages and strongholds since the mid-12th century, clearly not in the least concerned by the danger of Assassin retaliation. Joinville explains this by the fact that if a Hospitaller or Templar officer were murdered he would simply be replaced by another just as good, and the Assassins would have lost a couple of valuable fidais for nothing; not good business sense, as the Old Man must have sensibly concluded.

It was the Mamluk sultan Baibars who finally suppressed the Syrian Assassins, acquiring the last of their fortresses by 1273. Disheartened by the fate of their Persian brethren at the hands of the Mongols (who had destroyed Alamut in 1257) the Syrian Assassins had acquiesced to his demands for tribute, and very soon he appointed and dismissed their officers just as their master at Alamut had once done. During these last years the Assassins' special talents were at Baibars' disposal, and he took full advantage of them. In April 1271 he is reported to have threatened Bohemond VI of Tripoli with assassination (which is interesting since in the same year two Assassins were arrested attempting to murder Baibars at Bohemond's instigation!), and possibly the murder of Philip of Montfort in 1270, and certainly the attempted murder of Prince Edward of England in 1272 were carried out on his orders.

Even in the 14th century the Mamluk sultans were still using Ismaili assassins, but their strength was gone and they were now little more than a shady variety of civil servant. The Assassins had become, as one source succinctly put it, 'but a tale on men's lips and a legend in the world'. Even so, the Ismailis are still with us even today, and their spiritual leader, directly descended from Hasan-i Sabbah's immediate successor Buzurgummid, is no less a person than the fabled and immensely wealthy Aga Khan.

Chapter 7

The Byzantine connection

Incongruous though it may seem that Romans should have had anything what-soever to do with the Crusades, the fact remains that they did, and indeed were responsible, indirectly at least, for the whole Crusade movement. Nevertheless, most people do not associate Romans with the mediaeval era at all, usually stating blithely that the Roman Empire fell in 476, which is true enough; but that was only the Western half. The Eastern Roman Empire persisted for another thousand years, right up until 1453, and the only reason that most people remain unaware of this remarkable fact is that, by some quirk of historical convention, historians today refer to the East Romans as 'Byzantines', and to their empire as the 'Byzantine' Empire, curiously deriving this name from the town of Byzantion which had nevertheless been renamed Constantinople (modern Istanbul) as long ago as the 4th century! Although they spoke Greek rather than Latin and were of diverse ethnic origins, the Byzantines justifiably continued throughout this era to regard themselves as true Romans, *Rhomaioi*, and inasmuch as the so-called 'Byzantine' Empire was descended in a direct and uninterrupted line from the Eastern half of the Roman Empire their claim is irrefutable. The Moslems too referred to them as Romans and to their Empire as the lands of *Rum*, and indeed none of their contemporaries *ever* called them 'Byzantines'. For this reason if for no other I would personally prefer to call them East Romans but, alas, so well established is the 'Byzantine' convention that, paradoxically enough, for many their real name no longer rings true.

They had their own sophisticated systems of military organisation and tactics which I do not intend to go into in detail here, for the simple reason that to cover them adequately would take up as much as a third of this book, and their actual role in the history of the Crusades was not sufficiently great to justify this. Suffice it to say that they relied heavily on mercenaries by the end of the 11th century, although there were also regular regiments of native Byzantine soldiers (largely cavalry) receiving regular monthly salaries, those in the provinces also receiving grants of land on which to maintain themselves. The latter were called *pronoiai* and were rather like fiefs in that the holder, called a *stratiotes* or *pronoiarios*, had to provide military service with a predetermined number of men in exchange for his holding. The central guard regiments, based in Constantinople, were largely mercenary, the Vardariots (a Turkish regiment from Bulgaria) and the famous Varangian Guard of Scandinavians and, later, Englishmen, forming the nucleus. Their salary scale was probably similar to that of the Franks; I would guess at infantry receiving 2-3 nomismata per month, cavalry 8-12 nomismata, guard cavalry 12-24 nomismata, and Varangians 16-32 nomismata, with officers receiving more and mercenaries too probably being paid at a slightly higher rate, probably two nomismata on the basic or as much more as was necessary to ensure their services! A fuller description of Byzantine army organisation of this era can be found in *Armies and Enemies of the Crusades 1096-1291*. The Byzantine navy, on the other hand, which played a rather more active part in the Crusades than did the army, is described in some detail in Chapter 11.

The Byzantine connection with the Crusades ultimately dates right back to 638, the year that the all-conquering Moslems had made their victorious entry into Jerusalem. The rest of the Holy Land was in Arab hands by 639, Caesarea being the very last Palestinian Byzantine stronghold to fall. The loss of Syria was followed by Egypt, lost by 642, and Mesopotamia by 646, while further East the whole Sassanid Empire of Persia was completely overrun by 649. The Byzantine Empire had therefore become, in the short space of two decades, the eastern bastion of Christendom, standing virtually alone against the Moslems, a situation which was to persist—despite frequent fluctuations in the Empire's fortunes—for the next eight centuries. After two unsuccessful if prolonged Arab assaults on Constantinople in 668-675 and 717-718 it was not until 1071 that the Empire's status as the protector of Christendom was again seriously threatened. In that year the Byzantine army, ill-equipped and poorly trained as a result of severe cutbacks in military expenditure, was virtually annihilated by the Seljuk Turks on the field of Manzikert, near Lake Van in Armenia, a disaster from which the Empire never fully recovered. Over the next few years the Turks poured into the Anatolian vacuum that Manzikert had created, establishing the foundations of the Sultanate of Rum through which the pilgrims of the First and Second Crusades would later have to hack their way en route to Syria and Palestine. As Sir Steven Runciman observed, Manzikert was the single most decisive disaster in the history of the Empire: 'To the later Crusaders it seemed that the Byzantines had forfeited on the battlefield their title as the protectors of Christendom. Manzikert justified the intervention of the West.'*

That intervention was longer in coming than might have been expected, and when it did materialise it was largely at the prompting of the Byzantines themselves. The first competent Emperor to succeed to the throne after Manzikert was Alexius I Comnenus, made famous by the biographical *Alexiad* written in the 12th century by his daughter Anna. He was a shrewd politician as well as an extremely capable soldier, having fought his own way to the Imperial throne in 1081. By the middle of the last decade of the 11th century Seljuk power was on the decline and Alexius' armies were scoring some notable successes against the Turks on his borders. But the Empire was short of soldiers, its Anatolian heartlands, once the army's principal recruiting ground, still being in Seljuk hands. Alexius therefore sent ambassadors to the West, to the great Council of Piacenza called by Pope Urban II in 1095, to plead for mercenary aid in the never-ending struggle between Christian and Moslem. There was nothing new to the Byzantines about the idea of employing foreign mercenaries in this way—as mentioned earlier, almost their whole army was comprised of various mercenary

* *A History of the Crusades 1: The First Crusade*, Cambridge University Press, 1951.

1 & 2 *12th century Byzantine cavalryman and heavy infantryman in typical short corselets of scale and lamellar respectively; lances were generally some ten to 12 feet long and shields were normally kite-shaped.* **3** *Patzinak mercenary light cavalryman.* **4** *Varangian Guardsman armed with the characteristic two-handed Scandinavian axe; the shield could be round or kite-shaped.*

contingents, notably Patzinaks, Cumans and Varangians (by now comprised of Anglo-Danish emigrés as well as Scandinavians)—and Franks, largely of Norman or French extraction, had been in Byzantine employ since 1038, a notable Frankish leader, Count Robert I of Flanders, having supplied Alexius with 500 mercenaries as recently as circa 1090. Even so, it is unlikely that Alexius ever anticipated that the response to his appeal should have been so vast or so universal, and the resultant First Crusade was beyond his wildest expectations.

Alas, these crusaders were also beyond management, and in their overland march they looted and pillaged Byzantine territory almost at will, skirmishing on a number of occasions with the Patzinaks sent to escort them. The haughtiness of the Frankish leaders, among them Bohemond of Taranto, an erstwhile enemy of the Empire, did little to encourage mutual trust or understanding, and it is clear from the outset that both sides regarded the military alliance of West and East against the Moslems as one of temporary convenience. A series of misunderstandings, coupled with Byzantine diplomatic manoeuvres which the Franks neither liked nor understood, nurtured in the latter a growing contempt for their devious 'two-faced' allies which was to grow steadily throughout the 12th century and culminate in the tragic sack of Constantinople in the so-called Fourth Crusade. However, that is jumping ahead rather too far.

Insidious anti-Byzantine propaganda was generated en masse after 1096, much of it instigated by Bohemond who, disregarding promises made to Alexius that any ex-Byzantine territory recaptured would be held in fief from the Empire, failed to acknowledge Imperial suzerainty over Antioch, which he seized in 1098. Antioch thereafter remained a bone of contention right up until 1176, when the defeat of the Byzantines at Myriokephalon in Anatolia by the Seljuks put an end to the Empire's ability to lay claim to the ex-provincial capital. John II was the first Emperor to have had any success in that particular dispute, forcibly imposing Imperial authority over Antioch in 1138, after which a combined Byzantino-Frankish force went on to capture several fortresses including Athareb and Kafartab, even briefly laying siege to Aleppo and Shaizar; it was actually proposed that if the Imperial forces should be successful in capturing these two cities, together with Homs and Hamah, then the whole kit and caboodle should be assigned to the Franks as a new principality in exchange for the return of Antioch to the Byzantines.

The pro-Frankish Emperor Manuel had to reassert Imperial authority over Cilicia and Northern Syria in 1159, the year in which a formal alliance was finally established between the Empire and the Kingdom of Jerusalem. Although a proposed joint assault on Aleppo failed to materialise, the treaty fairly certainly remained in force. In 1161, for instance, a combined force of Byzantines from Cilicia and Franks from Jerusalem and Antioch under the overall command of a Byzantine general, John Kontostephanos, routed a band of Rumi Seljuks, and in 1164 a similar force, this time of Franks from Antioch and Tripoli, and Byzantines and Armenians from Cilicia (still nominally a Byzantine province) interrupted Nur ed-Din's siege of Harenc, only to be defeated and all but decimated.

The last actual joint venture was an expedition against Damietta in Egypt in 1169, doomed to failure from the outset by the Franks' initial lethargy and, later, their distrust of Byzantine motives. The entire Byzantine fleet of some 220 ships under the *Megas Dux* or Grand Admiral was involved in this affair, plus a large force of soldiers who were disembarked at Acre to march overland to Damietta alongside the Franks. Difficulties arose almost immediately because King Amalric was not ready to set out straight away, and since Emperor Manuel, anticipating a swift surprise attack, had only issued his fleet with three months' rations the Byzantines had almost exhausted their supplies even before the assault began, and their Frankish allies, although themselves well provisioned, refused to help them out (and they accused the *Byzantines* of being two-faced!). Urged on by their dwindling supplies the Byzantines repeatedly begged Amalric to chance a full-scale assault on Damietta's walls, but the king steadfastly declined; he pointed out the risks involved, in which he may have been acting on the advice of his nobles, who had put about a rumour that the Byzantines' zeal resulted from a desire to have Damietta for themselves. Inevitably in the face of such disaffection there was no hope of the venture succeeding and negotiations (opened by the Byzantines according to the Franks, and by the Franks according to the Byzantines) led to the besiegers being bought off with Moslem gold.

Disillusioned though he may have been, in 1177 Manuel nevertheless again offered the services of his fleet for a joint Byzantino-Frankish expedition against Egypt in conjunction with the crusade of a leading French nobleman, Count Philip of Flanders. Philip, however, inexplicably refused to participate, as a result of which the project was shelved. Since Manuel died only a few years later the Franks' last opportunity to establish a meaningful Latin-Byzantine relationship was lost. And, be it noted, through no fault of the Byzantines.

Relations between the two powers thereafter steadily worsened. The Franks never had understood how the Byzantines could enrol the same Turks in their army as they had themselves come out East to fight, and nor could they comprehend the political manoeuvres and skullduggery by which the Empire would make and break treaties with the Moslems as needs dictated. To the less subtle Franks such alliances with the infidel were perfidious treachery, and certainly it would be hard for any brash European to interpret complex diplomatic treaties that arranged the loan of troops to Moslem states—such as 20,000 men promised by John to Ilghazi of Mardin in 1121—as anything less than alliances against Outremer. But the fact remains that no such force was ever mustered or ever marched against the Franks. Such treaties were simply empty promises which bought the Empire time or safety without loss of life or territory.

The Franks, however, never saw them that way and were persistently outraged by the Byzantines' guile and duplicity. What made the situation even worse was the fact that the Byzantine church was schismatic and did not recognise the authority of the See of Rome, and that, together with the fact that the Empire controlled trade from the East, was sufficient excuse for a combined force of crusaders and Venetians to attack and pillage Constantinople in the infamous Fourth Crusade, setting up their own Latin Empire amidst its ruins. Admittedly the Empire of Romania, as it was styled, lasted only to 1261, but its very existence even for that length of time was of genuine disservice to Outremer in that it competed for the already insufficient manpower that was available to the Frankish East. The chronicler Ernoul specifically tells us that between 1205 and 1210 a hundred knights and 10,000 other Franks left Syria for the comparative safety of the Latin Empire.

The Fourth Crusade tore the very heart out of the Empire, and although it failed to completely overrun the Byzantines' possessions it nevertheless ended the Empire's career as a world super-power. The Franks could not have realised it, but they had also removed the one real deterrent against Moslem expansion. Certainly the Moslems themselves had never been in any doubts about the Empire's potential and they, unlike the Franks, had a healthy respect for the Imperial army; Ibn al-Qalanisi, a 12th century Damascene chronicler, reported in 1138 that when the Byzantine army withdrew 'all hearts were set at rest after their distress and fear', while Ibn al-Athir mentions that the Byzantines were the most formidable element in a Christian army which defeated Nur ed-Din outside Krak des Chevaliers in 1163, and a year later Nur was again particularly alarmed by the presence of Byzantine troops in the army he defeated at Artah. A little tolerance and understanding on the Franks' part, then, might well have ensured not only Outremer's guaranteed survival but also the Empire's, perhaps even to the present day. What a different world we might have lived in!

Chapter 8

Supply and attrition

In any war and any country the availability of supplies was and still is the single severest handicap on the movements of an army. In countries like Syria and Palestine the problem was compounded by the summer drought, which unfortunately coincided with the campaigning season, so that the principal consideration for every general was access to adequate supplies of water. Armies therefore mustered or encamped at wells or springs wherever possible, to which the enemy understandably made every effort to deny them access. The Moslems—and no doubt the Franks too—even resorted on occasion to poisoning the wells, but that was a move of desperation since it denied the water to both sides. Between watering places water had to be carried in bottles and skins, slung from the shoulder or the saddle-bow or carried by pack-animals. A 19th century traveller reported that the maximum load a camel could carry was six full water-skins, enough for three men for three days which, as we shall see in the next chapter, was the usual distance between watering places.

Its own ability to survive in such an arid environment was, of course, the principal reason why the camel was the main beast of burden in the Levant for both military and mercantile transport. Camels can go without water for prolonged periods according to the season, from two to three days in the heat of high summer and seven to ten days in the spring to four to six *weeks* in the damp, mild winter when their 'green' food contains a reasonable amount of moisture. This compares very favourably indeed with the poor old horse, which needs at least one drink every 24 hours without fail to remain in peak condition. Camels are also useful for smelling out sources of water, but since they can move faster than a man they are likely to beat you to it and soil and muddy the water before you can get there! They might drink it dry too, for a camel that has gone thirsty for several days is likely to drink as much as *25 gallons* of water at a time. Female camels can give four or five litres (one gallon) of milk per day in excess of suckling requirements, which is useful if there is no water available. The majority of camels used by the Franks, however, were males, which are capable of less endurance than the females and were consequently used only as beasts of burden. Females, on the other hand, were and still are used exclusively as riding animals, in which role they are capable of about 12 mph (20 km/h) flat out. They can keep this speed up continuously for many hours, and will in fact keep going until they die of either thirst or exhaustion. There are even Bedouin tales of camels travelling 90-125 miles (150-200 km) a day for several days on end, usually dropping dead on arrival at their destination.

Other beasts of burden were provided by mules and asses and sometimes even pack-horses, all used rather less by the Moslems than the Franks. Wheeled vehicles were hardly ever used at all except for the transport of siege equipment. Large numbers of animals therefore accompanied most armies on the march, a single supply caravan captured by the Franks in 1192 including as many as 3,000-4,700 camels plus 3,000 or more mules, asses and horses. In addition there were the herds brought along to feed the troops, meat obviously being kept on the hoof for as long as possible. These comprised cattle, sheep and (in Christian armies only) pigs. Camels were also commonly eaten by the natives, and the Franks too ate them when rations ran short, Ambroise, an eye-witness of the Third Crusade, recording that the meat was white and savoury. Mules, donkeys and horses were also eaten in desperation, although the meat of horses that died of their wounds was often eaten not through need but rather to avoid unnecessary waste.

The meat herds fed themselves by grazing, but the working camels often had their diets supplemented by dates, barley cakes or little balls of a kind of dough, horses similarly having their diets supplemented with grain in winter. Horses and mules were generally rather more of a problem, however, in that they required more food, and that of a better quality, than did the camels, so that foraging parties often had to risk their lives scouring the hostile countryside for grass and fodder with which to satisfy them. The author of the *Itinerarium Peregrinorum*, another eye-witness account of the Third Crusade, observes of such foraging that the fodder gathered was not infrequently washed with the blood of the foragers 'owing to their lack of caution'. Yet so important was their horses' fodder that as early as 1098, during the siege of Antioch, Raymond de Saint-Gilles had offered to pay for any horse that was lost while protecting a foraging expedition.

Horses were in fact a severe liability for the Franks. They were vital to their mode of warfare and therefore extremely valuable. The average *destrier* (knight's war-horse) cost 40 bezants, the most expensive costing up to some 160 bezants, compared to a maximum cost of perhaps 30 bezants for a pack-mule and probably about ten bezants for a camel. They were in addition extremely vulnerable, both to the weather and to Moslem arrows.

Knights were generally accompanied by three or four horses, and mounted sergeants by two, but that did not make the loss of even one of them any easier to accept. So it is no surprise that the feudal custom of *restor,* by which an overlord agreed to pay compensation to any of his vassals for equipment lost on campaign, rapidly evolved in Outremer into a system by which horses lost in combat were replaced at his expense. We have already seen how Raymond de Saint-Gilles guaranteed the horses of foragers in 1098, and circa 1110 we find Tancred, Prince of Antioch, told by his men during a battle that they feared for their horses' safety, similarly promising to replace those killed—a promise he had cause to regret, since his men lost 70 horses when they returned to the fray!

The Marshal of the kingdom, the Constable's lieutenant, was responsible for assessing and replacing horses, which were all meticulously catalogued by the government office known as the Grant Secrete, and all in all the system worked well; but it did not altogether prevent situations such as one recorded in 1192 when a force of 100 knights sent out from Jaffa to intercept some Moslem scouts was largely mounted on mules. Alternatively, horses killed or wounded in battle could be replaced by those captured from the enemy, although the

Moslems were less likely than the Franks to compensate for their losses in this way since their archery usually took an even greater toll of horses than men. In the Frankish army captured horses were distributed at the Marshal's discretion. One last little anecdote before closing on the subject of horses, and one which amply demonstrates the kind of demands that were placed on a mediaeval commissariat: it is recorded that when King Richard set out on crusade in 1190 he took with him as many as *50,000* spare horseshoes!

It was not uncommon for both Moslem and Frankish armies to set out without their train of cattle and camels, although for different reasons. With the Moslems the reason was that once beyond their own frontier their armies lived chiefly off the land, a means of sustenance which, although ideally suited to rapid movement, was nevertheless impractical if they had to tarry long in any one place, the produce of a single locality being soon exhausted. This problem became particularly acute for Moslems and Franks alike during sieges, as we shall see in Chapter 12. Moslems travelling without baggage were, incidentally, effectively travelling without armour since this was normally kept with their supplies, only being donned immediately before battle.

The Franks, on the other hand, would sometimes set up their camp first and then issue orders for supplies to be made available from the merchants of the local towns, who would visit the camp regularly to trade their goods, sometimes even accompanying the army when it moved on to its next site. It was not uncommon for merchants to similarly attach themselves to Moslem armies. We hear, for instance, that when, after the fall of Acre to the Franks in 1191, Saladin's field-army had to swiftly abandon its camp, the merchants—who had established a bazaar of 'several thousand' shops—lost much of their stock because there were not enough camels and horses to shift it all. Similarly William of Tyre records 'cooks and bakers in the enemy's army and those who provided the market with all sorts of commodities' during Saladin's second siege of Kerak in 1184. The need for pack-animals could also be obviated by supply from an offshore fleet, or by each individual carrying his own rations. Both Moslem and Christian sources agree that a single man could carry enough provisions to supply his own needs for a month. The *Itinerarium* tells us that they were carried in bags slung round the neck, and from other sources it is apparent that these would have weighed about 60 lb (27.2 kg), this being in addition to the individual's arms and armour. By contrast pack-mules could carry about 250 lb (113.4 kg) and camels about 500 lb (226.8 kg).

The basic diet of the average Levantine was bread, meat, wine and sometimes fish, supplemented by fruit and leguminous and root vegetables according to availability. Frankish armies on the march frequently substituted for the bread a kind of biscuit *(biscoctum),* also popular on shipboard. Wine was drunk in much the same quantity then as tea and coffee are today. It was technically taboo to the Moslems, of course, but drunkenness was in fact widespread amongst the Turkish military elite, and an amir who did *not* drink was considered exceptional. On the whole each individual had to provide his own rations, though in the case of Frankish foreign expeditions this responsibility might be assumed by the king. Sustenance for a month probably cost one to two bezants or dinars a man, and twice as much for a horse. We know that the sustenance of an army for a proposed foreign expedition of 1139 was to have cost King Fulk 20,000 gold dinars per month. However, costs inevitably varied according to demand (see page 119), although the prices of staples such as meat, grain, wine, fruit, oils and fish were apparently controlled to an extent by the local Court of Burgesses. Nevertheless, provisions always became more expensive in winter, and Joinville explains that this was because the sea was more treacherous in the winter so that only limited commerce could take place.

Winter was not a good season for campaigning in the Levant. Roads turned into quagmires in the torrential rain and became impassable. Food became scarce. An eye-witness of the Third Crusade encapsulated all the evils of winter campaigning in a single paragraph: 'We were discomforted by heavy rain and unwholesome weather, owing to which a great many of our beasts of burden died. So great was the tempest and so heavy the downpour of rain, coupled with violent blasts of wind, that the stakes of our tents were torn up and whirled away, whilst our horses perished of cold and wet. A great part of our food and biscuit was spoiled, and the bacon grew rotten. Our armour and corselets became fouled with rust, and no amount of rubbing could restore their original brightness; clothes began to wear out, and a large number of people lost their health and were afflicted with great ills.'

Mind you, the same chronicler relates how during the summer months 'many, fainting from the heat and outwearied by the strain of the long march, dropped down dead and were buried where they fell', so it was the general hostility of the climate rather than any particular season which was responsible for claiming so many lives. Franks from Western Europe inevitably suffered the most from Syria's environmental extremes, but the Moslems and other natives were not immune to such natural calamities as climatic variations, famines and epidemics. One source records that allegedly three-quarters of Egypt's population succumbed to a famine that was followed by pestilence in 1201-1202.

Disease seems to have taken its toll to a greater or lesser degree during most campaigns, but never more so than during a siege, where shortages of fresh food and clean water in the close confinement of an encampment or fortress resulted in a veritable breeding ground for germs and bacteria. In the crusader camp before Acre there died of disease Queen Sibylla of Jerusalem, the Patriarch Heraclius, several archbishops, bishops and abbots and quite a number of counts and other great nobles including Count Thibauld of Blois and Count Philip of Flanders. Since these were the elite of the host, and therefore the best fed and best cared for, the total of fatalities amongst the common soldiers and pilgrims must have been horribly high. What the specific maladies were that they succumbed to we cannot be sure, but it seems likely that sunstroke and malaria were both fairly rampant, while King Richard and King Philip were seriously ill with—and many other leaders died of—a disease described as *arnaldia* or *leonardie* which caused the hair and nails to fall out, probably a form of Vincent's disease or trenchmouth, caused by malnutrition and vitamin C deficiency.

In the circumstances under which most sieges were prosecuted there was little chance of entirely avoiding these and other fatal afflictions, and of course the longer the siege persisted the higher was the risk of contagion. No totally reliable figures are actually available for deaths by disease during any siege of this era, although at Damietta in 1218 we are told that in the course of about one month disease wiped out at least a sixth of the Frankish soldiers participating; it seems likely therefore that such losses could too easily reach as high a proportion as ten or 20 per cent of the total involved. The biggest killers of all, in field armies as well as siege camps, were fairly certainly typhoid, of which Richard nearly died in 1192, and *jusantirya* or dysentery. In addition epidemics of other then-fatal diseases such as meningitis, smallpox, quinsy, quartan fever and bubonic plague were not uncommon, sweeping through Syria and its adjoining lands on several occasions in the 12th and 13th centuries, usually in the wake of a famine or drought.

Despite the afflictions of disease the Franks of Outremer enjoyed a standard of medical care which was considerably more advanced than that of their European contemporaries. Hospitals existed in Jerusalem, Acre, Tyre, Tiberias, Nablus, Ascalon and Jaffa, the establishment of which was a direct result of the influence of the Arab medical institutions which existed in most Moslem cities. The best Frankish hospitals were those of the Knights Hospitaller, at each of which were four physicians and four surgeons. After a battle the wounded were loaded on to pack-animals and taken back to one of the major towns. If they were lucky they might receive treatment in such a hospital, as did the 750 wounded from the Battle of Montgisard who were treated at the Hospital in Jerusalem in 1177. This particular hospital had more than 1,000 beds, although John of Wurzburg reports circa 1165 that 2,000 patients were regularly treated there 'who are tended and restored to health daily at very great expense'. His optimism is perhaps misplaced, however, since he cheerfully goes on to say that 'sometimes in the course of one day and night more than 50 are carried out dead'!

Even so, a wounded man's chances of survival were better in the Hospital's hands than in those of one of the quack doctors he might encounter elsewhere. Usamah's anecdotes give us a glimpse of the sort of treatment to be expected from the latter, where amputation is prescribed as the cure for an ulcer on a knight's leg, the knight dying of shock as a result of the 'operation' (executed by two blows with a sharp axe!). It is therefore hardly surprising that the Franks generally preferred native doctors to their own. Even so, Frankish medicine as practised in Outremer was capable of bandaging, stitching and cauterising wounds with red-hot iron or white-hot lead, and of blood-letting, amputation and even dietary and limited medicinal treatments. Slight wounds were therefore generally no problem, but it seems a reasonable guess that probably ten per cent of slightly wounded men and perhaps 50 per cent of badly wounded men died, probably of loss of blood, shock, blood poisoning or gangrene, mostly en route for the hospitals.

The Moslems were one up on the Franks in having surgeons and doctors actually accompanying their armies in action, a tent being set up as an operating theatre close to the battlefield so that the badly wounded could receive immediate attention. Their losses amongst wounded men were therefore probably considerably lower than those of the Franks, whose medicine they rightly regarded as primitive. Their own medical science was based largely on classical Greek and Roman texts, and they were advocating cleanliness, the boiling of surgical instruments and reliance on medicines long before the Crusade era, even adding new drugs of their own, such as laudanum. A wounded Frank was therefore potentially better off as a prisoner of the Moslems than among his own people.

There was nothing comparable to the Geneva Convention at the time of the Crusades, and even if there had been it would have been contravened as regularly then as it is today. Prisoners-of-war were often executed (for example by the Moslems after Ager Sanguinus in 1119 and Hattin in 1187, by the Franks after the fall of Jerusalem in 1099 and of Acre in 1191), the motives apparently being a mixture of hatred, fear and revenge combined with a callous disregard for the sanctity of human life. Forty-five Franks captured at Beirut in 1190 and brought before Saladin at Acre were only spared because he did not wish his youngest sons, who were present, to 'become accustomed in their youth to the shedding of blood and laugh at it'! Those not executed were normally either ransomed or apportioned out as part of the booty to spend the rest of their lives as slaves. The usual price for slaves in the late 12th century was ten dinars for a man, five dinars for a woman (a price which, I feel sure, increased according to age and looks!), and one dinar for a child, ransoms therefore being calculated at the same basic rate. A sudden influx of slaves on to the market inevitably brought prices down; after Hattin in 1187 men were being sold for three dinars apiece, and one Moslem thought he had made a good deal in swapping one prisoner for a pair of sandals!

Captive leaders were nearly always held for ransom, although for various reasons some were confined in chains for the remainder of their days, occasionally being released by treaty or their captor's whim. Their ransoms were often huge; 270,000 dinars were demanded for Bohemond of Antioch's release in 1103, while the Franks asked 30,000 for the amir who had commanded Acre in 1191 and 8,000 for a lesser amir captured with him. Because leaders were so important in those days—considerably more so than now—very unequal exchanges sometimes took place; Baldwin d'Ibelin's release after Marj Ayyun in 1179 was in exchange for 1,000 Moslem prisoners *and* 150,000 dinars. Such huge sums of money, of course, helped considerably in the finance of armies. Some Moslem chieftains actually relied on ransom money to pay off their Turcoman or Bedouin mercenaries, and on at least one occasion some Turcomans, in butchering most of their prisoners, actually deprived themselves of their own pay!

One final strain on the durability of armies was desertion. Deserters are encountered in the sources on a large number of occasions, sometimes changing sides (and informing on their compatriots in so doing) but more often simply melting away and returning to their homes. During King Richard's advance towards Jerusalem in the Third Crusade, for example, most of the French crusaders soon lost heart and drifted back to Acre's brothels and taverns, from whence Richard had to retrieve them. Moslem armies, on the other hand, tended to be dispirited by wet weather and evaporated at the onset of winter, or else dispersed when it was time to collect the revenues of their iqtaat. After a defeat, of course, the number of desertions multiplied astronomically and it was only the ablest of generals who could rally a routed army for the continuation of a campaign, provincial contingents usually fleeing for their homes en masse without a thought for the consequences.

The actual potential of broken troops that a general might successfully rally remains questionable. There is after all a natural tendency for a defeated soldier, his morale shaken or broken, to ditch any item of equipment that threatens to impair his ability to flee as fast as humanly possible. Foot-soldiers are likely to abandon everything—shields, spears, pole-arms, bows and crossbows, the lot—and even horsemen would ditch anything that could not be sheathed, slung or cased, heavy troops ditching armour too; Moslem horsemen fleeing from the battlefield of Montgisard in 1177 threw away corselets, helmets and even greaves in their panic. The overall picture, then, is of a fair percentage of the vanquished being destitute of arms and armour. The victor, on the other hand, gathering such abandoned equipment as he could, would be extremely well-off for not only arms and armour but also horses, camels, tents, cash and everything else that the enemy's deserted encampment might subsequently yield. In the Frankish army the king customarily received a third of all such booty, the remaining two-thirds being distributed amongst the army, while in Moslem armies the ruling prince received somewhat less, only a fifth.

Currently the Wargames Research Group's rules do not allow for any kind of penalty on the performance of rallied troops other than minus three on reaction tests, and even this is an assessment of their morale rather than the completeness of their equipment. In the March 1979 issue of *Slingshot,* however, a reader sensibly suggested an adaptation of one of the rules in George Gush's *Wargames Rules 1420-1700* (also published by WRG), which, amending it to suit the Crusade era, I will paraphrase here: troops in rout will fling away all shields, lances, spears and two-handed weapons including staff-slings, plus half of their missile weapons in the case of mounted crossbowmen and infantry only (except for slingers), cavalry retaining all bows which can be slung or cased; also, 75 per cent of heavy infantry and 25 per cent of heavy cavalry will discard their armour if they fail to rally before leaving the table, these troop-types consequently becoming medium infantry and cavalry respectively until re-equipped to their old status. Obviously, all these figures apply only to *routed* troops, not those which withdraw in good order. In real life the cost of re-equipping an army was high, and a stipulation of this kind will hopefully ensure that it is realistically just as expensive for the campaigning table-top general.

As for attrition and natural wastage in a wargames campaign, I would recommend that you start by assuming that the Moslem and Frankish populations remain basically static, the latter being kept up to strength by a constant influx of pilgrims from the West, some of whom settle in fiefs or villages vacated by battle losses, disease or whatever. This can then be expanded, as you gain experience, into as complex a logistical arrangement as you may deem worthwhile. For example you may decide that x per cent of all pilgrims will settle each year, but of these only y per cent are of knightly status (and a lot of these may end up landless if there are insufficient vacant fiefs) and in total z per cent will die of disease within the first year. The effects of famines and pestilence—in Europe as well as the Levant—can then also be taken into account, as can the migrations of nomad hordes, droughts in Egypt and so on *ad infinitum.* The extent of your patience is the only limitation here.

Chapter 9

Communication

Despite the fact that reliable means of communication were essential to the survival of the Frankish states, with their exposed frontiers and isolated towns and strongholds, it was the Moslems who held the lead in this department throughout Outremer's existence. Their virtually uninterrupted maintenance of the old Byzantine *verudus* or Imperial mail system, preserved almost intact since the Arab Conquest of the 7th century, was partly responsible for this superiority, but the principal reason was without doubt the Moslems' sophisticated and highly effective use of carrier pigeons, which could carry a message far faster than any mounted messenger. A pigeon can cover 500 miles in a single day with relative ease, reaching speeds of up to 60 mph (96 km/h) even in windless conditions, and attaining 100 mph or more with a strong following wind.

The third Abbasid Caliph, al-Mahdi, apparently organised the first regular Moslem pigeon-post in the late 8th century, although it seems likely that the occasional use of pigeons as message carriers by the Arabs predates this event by a good many years, the very first use of carrier pigeons by anyone possibly dating back as far as the 8th century BC. Anyway, the pigeon-post flourished under the Abbasids, so much so that we hear of the best homing pigeons fetching between 700 and 1,000 dinars each in the market-place, and even the egg of a particularly fast pigeon could sell for as much as 20 dinars. By the time the Crusades began in the late 11th century, and for some time prior to that, pigeon-post services operated throughout most of both the Abbasid and Fatimid Caliphates' domains. Zengi introduced a pigeon-post to Mosul in 1160, and Nur ed-Din established a regular Damascus-Cairo pigeon-post in 1171, the latter based on a system of relay stations where the message was each time transferred to a fresh pigeon.

The Franks' first encounter with carrier pigeons appears to date to 1098, when Turkish emissaries from the Amir of Azaz, having successfully concluded an alliance with Godfrey de Bouillon, drew two pigeons from inside their tunics and despatched them to Azaz with the good tidings, causing much amazement and wonder amongst the Frankish observers. By the time Fulcher of Chartres wrote (1101-1127) the Franks had overcome their astonishment enough to have caught on to what this novel means of communication was all about. Fulcher supplies us with a succinct summarisation of the system: 'It is a custom of the Saracens living in Palestine to transport, from one city to another, pigeons to carry letters back to the city which was recently their home. These letters, written on paper tied to the pigeons' feet, instruct the finder and reader what is to be done.' Of course, they were not—could not be—very lengthy letters, so probably carried only the most essential details, although William of Tyre tells us that during one siege pigeons were released carrying 'a complete report' attached to their tails.

One very pertinent point in Fulcher's description is the fact that the pigeons would not fly just *anywhere,* but only back to the cot from which they had originally been taken. In effect, then, communication with pigeons was restricted to between two points—the cot *to* which the pigeons had been taken, and the cot *from* which they had come, and for returning pigeons to be re-used they had first to again be transported elsewhere; so it was impossible to have an endless supply. Even so, although its limitations are apparent, with a little pre-planning and a well-organised chain of relay posts the advantages of the system are fairly self-evident.

The Mamluk sultan Baibars appears to have established the most sophisticated pigeon-post service of this era. He arranged pigeon-cot stations along all the major roads of his domain, and the pigeons flew from one to the next in relay, being changed at each station as they had been under Nur ed-Din. Each of these relay cots could contain up to several hundred pigeons, while the pigeon-loft in the citadel of Cairo itself normally contained about 1,900 pigeons from all corners of the sultanate. Some were used to carry special or secret information for the sultan's eyes alone, and these carried a special distinguishing mark for identification purposes; whenever one of these arrived in the citadel cots no-one but the sultan was allowed to remove its message, and he was to be advised immediately of its arrival, whether he was asleep, eating or holding court. Arranged this efficiently, the pigeon-post was second to none.

Surprisingly, since they constantly saw those of the Moslems in use, the Franks did not make considerable use of carrier pigeons themselves, although the fact that we do sometimes find them being used by besieged garrisons does imply that some fortresses at least maintained their own cots; the Hospitallers had a pigeon-cot in Acre, for instance. Being easy to conceal about one's person (a modern conjuror shows *how* easy) the Franks apparently also used them on occasion for their spies to get information out of enemy encampments and towns, Baibars' troops killing one conveying a message from a spy in his camp to the besieged garrison of Montfort in 1271.

Which brings us to one final consideration; how easy was it to intercept a pigeon? The answer to this question must inevitably be 'not very', but that it was not impossible the above incident clearly demonstrates, as does the *Chanson de Jérusalem* which records how *all* the pigeons sent out by 'King Cornumarant' (a legendary figure probably based on Kerbogha of Mosul) were killed or captured. It also explains why the emissaries from Azaz mentioned earlier felt it expedient to despatch *two* pigeons with their news. It seems likely that pigeons were sometimes brought down by archery (mamluks from the steppes being particularly skilled at this, the Mongols being such marksmen that birds allegedly dared not fly when they were around); but personally it strikes me that the simplest way to bring a pigeon down is with a hawk, and both the Frankish and Moslem nobility were absolutely addicted to hawking, a whole section of the Assizes of Jerusalem being devoted solely to laws relating to this sport. The sources actually record one instance of a carrier pigeon being brought down by a hawk, at Caesarea in 1099, but that was by luck rather than judgement.

The main problem was therefore one of being in the right place at the right time and making sure of your bird—it would, after all, be embarrassing if not potentially disastrous to accidentally kill one of your own—and it seems apparent from the sources that luck had rather more to do with a pigeon's interception than skill in most instances. Even so, it is something that would need to be taken into account in a wargame campaign, perhaps by the introduction of a 'chance card' system or by rolling a combination of average dice; a relatively realistic ratio would seem to be something like one chance in 50 of intercepting a pigeon and one chance in 100 of a pigeon failing to arrive for any other reason—and it should be emphasised here that pigeons are quite capable of getting lost; if you look in the *Guiness Book of Records* you'll see that one released in Europe turned up 10,000 miles away in Australia, while another took over seven years to cover just 370 miles! Best advice would be that of the emissaries from Azaz—always send two.

The Franks' own favoured means of communication appears to have been by beacon, fire by night and a column of smoke by day. Beacons had been—and still were—much used by the Byzantines too, and the Moslem states seem to have established a sophisticated system comprising a chain of beacon towers right along the coast of Syria by the end of the 10th century, still in use in the Mamluk era when it was used to transmit warning of Mongol invasions. By this means news could travel all the way from Northern Syria to Cairo in about one hour.

The news thus conveyed must have been very simple, however, since fire-signals, by their very nature, had a very limited vocabulary and were unable to convey accurate or detailed information. A point of light in the distant darkness of night, or a thin wisp of smoke on the horizon by day, could effectively tell you no more than that a beacon had been lit. Why? Well, that you would have to go and find out for yourself. Of course you could have a very simple code, something akin to the North American Indians' smoke signals, but the myriad opportunities for misinterpretation that such a code presented would have probably soon discouraged its permanent adoption. So, best revert to the basics—lighting a beacon meant *danger*. But what sort of danger? Well once again you would have to go and find out for yourself, although you could be fairly sure (or at least, the Franks could) that it meant one of two things—siege or invasion, and either way the beacon was a call to arms. Its inability to transmit more detailed information, however, was probably the principal reason why the Franks entrusted their most important reports to mounted couriers.

It is the chronicle of Ernoul, who in the late 12th century was the Palestinian baron Balian d'Ibelin's esquire, which supplies us with the information that beacons were in widespread use amongst the Franks. He relates how 'there is a custom in Outremer that when the Saracens were known to have entered any part of the country, the first who had seen them lit a fire, until it was seen all over the country'. Of course this inevitably presupposes intervisibility between such beacons, which were presumably mounted on the highest towers of their respective castles, and certainly without such intervisibility communication by this means was, needless to say, impossible. Lines of known intervisibility between fortresses are shown on the maps in Chapter 13, and by judicious siting of simple beacon towers elsewhere the chain was probably far more extensive during the Crusade era—as we have already seen, a line of intervisible beacons along the coast enabled the Arabs to transmit fire-signals down the entire length of Syria's coastline, and doubtless the Franks were aware of and used the same beacon sites. Certainly Ernoul's report leads us to believe that the system was very extensive indeed,and presumably those sites which could not be reached by beacon were warned instead by mounted messenger; in 1187, for example, the king encamped at Sephoria was only made aware of Saladin's siege of Tiberias by a messenger despatched by its garrison, who seems to have taken about two hours to cover the 15 mile course. This compares very unfavourably with the few minutes that it would have taken for a beacon signal.

Having said all that, however, other than a passing allusion in a Moslem source to signal fires being lit at Krak des Chevaliers there is strangely enough apparently only one specific instance of a beacon-signal recorded in the Frankish sources, despite Ernoul's testimony of a widespread system. The instance is a good one though, and amply demonstrates the potential effectiveness of this form of communication. It dates to 1183 when Saladin began his first siege of Reynald de Châtillon's great fortress of Kerak in Moab; a signal beacon lit there told observers in Jerusalem *50 miles away,* probably via a relay of hilltop beacon stations, that help was needed, and the answering fire lit atop David's Tower apparently conveyed to the besieged garrison of Kerak the message that help was on its way. The fact that both parties accurately interpreted the sense of each other's signals may be taken as an indication that some form of code or perhaps a rudimentary system of optical telegraphy did indeed exist. One last thought—I wonder just how anyone observing a distant beacon decided whether what they saw was the actual point of danger or merely a link in the signal chain, passing on warning?

Such messengers as those sent out from Tiberias in 1187 normally rode the whole distance to their destination without relief or change of horse. Under ideal conditions, and travelling at no exceptional speed, it was possible for a horseman to cover an average of 30-35 miles in a single day by spending no more than six or seven hours on horseback, ie, an average speed of five or six miles an hour. However, bearing in mind the urgency of his errand a despatch rider was likely to travel at a far greater, not to say exhausting, pace. In 1836 an English officer carrying despatches at 'courier speed' from Basra to Beirut, traversing Syria's inhospitable Great Desert, covered the distance of 958 miles in 22 days, an average of about 44 miles a day, but only by sometimes spending up to 19 hours in the saddle without rest, and fairly certainly with the assistance of numerous fresh horses en route.

Communication within the crusader states being somewhat easier than in the Great Desert, it seems probable that our Frankish couriers could fairly certainly cover a somewhat greater distance, probably about 60 miles in a single day of about eight hours riding during the summer (more than halved in winter), which was probably about as much as the poor horse could endure in Syria's climate. They would have got a lot further more quickly if relays of horses were available along the way, but alas, although their messengers could undoubtedly acquire fresh mounts in towns and forts of substance, the Franks' administrative abilities did not stretch so far as to have relay stations at regular intervals en route. Here, then, the Moslems had another communications advantage, for they had inherited the established postal networks left behind by their Sassanid and Byzantine predecessors, with their relays of fresh horses and riders at fixed intervals along major artery roads.

Called the *berid,* from the Latin *verudus,* the service in use in the Crusade era was an amalgamation of both Sassanid and Byzantine systems, and though it functioned far less efficiently in the 11th and 12th centuries than it had in the past, largely due to decentralisation of government and lack of cooperation in the provinces, it was still vastly superior to anything the Franks had at their disposal. When, following the Mongol sack of Baghdad, Baibars restructured the berid to operate instead from Cairo, enough of its internal organisation remained intact for him to build on its foundations the most efficient postal network the Levant had yet seen, a sort of mediaeval Pony Express. His postmen (*beridiyin,* from the Latin *veredarii*) were handpicked mamluks, chosen for their tact, intelligence and discretion—not least because they doubled as spies (see Chapter 14); each wore a silver plaque round his neck for identification and a yellow scarf for instant recognition. They delivered twice weekly reports to Cairo from Damascus, Aleppo, Hamah, Kerak and, after their capture from the Franks, Tripoli and Safed, a letter from Cairo taking only four days to reach Damascus and five to reach Aleppo.

The roads these messengers travelled were themselves largely of Roman origin, some still well metalled for considerable distances or even their entire length, others in total disrepair, visible only by a faint outline and likely to turn into a quagmire capable of swallowing up men and horses during the rainy Syrian winter; the *Itinerarium* describes how, as the Franks advanced along the road from Ramla to Ascalon during the Third Crusade, it 'gave way beneath their feet—baggage, horses and men sank in the marshes, and the more men struggled the deeper still they sank'. Such conditions inevitably reduced a traveller's average riding speed considerably, from 30-35 miles a day in the summer to as little as seven or eight miles a day in the winter. Beha ed-Din, who wrote during Saladin's reign, records how it took 19 days to cover 150 muddy miles between Damascus and Jerusalem.

Reliable though Roman roads were, the problem was that they had not once been repaired since the Arab Conquest of the mid-7th century, and in the extremes of Syria's inhospitable climate many of them had virtually disintegrated. The Franks did little to improve their upkeep, even though part of the corvée, or obligatory unpaid labour owed by the peasants of the feudal estates, involved road repair.

It is hardly surprising to find that some major roads were actually impracticable for the passage of large armies (ie, forces of more than a couple of thousand men), although it is not now easy to establish which these were. The direct Toron-Judyn-Acre road was apparently one which was only suitable for small detachments, and the Sennabra-Acre road was apparently another. Reading the *Itinerarium*'s account of the Ramla-Ascalon road one's first reaction is to say that this was yet another, but the account refers to the winter months when most Syrian roads, even the best, were transformed into mud or marsh by the heavy rains. This particular road was in fact part of the Via Maris, the 'Way of the Sea', the most important road in Frankish Syria, stretching from Antioch all the way down to Egypt and well suited to the passage of armies.

The real problem was that most armies overflowed these roads to both left and right as well as marching along the 'road' itself, the limits of which were often ill-defined, and inevitably if the 'soft verge' on either side was overgrown, marshy or very uneven then the whole road was likely to be regarded as unfit for military use. Conversely what that means is that most roads probably *were* practicable for armies but not tactically suitable, ie, the army would have to be strung out over too great a distance, or would have to negotiate too many narrow passes, and so on. Faced by just such a problem during the advance to Nicaea in the First Crusade, Godfrey de Bouillon sent ahead of his army a body of 3,000 men with axes and swords to 'widen the path sufficiently' for the huge crusading army which he led, and undoubtedly such pioneer activities were resorted to on many other occasions. Some major fortresses, Belvoir for instance, were not even on major roads, although they might overlook them, but that did not stop them being invested by large armies.

Roads through the desert regions beyond the Jordan were another matter entirely. They were principally caravan routes, and although once again most tended to follow old Roman roads others, such as the 'Pilgrim's Road' to Mecca and Medina, were of Arab origin. These Syrian Desert routes had all been chosen with several considerations in mind, foremost of which was the availability of water. Admittedly *all* roads in Syria, and Anatolia, Sinai and Egypt too, were chosen with this primary consideration in mind, but in the arid desert regions it became an even more critical factor. Wells, springs and sometimes wadis could therefore be found at various points along most major roads, usually at no more than three-day intervals, both in Outremer and the surrounding Moslem lands. Wadis, however, were not a practical source of water for armies or large caravans—the water was near enough to the surface to dig up, but it would take an awful lot of digging to find enough for x thousand camels, horses and men!

A secondary consideration in choosing a route through the wild lands was the avoidance of bellicose Bedouin tribesmen who, though nominally Moslem, tended to undergo a lapse in their religious convictions whenever potential loot was close at hand, so that Moslems suffered from their depredations at least as much as the Franks and in fact probably more so. Such freebooting Bedouin, together with bandits of both Moslem and Frankish origin, were the main threats to communication by road, being prepared to attack not only pilgrims and merchant caravans but even military units. Narrow passes were their favourite ambush sites and often earnt appropriate names, for example the 'Valley of Thieves' or 'Valley of Running'. Security of the major roads was therefore a primary consideration of both Frankish and Moslem rulers, who established roadside forts and regularly patrolled their highways. This responsibility devolved in Outremer mainly on to the Military Orders, the Order of the Poor Knights of Christ (the Templars) being originally established for just such a purpose. Many of the Franks' roadside forts, situated principally at crossroads, fords and other danger zones, were likewise of Templar origin.

In time of war, of course, the Franks would raid the Moslems' caravans with impunity and vice versa, frequently gaining much wealth thereby; the great caravan that was jumped by King Richard during the Third Crusade yielded all kinds of luxury goods in addition to arms and foodstuffs, including gold, silver, rich brocades and silks, medicine, chess tables, silver pots and candlesticks. To raid a caravan in peacetime, however, was considered an act of war, and it was just such an ill-considered attack that sparked off the disastrous 1187 campaign.

Chapter 10

Strategy and tactics

Inevitably enough, Frankish strategy in Outremer was basically defensive, relying heavily on the establishment and retention of fortresses and walled towns. In the face of a Moslem incursion field armies were mustered (often by stripping those same fortified places of their garrisons) and carefully positioned in a place from where they could protect the largest amount of territory while at the same time restricting the movements of the enemy, who, thus frustrated in his aims, would hopefully turn for home.

The field army's principal function, in fact, was to interfere with any attempt by the Moslems to seize one of the Franks' strongholds. Since these were obviously undermanned, or even empty, as a result of their garrisons having joined the army (for example, just two sick men were left in Castrum Fabae when its garrison rode out to destruction at Cresson in 1187), the defeat of the field army itself invariably resulted in the fall of most of the fortresses in the immediate vicinity. The repercussions of a major defeat could be on a far greater scale, as the virtual extinction of Outremer following the Horns of Hattin proved only too clearly. Beha ed-Din states categorically that as a result of the Moslems' victory there 'Nablus fell into their hands, as well as Haifa, Caesarea, Saphoria, and Nazareth, for all these places had been left defenceless by reason of the death or captivity of their protectors'. It was obviously preferable, therefore, to avoid battle altogether if it were at all possible, defeating the enemy by strategic manoeuvre alone. It was doubtless this policy that prompted Usamah's otherwise inexplicable remark about the Franks 'who of all men are the most cautious in warfare'.

Moslem strategy, by contrast, was mainly offensive in nature. The Saracens obviously had far less to risk by accepting battle than did the Franks, and one of their principal aims in each campaign was to discomfit and, where possible, exterminate the Frankish field army. This would leave their undefended strongholds ripe for the plucking. The inherent problems of this policy, however, were twofold, in that bringing the Franks to battle in the first place was not particularly easy, while reducing even a grossly undermanned fortress could be time-consuming. And the one major shortcoming of any Moslem army, as we have already seen in Chapter 4 and elsewhere, was its inability to remain in the field for prolonged periods. They tended to disperse of their own accord if disaffected (as was often the case) or if the chances of success seemed improbable or distant, the onset of winter with its cold, wet weather usually resulting in the final dispersal of any Moslem army that lasted relatively intact through to October. Only the most able Moslem commanders could keep any forces at all in the field during the winter.

Although the tactics of the Franks in a set-piece battle in Outremer were similar to those employed at home in Europe, with the army divided into three or more divisions in line, echelon or column, climaxing in the delivery of the knights' decisive close-order charge that could 'make a hole through the walls of Babylon', such tactics could only be employed successfully against an enemy who would stand and take its full impact; and, alas, in this the majority of Moslem armies did not oblige, being largely of Turkish composition. Nevertheless under favourable circumstances Frankish knights could manoeuvre the enemy into a situation in which it was impossible to evade the charge (as at Arsuf in 1191), and on occasion even the Turks might decide of their own accord to stand up to it, despite the fact that man for man they were no match for the well armoured Franks in close combat.

Usually the Turks preferred to make the best possible use of their principal advantages over the Franks—their archery and their mobility—wherever possible avoiding direct contact with the Frankish cavalry. Horse-archers, of course, were the backbone of all Turkish armies, in Syria just as much as in Central Asia, and the Frankish chronicles are full of references to the effects of their archery, of their showers of arrows which fell 'as though rain was falling from the sky'. 'When the first rank had quite emptied their quivers and shot all their arrows,' writes William of Tyre of the Battle of Dorylaeum, 'the second, in which there were still more horsemen, came on and began to shoot more densely than one could believe. The Turkish squadrons at once flung themselves upon our army, and loosed such a quantity of arrows that you would have thought hail was falling from the air; hardly had the first cloud of them fallen, describing an arc, than it was followed by a second, no less dense.'

Fulcher of Chartres, writing of the Battle of Marj es-Safar (1126), reported that 'no part of the body or limb seemed safe against the shafts, so thickly did they fly'. Such a high rate of fire could be maintained, in fact, that Ambroise, who you will remember was an eye-witness, wrote of King Richard's advance to Arsuf that there was not as much as four feet of ground to be found that was entirely free of spent arrows. One of the Frankish dead at Ager Sanguinus had as many as *40* arrows in him, the Damascene historian Ibn al-Qalanisi reporting of the same battle that there were 'dead horses bristling like hedgehogs with the arrows sticking out of them,' and more than a century later Joinville thought himself and his horse fortunate to have been wounded by arrows only five and 15 times respectively at El Mansurah.

The successful maintenance of such withering rates of fire obviously necessitated the availability of sufficient ammunition. Each Turkish horseman carried at least one and often two or three quivers, each capable of holding up to 60 arrows; other arrows could be carried in the bowcase, stuffed into boots or belt, and so on. Little information is available regarding replenishing empty quivers on the battlefield, but at Hattin Saladin apparently had 70 camels laden with arrows, as well as 400 loads of spare ammunition for them, and such arrangements probably ensured the availability of an adequate supply of arrows on many other occasions.

At the same time, however, the effectiveness of Turkish archery should not be overestimated; during the whole four-and-a-half month siege of Tyre in 1111 the Franks lost only 2,000 men according to Ibn al-Qalanisi, despite the fact that he reports the Moslem garrison (which was, admittedly, far from exclusively Turkish in composition) to have discharged 20,000 arrows in one day's fighting alone! And it should also be borne in mind that Turkish arrows were relatively light and could strike—and perhaps penetrate—armour, even simple quilted armour, without actually wounding the wearer; at Arsuf, for example, Frankish infantry are recorded by Beha ed-Din marching along unconcernedly with up to ten arrows stuck in their armour. The cause for this was often that the arrows were too light and shot at too great a range. Several sources refer to the 'astonishing' range from which Turks sometimes opened fire, and later tests reported by Sir Ralph Payne-Gallwey, the eminent toxopholite, record Turkish bows being able to fire up to 480 yards—although at anything much over 100 yards their penetrative value was much reduced. The sources imply that at closer range their arrows became far more effective. Anna Comnena, for instance, records that they could pass clean through an unarmoured man.

Inevitably such archery was particularly effective against unarmoured horses, and the Turks were well aware of the important role of the horse in Frankish tactics. Writing of Hattin, Abu Shamah (who wrote in the 13th century) observed how 'the Frankish knight, so long as his horse is safe and sound, cannot be felled. Clothed from head to foot with a mail coat that makes him resemble a block of iron, he is not affected by repeated blows; but as soon as the horse is killed the knight is thrown down and captured. Although they numbered in thousands, there were no horses nor mounts in the booty . . . It was necessary that his mount fall . . . for the knight to lose his saddle.'

It was possibly for this reason that on rare occasions we find knights actually dismounting to fight. Bohemond's knights may have been ordered to dismount at Dorylaeum as early as 1097, and certainly the charge of Emperor Conrad's German crusaders before Damascus in 1148 was launched on foot. The troubador Ambroise even records an instance in 1191 of a Templar foraging party, surprised by 400 Turkish cavalry, dismounting and fighting back-to-back. Turks too are occasionally to be found dismounting to fight, incidentally, as at Arsuf where the *Itinerarium* records some 'who had of set purpose dismounted so as to aim their darts and arrows better'.

It was to protect the knights' horses until the moment of the charge that Frankish infantry usually preceded their cavalry, defending the knights 'like a wall' as Beha ed-Din puts it; Imad ed-Din, who was Saladin's secretary, uses a similar expression, describing Frankish infantry as 'a wall of arms'. At Jaffa in 1192 Richard formed up his infantry with spearmen in the first rank, shields to the front and spear-butts braced against the ground, with two crossbow-armed men behind each of them (one loading, one firing), a veritable 'wall of arms' indeed, one with which the Turks refused to close on that occasion. Louis IX's infantry employed much the same formation whilst holding the beachhead at Damietta in 1249, but in both situations the Franks were undeniably on the defensive. More usually they seem to have formed up in line in relatively close order, probably several ranks deep, those armed with bows and crossbows (constituting a large percentage of Frankish infantry) usually being to the fore so that they could return the fire of the Turks, who soon learnt a healthy respect for the crossbow in particular. Indeed, the presence of crossbow-armed infantry in Frankish armies may have been the principal reason why Turkish horse-archers often opened fire at such long range that their arrows had little real hope of penetrating armour.

William of Tyre, in his own account of Marj es-Safar, in fact credits Frankish infantry, presumably archers, with the same tactic as the Turks in that they 'turned their attention to wounding the horses of their adversaries and thus rendered the riders easy victims to the Christians [ie, the knights] who were following'. In the same account he also gives a good description of the role of infantry in close combat, relating how 'they instantly despatched with the sword any wounded or fallen infidel whom they chanced to find and thus prevented all possibility of escape. They lifted up those [of their own cavalry] who had been thrown down and restored them to the fray. They sent the wounded back to the baggage train to receive care'. At the same battle we also have one of the few references to Turkish infantry in action, Fulcher of Chartres describing Damascene infantry trained 'to spring up armed behind the horsemen, who when the enemy drew near descended and fought on foot; for so they hoped to disorder the Franks by attacking them with infantry on the one side and cavalry on the other'.

In addition to their archery the Turks had a second major tactical advantage over the Franks in their mobility, which enabled them to evade the Frankish charge and successfully employ hit-and-run skirmishing tactics. But above all it enabled them to attack the Franks on the march, showering their columns with arrows, suddenly closing and as suddenly falling back, and harassing in every way the army's advance. Attacked thus the Franks had no real option but to press doggedly on, relying on their solidity of array to deter the Turks and keeping so close together that 'if an apple had been thrown amongst them, it would not have fallen to the ground without it touching a man or a horse'. The infantry, whose iron discipline is demonstrated at its best in such running fights, marched on the outside of the column or on the flank nearest to the enemy, those in the rear (against which most attacks were directed) often having to march backwards in order to beat off the repeated Turkish attacks, the cavalry conforming their own pace to that of the infantry 'that the ranks might not be broken and the enemy given a chance to break in upon their formation'. Often, in fact, the infantry even carried their own dead on camels and pack-horses as they marched so as to conceal the number of casualties from the enemy.

As mentioned, the Turks concentrated on the rearguard when attacking a Frankish column, in the hope that it would be slowed down sufficiently to cause a gap between it and the main body which could then be exploited (as happened at Mount Cadmos in 1148 and nearly happened at Hattin in 1187). Heavy attacks were also often made on the vanguard in the hope that the whole column might thus be halted. In addition they would frequently sling their bows behind their shoulders and make short, controlled charges on the offchance that, in the words of Abu Shamah, the Franks would be 'carried away by blind fury' and 'would attack us and in this way would give us the opportunity to divide and break their mass'. Concentrated archery could likewise goad Frankish knights into an impetuous counter-attack, as it did at Arsuf. The Franks, however, learnt in turn to try and control their counter-attacks, the knights only charging out to drive the enemy away to a safe distance if he pressed too close, then rallying and falling back to the main column, a tactic which the author of the *Itinerarium* likens to beating off a fly 'which, though you may drive it off, will return directly you cease your efforts'!

Odo of Deuil, a participant in Louis VII's crusade, gives a good description of the organisation of a Frankish column on the march which includes all these points: 'Because the Turks were quick to flee our men were commanded to endure, until they received an order, the attacks of their enemies; and to withdraw forthwith when recalled . . . When they had learned this, they were also taught the order of march so that a person in front would not rush to the rear and the guards on the flanks would not fall into disorder. Moreover those whom nature or fortune had made foot-soldiers . . . were drawn up at the rear in order to oppose with their bows the enemy's arrows.' In fact severe penalties awaited any man who broke ranks. Examples of battles fought on the march include Hab, Mount Cadmos, Hattin and Arsuf. The column formation could also be used to retire off a battlefield in good order, as at al-Babein in 1167.

The contingents of the Military Orders were the best disciplined troops available to the Franks. Jacques de Vitry relates how they fought 'not rashly or disorderly but wisely and with all caution, being the first to attack and the last to retreat. They were not allowed to turn their back and flee, nor to retreat without orders'. In reality, however, knights of the Military Orders could be just as wilful and headstrong as their secular counterparts, if not more so; witness,for example, the actions of the Templars at Marj Ayyun in 1179 and Cresson in 1187, and of the Hospitallers at Arsuf. But, it should be noted, in the first two instances they were following the orders of their Grand Master, while the Hospitallers at Arsuf were following the example of their Marshal.

Because of their military prowess the Orders' contingents usually held the dangerous stations of vanguard and rearguard on the march. One cartulary of the 13th century states that it was actually customary for the Orders to hold these positions, and certainly the practice was common enough for the Mamluk sultan Baibars to march out on one occasion with captured Hospitaller and Templar banners in the van in order to fool the Franks. Examples of the practice to be found in contemporary sources include Templars holding the van at Mount Cadmos and, with the Hospitallers, the rear at Hattin and in the retreat from El Mansurah; Hospitallers the rear and Templars the van at Arsuf and in Galilee in 1204; and Hospitallers and Teutonic Knights the van at Caroublier in 1266. This custom may also be implied in de Vitry's words about the brethren 'being the first to attack and the last to retreat'.

The other principal use to which the Turks put their mobility was in feigning flight, a characteristic Turkish tactic. The feigned flight could assume one of three different forms; either a steady retreat lasting several days, designed to weary the enemy and draw him away from his bases; as bait for a pre-arranged ambush; or as deliberate provocation in the hope that the enemy would throw caution to the wind and charge in pursuit, thus disrupting his formation. As early as 1096 the Byzantine Emperor Alexius I cautioned the leaders of the First Crusade 'not to pursue the enemy too far if God gave them the victory, lest falling into traps set by the Turkish chieftains they should be massacred'.

The Franks too seem to have occasionally employed this ruse, Tancred apparently feigning flight at Artah in 1105, while William of Tyre describes in detail how Baldwin II successfully used this tactic against the Fatimids at Ascalon in 1125 in conjunction with a concealed ambush, despatching a decoy body of light-armed horsemen to lure the Moslems into his trap.

These 'light-armed horsemen' may have been Turcopoles, sometimes used in a light cavalry role by the Franks—at least, they seem to have sometimes preceded the knights. At Sarmin in 1115, for example, and at Ager Sanguinus, we find them in advance of the knights, on the former occasion at least fighting as horse-archers, but in both instances they appear to have been pushed on to the knights behind them. Even the *Livre au Roi,* a legislative compilation of circa 1197-1205, seems to imply that they were customarily placed in front of the knights, stating that the Constable's double-strength troop held the first place in battle *after* the Turcopoles, with the Marshal's troop and then the king's behind him. Another occasion on which they are recorded being employed as horse-archers in a skirmishing role takes place during the Third Crusade, when King Richard 'sent his archers forward in the van with the Turcopoles and crossbowmen, to skirmish with the Turks and strive to press them till he could arrive'.

Undoubtedly there are other unrecorded occasions too on which the Turcopoles fought as horse-archers, but this aspect should not be overemphasised, the infrequency with which it does occur in the sources tending to suggest that they were not particularly effective in this role; although he does not record how they fought, William writes of the Turcopoles at al-Babein that they were 'for the most part, useless'—probably as a result of Frankish misuse rather than military incompetence. It is quite probable that instead they often fought alongside the Frankish knights and sergeants. They are also occasionally recorded in a reconnaissance role as, for example, in the Rule of the Order of the Temple, which specifies that the Turcopolier was to send out one or two of his men to reconnoitre beyond the army encampment.

Although so far only Turkish tactics have been described, it should not be assumed that all Moslem armies fought in the same way, using horse-archers, skirmishing tactics and the feigned flight. The Arabs of Fatimid Egypt employed none of these, although small numbers of allied or mercenary Turkish horse-archers very occasionally appear in their armies (as at Third Ramla in 1105). Instead they fought with sword, mace and couched lance very much like the Franks, Usamah (himself a Syrian rather than Egyptian Arab) describing in detail how the lance should be held to best effect in the charge, held by the rider 'as tightly as possible with his hand and under his arm, close to his side, and [he] should let his horse run and effect the required thrust'. Their archers were infantry rather than horsemen, supplied mainly by Sudanese ghulams; like the archers of the Franks these usually preceded the cavalry in battle, and earlier sources testify that they were expert marksmen.

Ibn Khaldun, a 14th century author, states that the Fatimids employed two principal formations in battle, these being the 'Persian' tactic of advancing in line in organised divisions, and the Bedouin or Berber tactic of attacking in small, disorganised groups, and he observes that the Persian method was the more sure of victory in being well organised and 'as impregnable as a continuous stone wall or a strongly constructed fort'. As already mentioned, archers formed the first rank, with spearmen in the second and cavalry in the third, elite units usually forming the centre, where the army's main standards flew; the density of the formation depended on the strength of the enemy. Sometimes numerical superiority permitted an outflanking movement, and Bedouin are often encountered in this role.

For a set-piece battle the Ayyubids and Mamluks used a very similar formation, but usually without the infantry. They drew up in three divisions, consisting of centre, left and right, still with the elite units and standards in the centre (usually the al-Halqa and/or Royal Mamluks, with the amirs' contingents on the flanks). The Mamluks in addition placed auxiliaries on the extreme wings, usually Bedouin on one wing and Turcomans on the other. In battle it was not uncommon for one wing or both to give way, victors and vanquished dashing from the field in pursuit or rout and leaving the centre to resolve the battle; this occurred at Acre in 1189 and at Homs in 1281, for example. Skirmishers usually preceded the main body of cavalry, either Turcomans or the best marksmen, Imad ed-Din describing how at Hattin Saladin 'picked out the advance guard of archers' from each company, while at Arsuf the Frankish sources record light cavalry 'coming down at us in full charge and hurling darts and arrows as fast as they could' while the 'well-ordered phalanxes of the Turks with ensigns fixed on their lances' were drawn up beyond them. The Mamluks usually carried a lance in the charge, apparently having a preference for hand weapons despite the fact that they continued to carry bows in addition and were trained to act as either horse-archers or lancers as need dictated. Infantry still sometimes preceded the cavalry, but under the Mamluks they were extremely uncommon except in sieges, and the Mamluks themselves rarely, if ever, fought on foot.

Finally, I would just like to ensure that no-one, having read this book, goes away thinking that Crusading warfare was all brave deeds, noble combat and romance, as Hollywood and most historical fiction would have us believe. In reality it was just gory, violent and sordid. The following description of the battlefield of Hattin by Imad ed-Din, who was present and clearly disgusted and deeply moved by what he saw, should put paid to any notions you may currently hold. It is translated by Francesco Gabrieli in *Arab Historians of the Crusades* (Routledge and Kegan Paul, 1969):

'The plain was covered with prisoners and corpses, disclosed by the dust as it settled and victory became clear. The prisoners, with beating hearts, were bound in chains. The dead were scattered over the mountains and valleys, lying immobile on their sides. Hattin shrugged off their carcasses, and the perfume of victory was thick with the stench of them. I passed by them and saw the limbs of the fallen cast naked on the field of battle, scattered in pieces over the site of the encounter, lacerated and disjointed, with heads cracked open, throats split, spines broken, necks shattered, feet in pieces, noses mutilated, extremities torn off, members dismembered, parts shredded, eyes gouged out, stomachs disembowelled, hair covered with blood, the praecordium slashed, fingers sliced off, the thorax shattered, the ribs broken, the joints dislocated, the chests smashed, throats slit, bodies cut in half, arms pulverised, lips shrivelled, foreheads pierced, forelocks dyed scarlet, breasts covered with blood, ribs pierced, elbows disjointed, bones broken, tunics torn off, hair lopped, backs skinless, bodies dismembered, teeth knocked out, blood spilt, life's last breath exhaled, necks lolling, joints slackened, pupils liquefied, breasts flayed, spirits flown, their very ghosts crushed; like stones among stones, a lesson to the wise. This field of battle had become a sea of blood; the dust was stained red [and] rivers of blood ran freely . . . '

That was what mediaeval warfare was really like, and I defy anyone to find anything romantic about it.

Chapter 11

The naval scene

Throughout this era naval power in the Mediterranean was a monopoly in the hands of the Italian maritime republics. The Byzantines and Moslems had their own fleets too, of course, as after a fashion did the Franks of Outremer, but none of them had a navy that was capable of competing with the Italians on anything like an equal footing. Not that this had always been the case. Until the 10th century it had been the Byzantine navy which ruled the Mediterranean's blue waters, but periodic lapses—specifically in the 8th and 9th centuries—had often seen the Arabs in their place. The Imperial navy's latest decline had begun late in the 10th century, when constant and paralysingly expensive campaigns in Bulgaria and the East had left the Empire without sufficient resources to maintain its fleet, which in 992 resulted in the Byzantines employing Venetian vessels in a military capacity for the first time. This practise soon became so regular that the Empire's native fleet faded almost to the point of extinction; to meet a major attack on Constantinople in 1042 only a very small number of Imperial warships could be mustered, backed up by a motley collection of transports and hastily repaired hulks.

The condition of the Imperial navy at the beginning of the Crusade era was, undeniably, somewhat improved from this, but only as a result of the dynamic Emperor Alexius I's Herculeian efforts. He had reorganised the navy's command structure by incorporating the remnants of the provincial fleets into the Imperial fleet that was based in Constantinople, placing the entire force under the command of a newly created officer called the *Megas Dux* or 'Grand Duke'. However, even Alexius had to rely heavily on Venetian naval assistance and his efforts did not prevent the navy's steady decline from resuming once he was dead. His grandson Manuel redressed the balance for the duration of his own reign, constructing a fleet of considerable dimensions that is recorded as 220 ships during the attack on Damietta in 1169 but, like that of Alexius, this fleet too dwindled under his successors.

By 1196 there were apparently no more than 30 galleys still in service, and by 1203, when the fleet of the infamous Fourth Crusade began its assault on Constantinople, there was not even one large ship still serviceable, the fleet consisting of just 20 worm-eaten hulks laid up in a misbegotten state in the Golden Horn. The Megas Dux, a man called Michael Struphnos, appears to have been responsible for this, for at some stage—evidently for his own enrichment—he had stripped them and sold off everything aboard that was not nailed down, oars, anchors, masts, sails, rigging, 'and everything else belonging to the Roman navy which could possibly be turned into cash'. The only way the resultant hulks could be usefully employed thereafter was as fire-ships, and 17 of them were loaded up with wood shavings and pitch and launched against the crusaders' fleet. And that, for some years to come, was the end of the Imperial navy. Which brings us back to the Venetians, established in their own colony in Constantinople since 1084, because it was on them—and their rivals the Pisans and Genoese—that the Empire had to rely from circa 1100 onwards for naval support.

In this the Byzantines were not alone. The Frankish states of Outremer, clinging tenaciously to their narrow strip of land along the coast of Syria and Palestine, relied on the Italians' control of the sea-lanes for their very survival, and the Venetians and their compatriots knew it. The price one had to pay for their help was therefore high—the 50 Venetian galleys that accompanied the Fourth Crusade to Constantinople did so 'for the love of God' and *half* of all the loot and conquests that might result from it, not, one should hasten to add, in that order.

The assistance of their fleets in the capture of the coastal cities of Outremer between 1100 and 1124 required similar generous payment. There were 28 or 34 Genoese ships at the siege of Arsuf in 1100, 40 at Jebail and others at Lattakieh in 1103, and 60-70 at Tripoli in 1109; combined Pisan and Genoese fleets were present at Acre in 1104 and Beirut in 1110, providing 70-90 ships on the former occasion and 40 on the latter; and Venetian ships attended at Sidon in 1110 and at Tyre in 1124, where 70-120 are said to have been present. In exchange they were granted favourable trading concessions, autonomous rule over their own streets and quarters in each city, various forms of tax and customs exemption and other privileges, and up to a third of whatever booty was taken. For example, for their assistance in the siege of Tyre the Venetians demanded (and received) a street, church, baths and bakery in every town of the kingdom; the right to use their own weights and measures in all their business transactions; exception from all tolls and custom-duties throughout the kingdom; additional property in Acre; an annual payment of 300 bezants; and a third of the city of Tyre itself! Shylock, you may remember, was also a Venetian.

It was not long before such one-sided agreements had resulted in the establishment of Genoese communes in Acre, Antioch, Arsuf, Beirut, Caesarea, Jaffa, Jebail, Lattakieh, Saint Symeon, Tripoli and Tyre; Amalfitan communes in Acre and Lattakieh; Pisan communes in Acre, Antioch, Botron, Lattakieh, Tripoli and Tyre; and Venetian communes in the larger of these cities plus Jerusalem, in which the Genoese were also represented. Each was governed by its own consul or viscount, and although they were under no obligation to provide military service their residents usually assisted in the defence of those towns in which they had quarters. Further naval support, though sometimes given freely, often required further privileges in exchange; Bohemond IV of Tripoli, for example, had to grant his Genoese commune extensive additional trading concessions in 1205 for just two galleys and 300 seamen to man them.

The Venetian, Pisan and Genoese colonies in Constantinople, established respectively in 1084, 1111 and 1155, were the result of similar agreements with the Imperial government which likewise granted them extensive trading privileges and quarters in many other cities of the Empire such as Thessalonika, Adrianople and Corinth. In an agreement dating to 1187 the Venetians offered in return to supply 40-100 galleys at six months notice. Admittedly the Emperor was to pay for fitting them out, but their crews were to be provided by Venetian colonists living in Constantinople (of whom there were as many as 10,000 by 1171, plus 10,000 more elsewhere throughout the Empire), three out of every four of whom were liable for such service. These were to obey the orders of the Byzantine Megas Dux, despite having their own officers. In real emergencies where no time was available for the ships to arrive from Venice the colonists had to serve instead on whatever Byzantine vessels were available. When the danger was over Venetian ships could return home, where they were to be kept ready for further service should they be needed. Details of another agreement, this time with the Genoese in 1261, are also still extant. This was the Treaty of Nymphaeum where, in exchange for the city of Smyrna, a colony in the suburb of Galata, quarters and churches on Chios and Lesbos, an absolute monopoly, with the Pisans, of all commerce in the Black Sea and the usual trading concessions, they agreed to supply 100 galleys—but only so long as they were not used against the Pope or Genoa's allies. Only 50 of them were manned and armed, the Byzantines having to supply their own equipment and crews for the remainder. Thereafter it was the Genoese who were supreme in Byzantine waters.

Inevitably bitter rivalry existed between the various Italian city-republics, whose mercantile ambitions were in direct, fierce and bloody competition with one another. 13th century Venetian and Genoese ships in particular could rarely meet at sea without attacking each other and, alas for Outremer, when they imported their way of life into the East they imported with it their mutual hatred. Jacques de Vitry observed of the Italians that 'they would be very terrible to the Saracens if they would only cease from their jealousy and avarice and would stop continually quarrelling and fighting with each other. But . . . they more often join battle against each other than against the treacherous infidel.'

The worst of their internecine conflicts was the First Genoese War, the so-called War of Saint Sabas, which started out as a localised squabble between the Genoese and Venetians over ownership of the monastery of Saint Sabas at Acre and ended as a full-blooded civil war, with Genoese, Hospitallers, Catalans and an array of native barons led by the lord of Tyre on the one hand ranged against Venetians, Pisans, Provençals, Templars, Teutonic Knights and the Ibelins on the other. It began in 1256 and dragged on in one form or another for 32 years. After the Venetians had soundly trounced the Genoese fleet off Acre in 1258, and after the loss of allegedly 20,000 lives in fierce street-fights in the capital itself, involving the use of siege engines against the commune walls, the scale of military activities diminished considerably, although trouble always flared up again when squadrons of the opposing fleets made their seasonal trading passage into Levantine waters twice a year. After the Genoese had concluded the Treaty of Nymphaeum with the Byzantines in 1261 the main theatre of war was transferred to the Byzantine Empire, although engagements continued to occur anywhere and everywhere that rival ships encountered one another, resulting in major sea battles at Settepozzi in 1263 and Trapani in 1266.

Peace of a sort was concluded in 1270, but Pisa refused to participate and maintained the struggle against Genoa for a further 18 years until 1288, suffering a crushing defeat at Meloria in 1284 from which she never recovered. By 1294 Venice and Genoa were again in conflict in the Second Genoese War, and their persistent rivalry fanned the flames of a whole series of inconclusive wars which dragged on right up to 1381, when Genoa finally conceded defeat.

The Italians, then, could not always be depended upon to provide naval support, especially where such service was incompatible with their bigotries or commercial ambitions—which goes a long way towards explaining why Italian merchants actually *helped* the Moslems to repulse a Frankish attack on Alexandria in 1174! Similarly, and for the same basic reasons, the aid sometimes provided by the Sicilian fleet—for example in the attack of 1174 just mentioned, in which they allegedly provided 282 ships—could not be relied on, so all in all it was fortunate that the Frankish states could raise a few ships of their own when necessity dictated, albeit only by employing Italian vessels and pirates on a freelance basis. The 15 galleys placed under the pirate baron Gerard of Sidon's command at Ascalon in 1153 fall into this category, as do the 33 galleys collected in Tyre and Acre for the relief of Beirut in 1182. Five galleys and a number of lesser craft launched on the Red Sea by Reynald de Châtillon the same year to raid Meccan pilgrims were undoubtedly crewed by pirates.

The only evidence for any more permanent sort of armament dates to 1232, when King Henry I of Cyprus paid out money-fiefs to the Kingdom of Jerusalem's '*poulains* of the ports' for fitting out armed ships. The Franks' only other sources of naval aid were the fleets maintained by the Military Orders from about the mid-12th century, employed in the lucrative business of transporting pilgrims from Europe during peacetime but available as warships when the need arose. In an engagement before Tyre in 1187, for example, there were allegedly as many as 17 Hospitaller and Templar galleys (in reality probably only seven), apparently crewed by Pisans and Genoese. We know too that several large Templar warships accompanied Louis IX's Seventh Crusade to Damietta, and in 1278 12 Templar galleys are recorded in an attack on Tripoli.

Turning to the Moslems, at the beginning of the Crusade era the Fatimid Egyptian navy was still a formidable opponent, causing the newly founded Frankish kingdom frequent discomfort and unease in the early decades of the 12th century. Its principal bases were at Alexandria, Damietta, Ascalon and Aidhab on the Red Sea, with secondary bases at Sidon, Tyre, Acre and Caesarea which had all been lost to the Franks by 1124. Alexandria, Ascalon and Damietta in addition had their own shipyards where warships were constructed, often from pitch, iron and especially timber imported into Egypt by Italian merchants, of whom Saladin wrote in 1174 'there is not one of them that does not supply our land with materials of war'. This was a clandestine trade in which Venice at least had indulged since the 10th century, Egypt herself having always been destitute of home-grown shipbuilding timber.

A later source tells us that in total the Fatimid navy had once comprised 75 galleys, ten 'galleasses' or large galleys and ten transports, and these figures tally with those which occur in other sources. Fulcher of Chartres records that 25 Fatimid galleys were driven ashore between Jaffa and Egypt in a storm in 1105, William of Tyre adding that 2,000 oarsmen and sailors were captured as a result; in 1115 another Fatimid fleet off Jaffa comprised nearly 70 ships 'of which some were triremes, some were beaked ships [ie, they had rams] and some were freighted with supplies'; and in 1118 a Fatimid squadron which sailed to Tyre is described as 'a dangerous fleet of no small size'. In 1126 the Egyptian fleet is said to have comprised 22 'triremes' and 53 other ships, and at Ascalon in 1153 it is recorded as 70 large ships and some smaller vessels. Thereafter the Egyptian fleet declined somewhat, but Saladin rebuilt it soon after his accession and in 1179 it comprised 60 galleys and transports.

We frequently encounter Egyptian ships in action during the period between 1177 and the end of the Third Crusade (1192), during the earlier part of which several daring attacks were launched along the Syrian coast, including a combined operation against Beirut in 1182. After 1187, however, we rarely encounter Saladin's fleet in a victorious role. In that year the admiral of Alexandria himself was captured off Tyre with eight other amirs and seven galleys by the Frankish garrison's own fleet of seven (a figure alternatively quoted as 17 and 27). In this battle Conrad of Montferrat, self-appointed lord of Tyre, had used the age-old ruse of a feigned flight to lure five of the Egyptians' 12 galleys into the harbour and, raising the chain that barred the harbour entrance, captured them prior to sending out his own seven galleys against those of the Moslems, driving five ashore (which Saladin burnt for fear that the Franks would capture them) and capturing the other two*. In 1189 50 Egyptian ships broke through into besieged Acre, but the next year a larger flotilla was beaten there in a fierce engagement by a combined Piso-Genoese fleet of 50 galleys again under Conrad, losing several more ships captured or sunk before gaining the safety of the harbour. When the city finally surrendered in 1191 the many Moslem ships still at anchor in the port went to the Franks, diminishing Egypt's naval strength yet further, and the appeal for naval aid that Saladin sent out at about this time to the Almohade Sultan of North Africa, whose fleet was one of the most powerful in the Western Mediterranean, brought no response.

It is hardly surprising to find, then, that after Saladin's death in 1193 Frankish supremacy at sea went virtually unchallenged for the rest of the Crusade era. 'After the death of Saladin,' as one Moslem chronicler observed, 'the affairs of the fleet were given little attention.' There were so few volunteers for the navy that the authorities had to resort to press-gang methods to raise crews for their warships, seizing unsuspecting individuals off the streets who were locked up by night and chained to their posts by day. The term *ustuli*, meaning 'man of the navy', was even considered a form of insult by Egyptians!

The Moslem fleets that we *do* encounter in the 13th century are invariably smaller than those of the 12th century. The efforts of the Egyptian fleet at Damietta in 1218 were indecisive and unsuccessful because it had too few ships, and although 21 galleys were mustered to assist in the siege of Ascalon in 1247 most of them were lost as a result of poor seamanship, being driven ashore in a sudden storm. The flotilla that scored such a remarkable series of successes against the Franks' supply ships during the Seventh Crusade included very few galleys at all, being comprised instead largely of light skiffs transported camel-back to the Nile and used to ambush the Christian vessels as they proceeded upriver.

The only revival that the Egyptian fleet underwent in the course of the 13th century took place, inevitably enough, under the auspices of the ever-energetic Baibars, the only Mamluk sultan to take any kind of interest in the navy during the era of the Crusades. Having lost virtually his entire fleet (all but two of 11-14

---

* Most Levantine port cities of the Crusade era had long moles round their outer harbours with a central opening flanked by towers, between which a chain could be stretched for defensive purposes. As well as Tyre we know for certain that Acre had one, as did Jebail, Damietta and Constantinople. Attacks on ports usually involved capturing one of the flanking towers in order to lower the chain, as at Galata in 1203 and Damietta in 1218.

galleys) in a storm off Cyprus in 1270, he ordered the immediate construction of 20 more in Egypt and summoned the only other ships he had, five more galleys, from their station at Qus. Other sources say that he even built as many as 40 galleys, but either way they and their inferior seamen were no real threat to the Italians' domination of the Mediterranean which was all that enabled the Franks to resist the Mamluks for as long as they did. By circa 1285 the Egyptian navy had virtually ceased to exist, but even that and Italian naval supremacy did not prevent the Mamluks' final victory and the collapse of the Frankish states in 1291. Perhaps what Baibars had written to the King of Cyprus after the loss of the Egyptian fleet in 1270 was true: 'Your horses are ships. But *our* ships are horses.'

I don't know about horses, but some ships were certainly called *gamells* (camels) and others were called *colombels* (pigeons). In fact the ships in use in the Mediterranean came in many and diverse forms which can be simply (but not altogether accurately) divided into merchant vessels and warships. The typical merchant ship of this era was a sailing vessel about three times its beam in length, with two or three forward-raked lateen-rigged masts with yards as long or longer than the ship itself. The larger ships of this type, about 85 feet in length, had at least two decks plus forecastle and stern castle and usually mast-head fighting tops (small affairs shaped rather like barrels). Such a vessel was called in Italian a *buzus* or *navis*, terms which literally meant 'bus' and 'ship' respectively. In other sources they appear as *bucca* and *nes* or *nef*.

King Richard took with him 14 such *buccae*, 'vessels of vast size, wonderful speed and great strength', when he set out on the Third Crusade, each well equipped with a store of spare gear which included three rudders, 30 oars, two sets of sails, three sets of ropes, and two full sets of all other equipment except masts and ship's boats, plus as many as 13 anchors (such ships normally carrying ten to 20 anchors at a time). In addition they appear to have carried 40 war-horses, 40 knights and their arms and 40 foot-soldiers plus a crew of 15 sailors, and 'a full year's food for all these men and horses', so such vessels were clearly of considerable size. Average deadweight tonnage was some 200 tons, although some were even bigger. In 1264 the Venetians had a huge sailing ship with a 100-120 man crew called the *Roccaforte* or 'Fortress' which was of as much as 500 tons, a big ship even by 18th century standards and a giant by the standards of the 13th century. Such colossi probably first started appearing around 1240 or 1250. Venice apparently had only two in the 1260s, and probably there were less than six of *Roccaforte*'s tonnage in the whole Mediterranean at one time.

Smaller merchant ships were the longer, single-decked and two-masted *tarettes* or *esneccae* ('smacks') of about 100 tons which, with oars as well as sails, often accompanied warships as supply vessels, being easier to handle than the larger *naves* which were less able to beat to windward. Obviously all such vessels were better able to stay at sea for longer periods than the warships, whose limited cargo capacity dictated that they must put into port at fairly regular intervals for food and water (say every ten days), a hazardous occupation if you were off an enemy coastline at the time; Fulcher of Chartres records how a Fatimid landing party which put in for water near Beirut in 1126 was chased back to its boats by the local militia and lost 130 dead. On the other hand, since the merchant ships relied on favourable winds, and dependable pre-vailing winds do not exist in the Mediterranean, they were not often at sea themselves for more than a few days at a time before adverse winds or stormy weather obliged them to put in to harbour.

Under such conditions, and at their average speed of some five to eight knots, sailing ships could take up to six weeks on the voyage from mainland Europe to Outremer; the very fastest journey possible, direct from Marseilles to Acre with no island-hopping or coast-hugging, was some 15-20 days. Warships under sail went at much the same speeds. Under oars they could probably reach a top speed of about seven knots for short spurts, maintaining about four knots on short trips of two or three hours duration, and averaging about two knots on longer journeys. Contrary winds, of course, slowed them down too.

All the warships used in the Mediterranean during the Crusade era by Moslem and Christian alike were descended from or related to Byzantine types, many of them still in service with the Imperial fleet. From circa 500 onwards their generic name had been *dromon*, meaning 'racer' or 'runner', therefore indicating that they were ships of speed and automatically distinguishing them from the slower-moving merchant round-ships. In the Byzantine navy of the 8th-10th centuries this blanket term covered a number of distinctly different ship types, notably the *ousiakos, pamphylos, chelandrion* and *siphonophoros*. Since Mediterranean winds are almost invariably either too light or too fresh for manoeuvering heavy sailing ships in battle, these types were all oar-propelled so that they could manoeuvre regardless of wind speed and direction. They did have masts, from one to perhaps three depending on the size of the ship, and sails too, lateen-rigged throughout, but although these were curiously sometimes not struck before action all movement in battle was executed by oar.

In fact it was really only in the number of their oarsmen that the various categories of Byzantine dromon actually differed from one another. They were all much the same length (about 110-130 feet) and had two banks of oars one above the other on either side, each usually of 25 benches but occasionally up to 30 and sometimes as few as 20. The difference was that although the oars of the lower bank were always manned by just one rower, those of the open upper deck were manned by one, two or three men; the first therefore had an average crew of 100 oarsmen plus probably about 40 seamen, marines and officers (usually six) and was called an ousiakos because its upper oars were crewed by only one *ousia* or company. Ships with two men per upper oar were called *pamphyla*, and those with three men were the *dromones* proper, these types having about 55 and 70 additional sailors and marines respectively. The largest number of oarsmen we hear of on a Byzantine dromon is 230.

The chelandrion is a bit more of a mystery; it is the only term used by Moslem sources to describe Byzantine ships, and its use in the 10th century as a prefix for both ousiakos and pamphylos would tend to indicate that it was possibly an alternative term for 'dromon'. Then again, in Greek its name suggests some affinity with a tortoise, from which it could be inferred that the upper deck had some kind of protective roof or perhaps even another deck over it. Several sources agree that it had two banks of oars and 150 oarsmen and add that it was armed with Greek Fire siphons, so it seems likely that chelandrion, pamphylos and also siphonophoros could all in fact be names for the same type of vessel, *siphonophores* being siphon-equipped warships.

Byzantine ships were still using Greek Fire, that most hideous of mediaeval weapons, when the Crusades began at the very end of the 11th century. Anna Comnena reports how in 1103 her father the Emperor Alexius I equipped a squadron of his ships with siphons which shot jets of Greek Fire out through the mouths of gilded brass or iron lion-heads fitted on the prow of each vessel, 'so that it seemed as if the lions . . . were vomitting fire.' The Pisans against whom this fire was directed in the ensuing naval engagement off Rhodes were thoroughly demoralised by it 'because they were not accustomed to this sort of machine or fire which, naturally flaming upwards, in this case was thrown in whichever direction the firer wished, often downwards or crossways.'

The fire itself, called Greek Fire by the Franks but Sea Fire by the Byzantines themselves, had originally been invented circa 673 by a certain Kallinikos, a Syrian from Heliopolis in Byzantine service. In reality it was probably no more than an improvement on one of the various other incendiary mixtures which had been in use in the Mediterranean world for some time, and it seems equally likely that its composition underwent constant change throughout its history. The principal ingredients appear to have included naptha, bitumen, quicklime, sulphur, resins, turpentine and oil and its chief attribute—especially in naval warfare—was that because of the quicklime it could even burn underwater, which in turn obviously meant that water could not be used to extinguish it. This earnt it the alternative names Wild Fire and Wet Fire, and contemporaries believed that only sand, urine or vinegar could put it out. The siphons from which it was fired are described in an earlier source as covered in copper, bronze or iron and swivel-mounted to enable them to fire in any direction. A pair were normally situated in the prow but they are sometimes also to be found in the stern and amidships, in the latter instance probably being sited on the wooden castle that the very largest dromons carried there. We cannot be certain quite how these siphons worked, but most probably they involved a jet of water which simultaneously ignited and propelled the Fire at its target, the water jet being produced either by a simple pump or a syringe-mechanism (the Byzantine word for siphon, *klysteros,* also meaning syringe).

The one real mystery that remains is why this highly efficient ship-killing weapon, with which in the engagement off Rhodes mentioned above a single Byzantine dromon destroyed four of the largest Pisan warships in a matter of minutes, should have ever fallen into disuse. All one can assume is that knowledge of the chemical composition of this particular form of Greek Fire, always a closely guarded secret, became somehow lost or less widespread, and that with the steady decline of the Imperial navy during the 11th and 12th centuries its use similarly declined to the point where its potential in warfare was no longer recognised. After Alexius' reign and his brief revival of the Imperial fleet we hardly ever read of Greek Fire siphons again, the very last rather uncertain references to their use apparently dating to 1165 and 1171. Interestingly, Venetian ships in Byzantine service are twice recorded using Greek Fire in the 11th century, once in 1002 and again in 1084, but these are isolated instances in which the siphons and their crews were probably both supplied on temporary loan by the Imperial government. It would be interesting to speculate on what such a combination of Venetian seamanship and Byzantine flamethrowers on a long term basis might have meant to Frankish power in the Eastern Mediterranean.

Although the term dromon remained in use, occasionally appearing in the forms *dromund* or *dromond*, by the mid-12th century its meaning had changed. Its interchangeability with the European terms bucca and navis indicates that it was no longer regarded as a warship, and nor was it even necessarily a lateen-rigged, sail- and oar-powered Mediterranean-type vessel. Dromons of the earlier Byzantine type did nevertheless remain in service as warships but, as we shall see, under a new guise. The main reason for the dromon's own decline in the military field was basically that it was no longer the fastest type of ship around, while its very size and attendant cargo and troop-carrying capacity lent themselves ideally to the function of a transport, in which role we normally encounter *dromundi* for the remainder of their history until the word disappears entirely in the 14th century. The largest could apparently carry over 1,000 people as well as 200 tons or more of cargo. One wrecked in Egypt in 1182 allegedly had as many as 1,500 pilgrims aboard, and the same number of passengers is acredited by one source to the Moslem dromon which, as will be described further on, King Richard's ships sank off Acre in 1191, an episode which proves that even as a transport the dromon could still be a formidable adversary.

The dromon's successor, both as principal warship and generic term for all Mediterranean warships, was the small, swift *galea* or galley (from the Byzantine *ghalaia*, meaning 'swordfish'). Of Byzantine ancestry (it seems to first appear in Leo VI's time), the galley was originally used in reconnaissance, coastguard and observation or spying roles, where its speed could be employed to best advantage. Although it was usually of the same or similar length, the true galley differed from the dromons it was supplanting in having only one bank of oars—hence its alternative name of *moneres*—manned in the first instance by only one rower per oar, which inevitably reduced its tonnage and increased its speed accordingly. The galleys of the Crusade era, however, do not necessarily fit this description, and in a fair number of instances what the Frankish chroniclers are describing as a *galea* is in fact no more than a rechristened dromon; this is particularly obvious when they are described as 'triremes' as in Fulcher of Chartres' history, or when very large numbers of oarsmen or upper and lower banks of oars are mentioned. For example, in the battle between Conrad of Montferrat and Saladin's squadron off Tyre in 1187 we are told how the Moslems boarded one of the Frankish *galeae* and drove the oarsmen from the upper deck, taking their places at the oars. The Franks continued to hold the lower deck, however, and rowed against the efforts of the Moslems above them so that the ship was jerked one way and the other until the Franks eventually rallied and retook the upper deck.

Some of the terminology used to describe various types of galley also betrays that the ships in question are in reality of the dromon class. Italian fleets included ships called *zelandrie* and *galandrie*, names which are obviously corruptions of the Byzantine chelandrion, of which the latter variant interestingly incorporates the word galea too. Another type of Frankish galley called a *sagitta* or *saete* ('arrow'), a very fast vessel with up to 48-60 long oars, was sometimes called a *pamphilo* or *panfilo*, even though it was actually smaller than the original pamphylos. The smallest fighting galleys one normally encounters were called *galeotta* or *galeotes*, 16-20 oared vessels, while the largest galleys were called *galions* or *gatti*. Twenty-eight Venetian gatti recorded in a naval victory over the Egyptians at Ascalon in 1123 are described as 'larger than a galley and manned with 100 oars, each one worked by two rowers', which again sounds rather like a dromon with two banks of 25 oars a side.

Returning to the galley proper, in terms of a ship with only one bank of oars, these were usually built in or close to the proportions of 8x (length) × x

(breadth) × $^x/_3$ (draft), with a lateen-rigged mast—usually just the one—of $4x$ height, situated at a distance of about a third of the ship's length from the prow. The sail and yard were both normally struck when the galley made ready for battle although, as with the dromon, this was not always the case. The oars, of which there were normally from 24 to 30 a side, had their tholepins on a *telaro* or outrigger, a strong frame above deck height and rectangular in plan with sides which extended about two or three feet over the water on either side of the hull. A *corsia* or walkway ran fore and aft along the centre of the outrigger, sometimes with a *castello* or wooden tower halfway along, and in battle marines and soldiers stood between the oars on a platform which ran along the *apostis* or long edge of the frame. This had a guard-rail to which shields and possibly wooden mantlets called *pavesades* were added in action to protect the otherwise exposed oarsmen.

By the end of the 12th century at the latest the rowers' benches were angled so that their inboard ends were further aft than the outboard ones, so as to enable two men sitting on the same bench to each handle their own oar. It is this arrangement which is normally intended by the word 'bireme' in mediaeval sources, and it can be seen quite clearly in many illustrations from the 13th century onwards where the oars are grouped in pairs. Sets of three to five oars are even claimed by Vincent de Beauvais, who wrote circa 1250, and although his optimistic claim is rather premature we know from another source that from circa 1290 and in fact even earlier some galleys started to have three oars per bench, and that by about 1320 some did indeed have four or five. Rowing three to a bench was called *ad terzarolos*, and the sources make it clear that galleys manned thus were faster than those with only one or two oarsmen per bench. Jean d'Ibelin's galley at Damietta in 1248, which 'seemed as if it flew, so did the rowers urge it forward with their oars', may have been of this type even at this early date, especially since it had allegedly as many as 300 rowers, an average galley of the 13th century usually only having about 150. In Venice the smallest galleys could have crews of less than 60 men, but by Venetian standards such ships were classified as 'unarmed', ie, they were not warships.

One final class of ship, and one which was particularly important to the Franks after the 12th century when most crusaders travelled to the Holy Land by sea, was the horse-transport. This differed from the other types of warship in being—like most merchant ships—operated by sail alone. But it was still, yet again, of Byzantine origin. These transports were sometimes called by their Byzantine name of *onerariae*, but more commonly they were described as *oxorii*, *ippagogi*, *ursers* or *huissiers*. The French name *huissier* (Italian *uscieri*) derived from the characteristic feature of such ships, the door (French *huis*, Italian *usci*) for embarking or disembarking the horses. 'For,' writes Robert de Clari, a knight of the Fourth Crusade, 'the transports were built in such a way that there was a portal which could be opened and a bridge that could be thrust out by which the knights could go out to land mounted', although de Clari's fellow-crusader Villehardouin says that the horses were led out before being mounted. William of Tyre writes of Byzantine onerariae in 1169 that they had 'stern-openings for unloading', and the door seems to have most commonly been in the ship's side near the stern, the ship normally having to be beached before disembarkation could take place.

Once the door had been opened and reclosed the huissier could not put to sea again without some work first being carried out to ensure it had been made watertight. Joinville tells us of his own embarkation that 'they opened the portal of the ship and put inside all the horses we were taking overseas; and then they reclosed the door and caulked it well, as when a cask is sunk in water, because when the ship is on the high seas the said door is entirely under water.'

Capacity of an huissier appears to have been 40 or, at the very most, 60 horses and about 30-80 men plus a crew of some 15-40 sailors. In size it resembled a tarette. Indeed, Moslem horse-transports (carrying a maximum of 40 horses) were actually called *tarridas*; like the huissiers, to which they were no doubt identical, the embarkation door of the tarrida was towards its stern.

Those of you who are still with me after all that may have noticed that thus far little mention has actually been made of Moslem ship types. There are two good reasons for this. The first is quite simply that little such information is available, except for such odd snippets as the fact that Moslem galleys were called in Arabic *shiniyyah* and large galleys of the galion type were called *butsah*, derived no doubt from bucca. And the second reason is that the information which *is* available proves beyond a shadow of a doubt that Saracen ships were identical to the lateen-rigged vessels used by the Franks, being copied from the same Byzantine originals. For instance, Saracen blockade-runners at Acre needed only to change their clothes, shave off their beards Frankish-fashion and let pigs run around on their upper decks (Moslems being forbidden to touch pork) to convince the Franks that their ships were Christian ones. Similarly in 1270 it was proposed to paint some Mamluk galleys black and put crosses on their sails so that they could pass for Frankish vessels. In broad terms, then, the above paragraphs apply equally well to Moslem ships.

Most of the detailed information that we have on Mediterranean sea-fights of the Crusade era is derived from descriptions of battles between rival Italian fleets, particularly the Venetians and Genoese, but there is enough incidental evidence available to prove that naval battles between Christian and Moslem fleets were much the same. Generally they involved combining to best advantage the two categories of ship described above—the slow, unmanoeuvreable merchantman and the swift warship—their roles being respectively those of defence and attack. Thus the Venetians at Durazzo in 1081 and Passaron in 1084 formed their large ships into a so-called 'sea-harbour' by stretching cables from vessel to vessel, probably a crescent-shaped formation facing towards the foe and protecting the flanks of the galleys gathered within it. Such high-sided merchantmen, with their castles fore and aft and often equipped with stone-throwing artillery forward or amidships, posed a formidable problem for attacking galleys, which were subjected to a withering barrage of crossbow bolts, stones, timber stakes and other missiles against which, since they came from above, they had little protection. For instance in 1264 the huge *Roccaforte* mentioned earlier held off as many as 16 Genoese galleys after taking aboard the crews of the 18 smaller Venetian ships which had accompanied her. Similarly, as we shall see below, a single very large Moslem ship held off allegedly as many as 40 Frankish galleys at Acre in 1191. If possible the enemy would cripple such ships by slashing and scything their sails and rigging with broad-headed arrows and long-handled cutting weapons, or by divers boring holes in their hulls or otherwise disabling them. Some would be sunk instead by ramming since many galleys were still fitted with rams, a point to which we shall return anon.

Fleets were marshalled by simple signals transmitted by flags or lights, orders otherwise being issued by hailing, by ship's boat, or possibly by trumpet. The ships normally formed up in line or occasionally in two lines, sometimes curved with the wings either advanced like horns, as in the Venetian 'sea-harbour', or refused. If possible they protected their rear by drawing up close to the shore so that in fact the majority of sea-fights were really coastal engagements. The Genoese fleet at the Battle of Meloria against the Pisans in 1284 formed up in two lines, with 63 galleys and eight pamphilos in the first and 30 more galleys in the second. Although the second line had struck its sails the first had left them unfurled, possibly to conceal the presence of the second line since numbers could only be identified by the counting of masts; certainly the Pisans did not realise that there *was* a second line until it was too late to turn back.

We hear of sails being left unfurled on other occasions too, apparently to utilise a favourable wind as opposing fleets bore down on each other. In the engagement between Venetians and Egyptians off Ascalon in 1123, for example, where the former had divided their fleet in two and succeeded in sandwiching the unsuspecting Moslems, the latter only became aware of the squadron in their rear when they saw them loom up 'with sails unfurled and oars straining'. The squadron to their front, incidentally, was made up of the Venetian fleet's largest ships, four very large merchantmen and the 28 gatti, so that the Egyptians were successfully deceived into thinking it to be a merchant caravan carrying pilgrims from Cyprus. One other instance of unfurled sails which should be noted is the Battle of Lajazzo in 1294, where a sudden head breeze caught the unfurled sails of the Venetian ships and turned them broadside on to the Genoese, with the result that the Venetian battle-line was thrown into total confusion. The Genoese, incidentally, apparently on this occasion adopted the Scandinavian custom of lashing their ships together into a huge floating platform; in the subsequent engagement they captured or sank 25 out of 68 Venetian galleys.

Battle itself opened with an exchange of missiles, usually arrows and cross-bow-bolts, accompanied by stones where ships fitted with mangonels were present. As the ships drew closer pots of flour and powdered quicklime were also hurled, to blind the enemy, and pots of liquid soap to make his decks too slippery to walk on. Incendiaries—fire-arrows and naptha grenades—were also used by Christian and Moslem alike, hides and vinegar-soaked felt blankets being draped over the ship's sides as protection against them, the ship then being known as 'padded' (*imbarbottata*) or simply as *barbotte*. Ships drawing alongside to board ran the added risk of having lengths of stout timber dropped through their decks from the enemy's mast-heads, either from the fighting tops or from the ship's boats which were sometimes manned with archers and hoisted up between the masts in battle. But thereafter, once the ships had collided or grappled, it was a matter of seizing the enemy's vessel by brute force in a bloody hand-to-hand mêlée, rowers abandoning their oars and joining the grim struggle.

A classic description of such a ship-to-ship action is given by Ambroise, that garrulous chronicler of the Third Crusade. The whole episode is worth quoting at length for the myriad of other details it provides:

'At last,' writes Ambroise, 'on this side of Sidon near Beirut, they [the English fleet under King Richard] saw a certain ship some way off which was filled with Saladin's best soldiers, the pick of all his pagan realm, which was bringing aid to the besieged in Acre. Seeing that they could not make straight for Acre because the Christians were so close, these Saracens had pulled out to sea a little to wait for a chance to make a sudden dash into the harbour. But

Richard, who had noticed the ship, called up Peter des Barres, one of his galley commanders, and told him to row over to it and enquire who its commander might be. The word that came back was that the ship belonged to the King of France; but Richard, as he urged his own ship closer, could not hear a single word of French from it nor see any Christian flags or banners. And as they approached he began to wonder at its size and its firm and solid build. It had three very tall masts and its smooth sides were covered here and there with green or yellow hides [as a defence against Greek Fire]; and it was so well rigged, provisioned and fitted out that it could not have been bettered.

'A man present aboard the king's ship said that he had been at Beirut when this vessel had been loaded [he was undoubtedly a Frankish spy]. The cargo he had seen carried aboard it comprised 100 camel-loads of arms of every kind, crossbows, bows, spears and arrows. There were also seven Saracen amirs and 800 chosen Turks aboard [other sources say there were 650, 700 or 1,500 aboard], not to mention such a quantity of food that it defied calculation. There was a stock of Greek Fire grenades too, as well as 200 deadly snakes intended to wreak havoc amongst the Christians.*

'The king now sent over more messengers, to enquire more particularly who the strangers were; this time they received a different reply, that the strangers were Genoese bound for Tyre. While most were left feeling uncertain as to what this contradiction might mean, the man from Beirut kept on saying with confidence that the ship was a Saracen one. He told the king that he could cut off his head or hang him if he could not prove that what he said was true. "Now that they are scurrying away," he said, "send a second galley after them, without it giving them a single word of greeting; that way we'll see just what their intentions are and what faith they hold."

'So at the king's command another galley started after the strange ship at full speed. And as it drew alongside, without offering any word of greeting, the sailors of the strange ship began to hurl arrows and darts against the galley crew. On seeing this Richard gave his galleys the order for an immediate attack. Missiles fell like rain on both sides and the strange ship now went more slowly, for its oarsmen had to slacken their efforts [in order to protect themselves] and there was very little wind. Yet though our galleymen rowed round the enemy again and again they could not see a good opening for an attack, so strongly was the vessel built and manned and such an uninterrupted barrage of darts did it lay down. Our men, on the other hand, were suffering badly from the Saracens' fire, falling as it did from such an extraordinarily high-sided vessel, for with gravity on its side a dart from above does considerably more damage. For this reason our men began to falter and fall back, wondering what King Richard would deem the best move to make under these circumstances. But he bellowed at them, "What? Are you going to let that ship get away unharmed? Shame upon you! After so many victories you're surely not going to let sloth take over and just give up like cowards? Every last one of you will deserve no better than to be hanged or executed if you let them escape!"

'When they heard this some of the galleymen thought it wise to make a virtue of necessity and, diving overboard and getting under the enemy ship's hull,

* Venomous snakes, scorpions and the like had been employed in sea battles since the Punic Wars. They were thrown on to the decks of enemy vessels in open baskets, their presence thereafter tending to somewhat distract the afflicted seamen from other matters requiring their urgent attention.

bound her helm over with ropes so that she veered round to one side and her progress was thus hindered. Others, bringing their galleys skilfully alongside, grabbed the enemy's rigging and made to leap aboard. But the Turks were ready and quickly slew them, lopping off one man's arms, another's hands or head, and pitching their bodies into the sea. The sight of this roused the other Christians to greater valour, and scrambling over the ship's bulwarks they hurled themselves upon the Turks, giving no quarter to any who offered resistance.

'But the Turks, strengthened by desperation, made furious efforts to repel the galleymen, succeeding in cutting off a foot here and a hand or head there, whilst their opponents drove them steadily back to the very prow of the ship. Upon this other Turks came rushing up from the lower deck of the ship and, joining their companions, put up a fierce resistance, being determined to drive off their foes or die bravely like men. So the fight raged on and warriors fell everywhere on both sides until at last the Turks, surging forward with sudden energy, forced our men back and drove them off the ship. Our men withdrew to their galleys and pulled away and began once more to row round the vessel looking for a suitable opening to attack.

'Meanwhile the king had realised that it would not be easy to take the Turkish vessel intact with all its stores and arms without further endangering his men, and he gave orders for each of the galleys to prick the enemy with its spur [ie, its ram]. So the galleys drew back a little, then once more surged forward under the impulse of many oars to pierce the enemy ship's sides. In this way the ship was stove in and, taking in water, began to sink. To avoid going down with her the Turks leapt overboard into the sea where they were all killed or drowned. But the king spared 35 of them [an alternative source says 200], to wit the amirs and those who were skilled at making siege engines. The others all perished, the equipment was all lost, and the serpents were drowned or tossed about here and there on the waves.'

A Moslem source gives us the added details that the Frankish galleys totalled 40 in number and that the 'Turks' succeeded in burning and sinking one of these, together with its crew, with their Greek Fire; he also says that on their captain's orders the Moslems scuttled their own ship to prevent its supplies from falling into Frankish hands, making no mention of the latter using their 'spurs'. Which brings us back to the enigmatic ram—enigmatic because so many modern authorities claim that (a) it was not much used, and (b) that it was now a ship-crippling weapon, not a ship-killing one. Stopping to consider the evidence in detail, however, neither of these points hold water, if you'll forgive the pun. Many—but not all—warships were quite clearly fitted with the ram: Fulcher of Chartres repeatedly mentions 'beaked ships' and goes out of his way to differentiate them from other oared warships, which he generally calls 'triremes', probably indicating dromon-type ships with three men per upper oar; William of Tyre also mentions 'rostrated' or 'beaked' ships on several occasions, and he records how in the Venetian victory off Ascalon, Doge Domenico Michiel's own vessel rammed and overturned that of the Egyptian admiral, one of several vessels sunk by ramming on this occasion; in the Third Crusade King Richard's own galley is described as long and low on the water 'with a sharp spar at the bow called a spur'. The evidence of Ambroise and William of Tyre, then, proves beyond a shadow of a doubt that the spur, as the ram is usually referred to, was still very much a ship-killing weapon, and if it was 'not much used' it is hard to conceive why so many galleys were thus equipped.

Strangely, however—and this is very clear from contemporary illustrations—the spur was always well above the waterline, usually at about the height of the telaro or outrigger frame, and where it succeeded in sinking a ship it was quite obviously more a matter of its impact rupturing the vessel's framework over a large area rather than punching a neat hole through which water could enter the hull. Its location at telaro-level suggests, in fact, that the ram was possibly intended to smash the outrigger frames of opposing galleys and thereby cripple them—hence theory (b) above—the shearing off of an enemy's oars having been a recognised naval tactic since classical times.

Certainly less ships appear to have been sunk now than in the naval battles of antiquity. More often they ran aground or were captured. For instance at Meloria only seven Pisan galleys were sunk, while five or more ran aground and as many as 30 were captured by the Genoese. Their total losses accounted for something over half the fleet, and 50 per cent casualties were not unusual in naval engagements. At Acre in 1258 the Venetians sunk or captured 24 galleys out of a Genoese fleet of 50 galleys and four great merchantmen, 1,700 Genoese being killed and probably as many captured. Some victories were even more total. The Egyptians defeated at Ascalon were almost annihilated; only four galleys, four gatti and one 'huge vessel' were captured, the remainder—probably some ten or 15 vessels—being nearly all sunk. Defeated crews were more often than not butchered in the fight or drowned after leaping overboard, the weight of their armour and other equipment dragging them under. Those who survived were taken captive either on board or when they had swum ashore. If they were unlucky they might be mutilated or executed, but the luckier ones ended up in prison or as slaves and some at least stood a chance of being ransomed. Venetians captured by Genoese, or Genoese captured by Venetians, frequently fared less well.

Chapter 12

Siege warfare

In the words of one of the leading scholars of the Crusade era, 'in a country where shortage of manpower was a constant feature of existence, stone walls had to replace warriors in the permanent and arduous task of defence.'* In fact, as we have already seen, in Outremer the vast majority of the Frankish population actually dwelt in castles or fortified cities, and even the manor-houses, mills and monasteries of the rural areas were fortified or had their own defensive towers. Well over a hundred fortresses and fortified towns are known to have existed in the Kingdom of Jerusalem alone, and in the whole of Outremer there were probably at various times more than 300 fortified sites in Frankish possession, ranging in scale from the humble, square towers that were a typical feature of open towns and villages, right up to the double-walled city of Acre and the massive complex of Krak des Chevaliers in the County of Tripoli. Some were originally constructed to blockade Moslem strongholds, others to guard frontiers, roads, fords and bridges, to cut lines of communication, or to control newly-conquered regions, and yet others to restrict the movement of raiders through the Frankish domain. A large number acted in addition as administrative centres or places of refuge in troubled times, and many had permanent garrisons and could be used as bases for counter-raids. Their area of influence was any point within a day's ride, therefore anywhere within a 15-35 mile radius of the castle depending on the nature of the surrounding countryside.

On the construction and style of the castles themselves it is too easy to make misleading generalisations, and too many people already have done. Rather than join their ranks I would refer the reader instead to any one of several excellent books on the subject written with authority by experts who know their subject, particularly *The Crusaders in the Holy Land* by Meron Benvenisti, *Castles of the Crusaders* by W. Müller-Wiener, *Castles and Churches of the Crusading Kingdom* by T.S.R. Boase, and chapter VII 'The Crusaders' Castles' in R.C. Smail's *Crusading Warfare 1097-1193*. Here we are concerned *not* with the architecture and ingenuity of the castle's defences, but rather the ways and means by which they could be overcome.

First we can divide up the ways of attacking a castle into three separate categories, which involve going over, through or under its defences; a fourth category combined deception, cunning or treachery with any one of these, most

* Joshua Prawer, *The Latin Kingdom of Jerusalem*.

commonly the subversion of dissatisfied elements within the garrison. Of course, most sieges involved the employment of every means available by the besieged as well as the besiegers, and not all necessarily depended on some form of actual attack. However, Franks and Moslems alike would always first attempt a direct assault on the walls with ladders and grappling hooks—after all, you never knew your luck, and if there was an element of surprise on the attacker's side he might even (and occasionally did) carry the defences in his first rush, particularly if the garrison was understrength or depleted. If the attack failed, though, what was he to do next?

The attacker's first option, and the one which for us springs to mind almost automatically when we imagine a mediaeval siege, was to entrench his camp with ramparts and ditches and sit down and wait, ensuring as he did so that he had successfully cut off all communication between the garrison and the outside world—ie, nothing could get in and no-one could get out. The idea was to starve the castle into submission, and it often worked, but it was nevertheless a tactic that was rarely as successful in Syria as it was in Europe. There were a number of reasons for this, not least of which was the fact that crusader armies at least were often too small to successfuly blockade a large fortified city. Nor did the castles of Outremer have as many mouths to feed, because not only was the garrison usually understrength but there were not as many refugees to cater for either since, as we have seen, the majority of the rural population were Moslems who had nothing to fear from the approach of their co-religionists. The principal reason, however, was quite simply that most of the major castles made full provision for just such an eventuality; al-Marqab's cellars, for example, could feed a garrison of 1,000 men for five years, and the incredibly vast storage spaces similarly available in other castles can still be seen today. In addition many were equipped with their own oil-presses, granaries and mills and all had wells or large cisterns in which to collect water.

This means of 'attack' nevertheless succeeded on a number of occasions, such as when the garrison of Kerak, having eaten every last horse and dog, surrendered to Saladin in 1188 after a siege of more than a year, to be followed in 1189 by Krak de Montréal after an even longer siege, many of its garrison having gone blind through lack of salt. In both these instances, however, the Moslem besiegers already held the surrounding countryside and had been regularly replaced by fresh contingents, while there had been absolutely no risk of a Frankish relief force disrupting their operations, the Franks having neither the men nor the leaders available to raise such a force. Under other circumstances, where the surrounding territory was in Frankish hands and there *was* the risk of an army marching to the rescue, sieges of this duration would have been impossible; either the besieging army would have been forced to raise its siege and march away or, unable to gather adequate supplies from the locality, it was likely to itself run out of food long before the besieged garrison did (as happened, for example, to a Moslem army at Edessa in 1110).

If circumstances were not right to achieve victory by famine, then alternative means had to be found, which brings us back to our three methods of breaching the defences, by going over, through or under them. The attacker, you will remember, has already had one attempt at going *over* the walls in his first mad rush, and it has presumably been singularly unsuccessful, as on the whole such assaults were. Now, however, the problem would be approached more scientifically, and this was one particular area in which, if they did not already, the Franks soon came to surpass their Moslem rivals.

After grappling hooks it was scaling ladders which were the simplest means of ascending a castle or city wall, and both are likely to have been used in the initial assault; which, if the fortress in question was adequately garrisoned, was probably the reason the attack had failed since this form of assault was both the easiest to repulse and the most costly to mount. Where it did succeed it was largely because the garrison was insufficient to man every section of the walls, or because the attackers were present in such numbers that they could attack any number of points simultaneously and simply shrug off the dreadful losses in which this would have resulted.

The advantage of large forces was usually with the Moslems, and this fact possibly explains why on the whole they stuck to the scaling ladder form of assault while the Franks tended to rely instead on the siege-tower, the celebrated belfry or *berefridum* (also called a *belfragium* or *beffroi*). Arab sources only seem to record the Moslems using such siege-towers, which they called *burj* or *dubbaba,* on a very small number of occasions, such as at Kerak in 1184, Tyre in 1187 and Caesarea and Arsuf in 1265. Frankish sources mention a few more instances, but clearly this was not a type of siege engine which the Moslems favoured.

The belfry was basically a tall wooden tower. Some were used in a static role, either to guard the besiegers' camp or to act as a counter-castle from the top of which it was possible to rake a specific portion of the defenders' walls with heavy fire (as did King Richard's belfry *Mattegriffun,* used on Sicily and later set up before the gates of Acre in 1191). More usually, however, they were mounted on wheels which were often called *pedes* or feet. They had several internal levels (called *caenacula* or *solaria*) interconnected by ladders, each level being pierced with embrasures through which archers could fire, and there was a drawbridge situated near the top at a point higher than the walls against which the tower was to be used. They took some time to build (two used at Tyre in 1111 were about 11 weeks in construction), and involved in their manufacture a considerable amount of wood, such a rare commodity in Syria that towers used in the capture of Jerusalem in 1099 were actually made from the timbers, ropes and nails of Genoese ships that had been dismantled at Jaffa and transported overland to the besiegers' camp. Otherwise the surrounding countryside had to be scoured and timber dragged in from miles around by horse, ass and camel. One source even tells us that three towers constructed at Acre in 1190 were built of wood 'brought from abroad, for a very specific kind was needed for them', and the Venetian ships attendant on the siege of Tyre likewise brought 'very long timbers' with them from Europe for the construction of siege-towers.

The belfry's actual height, and the number of floors it contained, varied according to the height of the walls opposed to it, but the tallest on record during this era appears to be that constructed at Lisbon in 1148 by crusaders en route to Syria, which was 95 feet tall, while the three at Acre come very close behind at 90 feet. These were probably about 25 feet square at the base, tapering slightly to about 15 or 20 feet square at the top. A belfry used by Amalric I's troops at Damietta in 1169 may have been even taller than any of these since it had seven storeys compared to five in the Acre belfries. In action these storeys were crowded with soldiers—the three towers at Acre allegedly each carrying as many as 500 men—as well as shields, armour, arms and other supplies. The men were presumably the same ones as pushed and pulled the tower into position against the walls, an operation sometimes carried out by men actually within the tower, but otherwise achieved by men outside with ropes in full view of the enemy on the battlements, who were hopefully distracted from firing down on them by covering fire laid down both from the ground and the top of the approaching belfry, which sometimes even carried its own catapult.

The crossbowmen and archers on the ground fired from the shelter of mantlets variously called *circleiai, plutei, crates* or *hourdis,* usually rectangular in shape and made of wood or interwoven branches covered in leather, each capable of covering several men. During his illness before Acre King Richard of England himself passed the time by taking pot-shots at the Moslems with his crossbow from behind such a mantlet.

However, we have jumped a little too far ahead, because before the ponderous belfry can make its final approach, amidst a barrage of missiles and incendiaries, one major obstruction has yet to be overcome. Nearly all of the larger fortresses and walled cities had one or more broad, deep ditches right round them (Tyre had as many as three), and there was no way that a belfry could get to the walls without someone first filling these. Fascines, piles of earth, rubble and debris, and even the bodies of dead men and horses were used for this, and a substantial volume of material must have been needed to fill an adequate section of ditch that could be between 25 and 65 feet wide and 20 to 40 feet deep. At the siege of Jerusalem we know it took one whole night and until evening of the next day to achieve this, the sappers suffering heavy casualties all the while from the Moslem garrison's fire, in the face of which murderous barrage they were encouraged by the promise of a denier for every three stones that they cast into the ditch.

The garrison's main defence against the belfry itself was fire, and unfortunately for the Franks the Moslems were well versed in the science of pyrotechnics. As the tower came nearer and nearer to the walls a hail of incendiaries of all types was usually launched against it—burning faggots, fire-arrows, white hot bolts and stones, jars of naptha, and grenades filled with Greek Fire. Admittedly the latter was not of the same recipe as the 'Sea Fire' originally invented for the Byzantines by Kallinikos, but it was no less effective and equally hard to extinguish. The best description we have of this Greek Fire in use comes from Jean Sire de Joinville's chronicle of the Seventh Crusade, which, although frequently quoted, deserves to be repeated again. 'In appearance,' he writes, 'the Greek Fire was like a large barrel of verjuice, and its fiery tail was the length of a long lance. In coming it made a noise like heaven's thunder. It seemed like a dragon flying through the air. So great a light did it emit, because of the great abundance of fire that made the light, that one could see as clearly throughout the camp as if it had been day.'

On the occasion Joinville is describing the fire was being aimed at two belfries that the Franks had erected before Damietta, and soon afterwards they were both burned to the ground together with the men in them, a hideous form of death the very idea of which Joinville makes it quite clear terrified both he and his men. An early 12th century Moslem author gives us a fairly clear idea of what happened once a belfry was ignited. Speaking of one in use at the siege of Tyre in 1111, he says that it caught fire amidst a cascade of burning oil, pitch, resin, woodshavings and cane-bark as it came up to the wall. 'The fire grew and spread, overcame the two men working at the top of the tower, killing one and forcing the other to go down, enveloped the top storey and crept down to the next, then the next, consuming the wooden frame and overcoming the men that were gathered on the platforms.'

As protection against such incendiaries most towers were covered with a variety of materials intended to repel or reduce the risk of fire. These included mud, felt matting soaked in vinegar or urine, the skins of freshly slaughtered animals, and even sheets of metal, a four-storeyed belfry at Acre allegedly having its top three storeys covered in lead, iron and copper. In addition jars of vinegar and water stood ready on each storey in case they should be needed. Such protection as the mud, felt and green hides provided was also useful as padding against stones shot from the defenders' mangonels and catapults, and although we do occasionally read of belfries badly battered by artillery fire we only rarely actually find one being knocked to pieces by this means. Alas, such precautions were rather less successful against fire, and you'll read of any number of siege-towers protected by every means available still going up like roman candles after a direct hit with naptha. But if the belfry once reached the wall then it was as good as all over for the defenders, because once the tower's occupants had stormed on to the battlements across their lowered drawbridge other men on the ground would start raising ladders against the same threatened sector and swarm up in support of their compatriots, and only rarely did such assaults fail.

Going *through* a castle's defences was another matter entirely, but even here the belfry could be of service for it often incorporated a battering ram in its lowermost storey, and the ram was the simplest means of effecting a breach in castle walls. The Franks called it a *mouton* (mutton), *eue* (sheep), or *bellier* or *aries* (ram), and the Arabs similarly called it a *kabsh,* also meaning ram. The *Itinerarium,* describing the siege of Acre, tells us that 'it is usually called *aries* because it destroys the solidity of the wall's fortifications by repeated and rapid blows, like a ram,' the idea being that the repeated pounding cracked and loosened the mortar of the wall to such an extent that in time it would simply crumble and collapse. It could obviously be even more effective against a door.

The ram itself was made from a single tree up to 90 or 100 feet long and had an iron head weighing 20 pounds or more. It was usually housed in a vault-roofed penthouse mounted on wheels and sometimes armoured with iron plates, one used at Acre allegedly carrying iron armour that weighed 7,500 pounds. Such penthouses, called 'cats' (*chats, cattes,* Arabic *sanura*) or tortoises (*testuda*), were also used for a wide variety of other activities, such as protecting the sappers who had the unenviable task of filling the castle ditch. The ram was suspended from its roof by ropes or chains, on which it would be swung back and forth against the wall by a crew of as many as 60 men, the cat's wheels often being removed to avoid any form of recoil caused by the swinging motion of the ram. All that the besieged could do in response was cascade stones and incendiaries down upon the cat—the ram at Acre, for example, despite its armour, being successfully smashed by huge stones dropped from the battlements which went right through its iron roof, its wreckage then being consumed by incendiaries. The garrison could also lower timber baulks or mattresses of straw, cotton or faggots to hinder or absorb the blows of the ram, as the Moslems did at Jerusalem. A Moslem officer involved in the defence of Tyre in 1111 showed considerable ingenuity in inventing a type of iron hook which, lowered from the walls, was manoeuvered to catch on the rams housed in one of the Franks' belfries. As a result the Franks were forced to cut down their own rams for fear that the Moslems, by hauling on the ropes attached to the hook, would overturn the whole tower, which they very nearly did.

A variant of the ram was the bore, a type of engine known in the Near East since ancient times. Usually called by the terms *truie* (sow) or *sus rostrata* (rostrated boar), it differed only in having a pointed head with which a hollow could be gouged out of the wall.

The second means of attaining a breach was to knock holes through the walls with stones fired from an assortment of 'artillery' pieces. The various categories of engine, sometimes not easy to distinguish from each other in contemporary sources, were apparently the petrary, mangonel, ballista and *trébuchet.* Of these the first three were evolved from classical originals, the latest models of which were still in use with the Byzantine army under the names *petrarea, manganon* or *manganika* and *toxoballistra* respectively. The two former were, in fact, alternative names for the same type of engine, the only difference being—according to Byzantine sources—that while manganon denoted a particular type of machine, petrarea indicated that it was one of the heavier models of its kind (the Byzantines also having a lighter mangonel called an *alakation*). The most common term for such engines in crusading sources is *petrariae* or *perrières,* literally 'stone-throwers', also frequently employed in a less specific sense to describe siege artillery in general, including trebuchets.

Like the old Roman *onager,* the petrary operated on the principal of torsion, the energy source being a tightly twisted skein of rope which was wound round a horizontal beam. The firing arm was fixed at right angles to this, and pulled right down to the ground. When the arm was released the torsion in the skein whipped it forward and up to strike a crossbar, upon which its missile, located either in a sling or a spoon-shaped receptacle, would fly on towards the target. Its trajectory was very high and it was apparently not as accurate as the trebuchet, but it was a powerful machine and could fire stones of considerable weight to some distance, modern tests indicating that 50 lb rocks could be thrown about 200 yards.

The ballista, resembling an overgrown crossbow mounted on a stand, was far more accurate but was really only practical as an 'anti-personnel' weapon, firing iron bolts which, although capable of killing two or three armoured men at a time under favourable conditions, were useless against stone walls. Hardly surprising, then, that they are normally encountered in use by the besieged rather than the besieger. Krak des Chevaliers, for example, had embrasures that were specifically designed for *ballistae,* and the keep of the Templar fortress of Tortosa carried an unknown number of such weapons, to the effectiveness of which is attributed Saladin's repulse from its walls in 1188. The Moslems used ballistas (which they called *arradat*) to shoot Greek Fire grenades, and a stone-throwing variety was also in use, but the size of its missiles would have been restricted. It may have been ballistas of this sort that Richard of England and Philip of France used during their siege of Acre.

Interestingly neither the petrary nor the ballista appear to be much illustrated, if at all, in contemporary sources. However, not so the trebuchet, which is invariably the type of engine depicted in every 12th or 13th century illustration of a siege that I have ever seen.

In use by the Arabs (who adopted it from the Byzantines) by 665 at the very latest, the trebuchet consisted of a base with two uprights housing an axle on which was fixed a long, revolving arm with a sling at one end. For firing the arm was wound down by a windlass until the sling rested on the ground, so that the other end of the pivotted arm was hoisted up into the air. The earliest trebuchets were apparently set in motion by men pulling in unison on ropes attached to the upper end of this arm; totally improbable, you may think, but there are innumerable contemporary illustrations and even some written sources that confirm it. We are told of this type of trebuchet that it cast smaller stones than other types but was quicker-firing in that loading and discharging was so simple. Although this form persisted until at least the end of the 13th century, by about 1200 at the latest a counterweight was being substituted. This was probably a Frankish development, or so we must assume from Moslem nomenclature, where the counterweight trebuchet—the heaviest calibre of engine that was used—is called simply *Farangi,* or 'Frankish'.

The Franks themselves had adopted the trebuchet from the Moslems in the 12th century, possibly by as early as circa 1100 in Spain, a fact which has led to the mistaken assumption that it was only first invented at that date. Interestingly the Arabs called it by the name *manganiq,* which we have already encountered in its Byzantine form *manganika* and its Frankish form mangonel *(mangonelle),* although as you will remember these were apparently torsion-operated stone-throwers of an entirely different type. Engine nomenclature, however, was clearly an imprecise science, and one conclusion that could be drawn from manganiqs being trebuchets, and trebuchets being perrières, is that the trebuchet was in fact the *only* stone-throwing siege engine in use during the mediaeval era, this fact being disguised by the frequent employment of older, obsolete terms to describe it.

Like the mangonel or petrary the trebuchet operated on a very high trajectory, but it differed in firing heavier missiles and being extremely accurate, capable of dropping missile after missile within a remarkably small target area. An authority of the late 13th century remarks of the trebuchet's accuracy that 'their aim is so sure that one may, so to say, hit a needle', and against the dense walls of an enemy fortress this was a very desirable attribute indeed. Range may have been adjustable by varying the counterweight but was probably a maximum of about 300 yards. At the 5th National Catapult Contest in the USA in 1976 a 61-foot high trebuchet reconstructed by American enthusiasts fired 100 lb rocks some $565\frac{1}{2}$ feet, or $188\frac{1}{2}$ yards. The ranges achieved with lighter missiles on this occasion are of interest: 10 lb 693 feet; 20 lb 720 feet; 30 lb 735 feet; 40 lb 748 feet; and 75 lb 623 feet. In fact adjusting an engine's range by varying the weight of its missile was general mediaeval practice.

The number of such engines used at any siege varied, artillery most often being constructed on site and burnt when the siege was lifted. One source claims that King Richard and King Philip had as many as 300 mangonels and ballistas at the siege of Acre in 1191, but this seems highly improbable. More reliable figures are the 18 large manganons of Emperor John II at Shaizar in 1138; Louis IX's 18 engines and the Moslems' 16 at El Mansurah in 1250; the three Farangi, three *qarabughas* ('black bulls') and four *shaytans* ('devils')—both smaller-calibre weapons—of the Mamluks at al-Marqab in 1285; and the 72 or 92 engines including 15 Farangi employed in the final siege of Acre in 1291, two of which were so huge that they each filled 100 ox-carts when dismantled. The Moslem historian Abul-Fida, who was an eyewitness of the fall of Acre, states that more engines were used on this occasion than had ever been used against town or fortress before. Certainly the Mamluks seem to have used more artillery in their sieges than anyone else in this era, probably employing on average about twice as many engines as their Ayyubid predecessors, only the Ilkhanid Persians (who generally used some 20-25 manganiqs in a single siege) coming close to equalling them. The crews of 19 engines involved in the Mamluk siege of Tripoli in 1289 totalled 1,500 men, or about 80 men an engine.

The ammunition they fired varied considerably, from returned emissaries, dead horses and prisoners' heads to incendiaries and huge stones, much bigger than those fired by the reconstruction mentioned above. The troubador Ambroise records one that fired stones which it took two men to carry and other sources mention missiles of 200 to 300 lb. Rocks fired by Saladin's manganiqs at Saone in 1188, which can still be found within the castle's ruins today, weighed up to 600 lb. A Byzantine trebuchet recorded in Emperor Romanus IV's siege-train in the Manzikert campaign is even recorded as throwing stones of ten *quintals* weight, equivalent to about 750 lb.

Obviously the impact of such stones, descending from the heavens at such velocity that they could penetrate a foot deep into the ground, must have been devastating. Nevertheless, solid stone walls of the type used in castles could withstand a fair old battering and still stay up, although people and lesser structures such as houses or siege-towers fared rather less well: a mill-stone hurled by Frankish engines into Shaizar in 1157 completely demolished an entire building, while a single huge stone fired from one of King Baldwin III's engines at Ascalon killed as many as 40 men. There were fluke shots too, of course, and Ambroise records how on one occasion a knight hit in the back by a manganiq missile was not even so much as bruised, when normally a man struck thus would have been hard to scrape together, as some sources delight in telling us.

Of course the besieged as well as the besiegers used such weapons, and occasionally artillery duels could develop. We know that at Acre King Philip's trebuchet *Malvoisin* ('The Bad Neighbour', a traditional and rather logical name for a siege-engine) was repeatedly being put out of commission by pots of Greek Fire fired by its Moslem counterpart, 'The Bad Kinsman', on the city walls; and when the Byzantines were laying siege to the Cilician Armenian fortress of Anzarba in 1137 so many of their own engines were being picked off by the defenders' artillery (again using combustible missiles) that the rest had to be emplaced behind mud-brick earthworks.

While all this was going on above ground the besiegers would normally also be burrowing about beneath the surface like frenzied rabbits, working away at the very foundations of the fortress under attack. This, of course, was the third means of circumventing its defences, by going right under them, and in this the Moslems appear to have surpassed all-comers. The engineers of some Moslem districts, particularly those of Aleppo and Khorasan, were especially noted for their proficiency in this field, so much so that they were even pressed into service by the Franks when captured (Richard using Aleppene sappers captured at Acre in his assault on Daron in 1192).

It was Aleppene and Khorasani sappers (Arabic *naqqabin*) who were responsible for the fall of Edessa in 1144. A Moslem source describes the process as utilised on this occasion, telling us how they 'made saps in a number of places which they had selected as suitable for their task. They proceeded with their sapping, digging away through the bowels of the earth until they were beneath the very foundations of the wall. These they shored up with stout timbers and special devices, and when this was done it only remained to set fire to them . . . When fire was applied to the supports it ignited and destroyed the timbers, and straightway the wall fell down.' The fire beneath the foundations was sometimes accompanied by an artillery barrage above ground, and the resultant breach was normally stormed before the dust had even settled. Inevitably the mine could occasionally fail. A portion of Acre's walls, undermined by King Philip's sappers in 1191, keeled to a dangerous angle but failed to fall flat, with the result that the Frankish storming party was soundly repulsed.

To avoid the need for protracted tunnelling the mine was usually started fairly close to the wall, often within missile range, the adit being protected by earthworks or a *catte*. The mines usually progressed at considerable speed—Le Chastellet was mined in just five days—and as a result frequently caught the defenders by surprise so that there was rarely much chance of their doing anything about them. Where they did have time the garrison could dig a counter-mine in the hope of intercepting the enemy's tunnel, in which case a subterranean mêlée would ensue, but this was not often attempted. An alternative solution was for the defenders to throw up a barricade or second wall behind that which was being undermined, but obviously this was time-consuming and really no more than postponed the final outcome. In fact the only sure defence against mining was to build on solid rock in the first place. Some coastal castles and fortified towns were fairly safe in being built instead on sandy soil, where tunnelling to any depth would cause ground water to flood the workings. Sea-water moats added further protection in just two or three instances, as at Château de Mer in Sidon.

After famine it was the mine, without doubt, that was the greatest psychological strain on the defenders of any fortified site. After all, the morale of the garrison was an important element in a castle's ability or inability to withstand a prolonged siege, and listening to the muffled thud and scuffle of picks and shovels reverberating through the walls day after day must have been enough to unnerve many a stout-hearted warrior. At Habis Jaldak in 1182, for example, the elite Moslem garrison surrendered simply because their nerve had been broken by the knowledge that the Franks were slowly digging their way in. In an even more famous episode at al-Marqab in 1285 Sultan Qalaun, after having had his sappers dig mines beneath the keep, invited the castle's Hospitaller commanders to come out and examine their progress; they did so and concluded that further resistance was useless (as Qalaun had hoped they would) and consequently surrendered the castle into the besiegers' hands unscathed.

In fact the insidious effects of what has been neatly described as 'castle-mentality' were probably the defenders' greatest enemy. 'However massive their construction and ingenious their design,' writes Dr Smail, 'crusader castles and their garrisons could be subjected to both material and moral pressures; and of these the moral were the more destructive.'* After all, the garrison could do little more than stand behind their walls and wait for the enemy's next move. They could launch the occasional sortie against the besiegers, possibly burning the odd siege-engine or capturing a few incautious souls, but any momentary successes thus achieved realistically counted for little in the overall pattern of the siege. Besides, the besiegers' camp might very well itself be surrounded by

* *The Crusaders in the Holy Land*, Thames and Hudson, 1973.

defensive ramparts and ditches against such attacks—the Franks at Acre had long, deep and wide trenches round the whole city, braced with timbers and with a palisade of stakes or shields where possible. In addition nets and traps were often set against such sorties launched at night, so all in all the chances of success were limited; and an unsuccessful sortie was obviously going to seriously harm morale rather than boost it. No, the besieged basically had little option but to watch and wait, a passivity which must inevitably have engendered in them the 'peculiar nervous instability' which one scholar describes*, that must in turn have encouraged fear, irrational panic and susceptibility to both rumour and dark despair.

Probably the most crucial factor in garrison morale was whether or not there was any chance of relief. To be isolated and surrounded, without the slightest hope of rescue, must have led to the very deepest despair of all, and it was undoubtedly the knowledge that no army could be raised for their relief that resulted in the prompt surrender of the vast majority of the Franks' strongholds after the Horns of Hattin. The boost in morale that the proximity of a relieving army encouraged, on the other hand, could lead to energetic resistance against the most fantastic odds. Take the city of Tyre, for instance, which had been prepared to give in to Saladin prior to Conrad of Montferrat's timely arrival in 1187; and the city of Acre which, although it had capitulated to the Moslems in a single day after Hattin, held out against the Franks for nearly *two years* between 1189 and 1191 simply because of Saladin's constant proximity beyond the besiegers' camp.

It has probably become apparent by now that the Frankish investment of Acre is in fact a classic example of the mediaeval siege, involving just about every element of siegecraft including one which we have not yet considered, this being supply. Although we *have* looked briefly at the circumstances of the besieged in this respect, the plight of the besiegers could be—and often was—a matter of considerably greater concern. After all, it goes without saying that 99 times out of 100 the fortress being besieged is going to be in enemy territory, where foraging, unless in the immediate vicinity, could be a very dangerous means of sustenance. The Franks besieging Jerusalem in 1099, for example, had to travel six miles for water, and many fell victim to Moslem ambushes organised along the paths to the springs. On the other hand we have seen that the environs of many Syrian cities boasted extensive orchards and gardens, easily capable of supporting a besieger for many weeks; the Frankish army that laid siege to Damascus during the Second Crusade deliberately sited their encampment by the springs and orchards beyond the city walls and were amply supplied therefrom until treachery led to them moving on to a secondary site.

However, sieges of lengthy duration, such as that of Acre, inevitably resulted in considerable shortages, to the point where at Antioch in 1098 one crusader in every seven was close to dying of starvation before supplies arrived from Cyprus. One chronicler even claims that at Damietta in 1219 as many as 100,000 crusaders died of hunger in a single month, but one can be fairly confident in ascribing his figures to the results of standing too long in the Syrian sun.

Cyprus also provided extensive supplies to the besiegers of Acre after Richard's capture of the island in 1191. The *Itinerarium* reports how he had 'appointed energetic men to be his wardens and captains in Cyprus, leaving

---

* Robin Fedden with John Thomson in *Crusader Castles,* John Murray, 1957.

them instructions to send after him whatever victuals were necessary, to wit wheat, barley, and the meat of all the animals in which Cyprus abounded.' These were dearly needed earlier in the siege, since the besiegers, themselves surrounded by Saladin's army, had been running desperately short of food. A silver denier bought only 13 beans or a solitary egg*, while a four bezant sack of corn rose in price to as much as *100* bezants (not least because avaricious Pisan merchants were deliberately hoarding grain in the hope of forcing prices even higher).

Those unable to afford such prices had no option but to steal, scavenge or die. The common soldiers were reduced to eating grass like cattle and chewing bare bones like dogs, while many knights slaughtered their own priceless horses for meat, a desperate measure indeed which we nevertheless encounter repeatedly in the sources, as for example at Antioch in 1098 and Montferrand in 1137. The famine at Acre was effectively ended only when a grain-carrying ship fortuitously reached the camp shortly before King Philip's arrival. The overall size of the crusading army involved in this enterprise, incidentally, resulted in horse-driven mills and a windmill being constructed in 1189 to ensure that enough flour was produced for its needs, the windmill apparently being the first ever seen in Syria.

---

* Just to show that inflation is nothing new, when famine struck Louis IX's camp in 1250 an egg cost not one denier but *12*.

Chapter 13

A gazetteer of fortified sites

As I mentioned at the beginning of the last chapter, more than a hundred fortified sites are known to have existed in the Kingdom of Jerusalem, while at least 300 and probably many, many more were at one time or another in Frankish possession throughout the whole of Outremer. It is impossible now to discover where they all were, or what they were all called, and archaeology and contemporary documents between them provide us with dozens of sites without names and names without sites.

In addition we know little of the history of many, some of them not unimportant. The following list, therefore, is in no way comprehensive, but it covers most of the major fortresses and, in the cases of Jerusalem and Tripoli (for which more information is generally available), many of the lesser ones too. Heavily fortified monasteries, of which there were quite a few, are not included.

Intelligent use of this gazetteer should, I hope, enable a wargamer who has elected to refight a particular campaign, or alternatively invented a scenario of his own choice, to establish who held which castles during the year(s) concerned. It also gives garrison strengths wherever possible, but such information is unfortunately extremely rare. It should be noted in this context, incidentally, that castle garrisons contained very few knights and were probably largely comprised of native mercenaries, even those of the Military Orders. Those knights present performed the functions of officers.

This gazetteer is compiled from a Frankish viewpoint and in most cases the names given are those used by the Franks themselves in the 12th and 13th centuries, the Frankish name being otherwise given in brackets where I have been able to discover it. Many castles, however, had more than one Frankish name and a Moslem appellation besides, and in other cases many variants of the same name can be found in different sources. Wherever possible I have given the main alternatives, but a certain amount of confusion is nevertheless inevitable since no two books on the Crusades give the same names. The number preceding each entry keys it into the maps.

The Gazetteer

Note The 'dismantling' of a fortress frequently mentioned herein usually involved the breaching of curtain walls, pulling down of towers and burning of gates. The fortress was therefore left substantially intact, and a contemporary saying was that 'a ruined castle is one half-built'. Captured garrisons were either allowed to depart with or without their arms and belongings (sometimes after payment of a ransom), or else butchered, even if their surrender had been conditional on the besiegers sparing their lives. Unless indicated otherwise all the sites listed are fortresses, either castles, towers, or sometimes fortified citadels within open towns. Walled towns generally had their own citadels.

1 Acre (Saint Jean d'Acre, Accon, Ptolemais) Captured by Baldwin I in 1104, this heavily fortified town was surrendered to Saladin shortly after the Frankish defeat at Hattin in 1187. In 1189 King Guy began a two-year siege, in which King Richard of England and King Philip II Augustus of France joined him during the later stages with the troops of the Third Crusade. The Moslem garrison started out at about 10,000, had declined to 6,000 by mid-1191, and less than 3,000 were captured with the city at its fall in July 1191, of whom Richard had 2,700 executed. Thereafter Acre served as the capital of the Kingdom of Jerusalem until its fall to Sultan al-Ashraf a century later in 1291, when its (insufficient) Frankish garrison totalled at its fullest strength 900-1,000 knights and 14,500-18,500 foot-soldiers. By the mid-13th century it was the most strongly fortified city in the Latin East.

2 Adamodana An Armenian fortress granted to the Teutonic Knights in 1211 and in their hands until captured and burnt by the Mamluks in 1266.

3 Adana A walled town captured by Tancred in 1097 but lost to the Byzantines in 1099. Tancred recovered it in 1101, but the Byzantines retook it again in 1104, and thereafter it changed hands fairly regularly between Armenians, Byzantines and Franks, with the latter in possession 1108-1132 and briefly in 1136, 1143-1144 and 1185. The Armenians held it from circa 1170 onwards, although it was sacked by the Mamluks in 1266.

4 Aintab Captured in 1097. Sold to the Byzantines with five other Edessene forts (Birejik, Duluk, Ravendel, Samosata and Turbessel) in 1150 after conquests by Nur ed-Din had isolated the remnants of the County of Edessa. Lost to Sultan Masud of Rum in 1151, who lost it in turn to Nur ed-Din in 1156. Much rebuilt under the Mamluks, it was briefly occupied by the Mongols during their invasions of 1280 and 1281.

5 Akaf A natural grotto like Le Cave de Tiron, fortified by the Templars and surrendered to Shirkuh in 1165 or, more probably, 1166. King Amalric I hanged the 12 Templar brethren of its garrison responsible for surrendering the fort without his permission.

6 Albara, Barra A walled town captured by Raymond de Saint-Gilles in 1098. Abandoned in 1104 as untenable in the face of a Moslem invasion but reoccupied in 1105. Lost in 1123 but recaptured soon after, the Franks surrendered it to Timurtash of Mardin in 1145 after withstanding a siege by his rival the atabeg Zengi of Mosul.

7 Albe Captured in 1109, this small fortress was destroyed by Baibars' amirs in 1266. They took it deserted, the garrison having abandoned it after the fall of neighbouring Tuban. The garrison was then overtaken and killed.

8 Albistan A small fortress held by the Franks from 1103 until 1105, when the local Armenians called on Moslem assistance and massacred the garrison of 300. It appears to have thereafter reverted to Frankish hands to be finally lost in 1111.

9 Aleppo (Halapia) A fortified city in Moslem hands throughout this era. Sacked by the Mongols in 1260, 1261 and 1280.

10 Alexandretta, Alessandria, Isso A port with a small sea-fortress captured in

1097 and assigned to the Templars in 1155. Lost 1188, recovered 1211 and finally lost to Baibars in 1268.

11 Antioch A heavily fortified town with Byzantine-built walls and citadel captured after a six-month siege in 1098, when its Seljuk garrison is reported as an improbable 2,000 askaris, 4-5,000 other cavalry and 10,000 infantry. Occupied briefly by the Armenians 1194, 1208 and 1216. Lost to Baibars in 1268.

12 Anzarba (La Nouvelle Troie) This fort was much-contested. It was held by the Franks 1098-1099, 1101-1104, briefly in 1130 and 1131, and finally in 1143-1144, the rest of the time being fought over by the Byzantines and Armenians, finally passing to the latter in 1173. Heavily rebuilt and refortified in 1188 to become possibly the strongest of all the Armenian fortresses.

13 Apamea A fortified town and citadel captured by Tancred, regent of Antioch, in 1106, and lost to Nur ed-Din in 1149. It was dismantled soon after, being in ruins when the site was briefly reoccupied in 1157. Thereafter in Moslem hands, although the Ilkhanid Mongols held it for a short while in 1271.

14 Araima, Aryma An ex-Byzantine fortress partially rebuilt by the Franks. Seized from Raymond II of Tripoli by a rival in 1148 it was razed by his Moslem allies in 1149. Rebuilt, it passed to the Templars before 1152, was apparently dismantled by the Moslems in 1171, and again rebuilt by the Franks soon after. It remained in Frankish hands after Hattin, finally falling to Baibars only in 1271.

15 Arcas This fortified town was captured by William-Jordan, Count of Cerdagne, after a three-week siege in 1109. It was briefly recaptured by the Moslems in 1138 and again in 1171, the latter despite having been assigned to the Hospitallers in 1170. Lost in 1188, it was probably recovered in 1192. It appears to have passed to the Templars at some time before it was finally lost to one of Baibars' amirs in 1266 after its garrison had abandoned it following the fall of Albe and Tuban. It was subsequently dismantled.

16 Arsuf (Arsur) A fortified town captured by Baldwin I in 1101 and lost after Hattin 1187. It was recaptured by King Richard immediately after the Battle of Arsuf in 1191 and sold to the Hospitallers in 1261, becoming one of their key fortresses. However it fell to Baibars only four years later and its garrison of some 1,000 men, including 260-270 brethren, was killed or captured. Baibars demolished its fortifications.

17 Artah Captured in 1097, this fortified town was handed back to the Moslems by its Armenian population in 1104. Tancred recaptured it in 1105. It fell to Nur ed-Din in 1147, was recovered soon after, but was lost for good in 1149

18 Arzghan Captured in 1098 and strengthened in 1132, this fortress was lost to Nur ed-Din in 1149. It was recovered in 1159 but finally lost, again to Nur, in 1160.

19 Ascalon (Escalone) A strongly fortified town, called by the Moslems 'The Virgin of Syria' because it could not be taken! Its Moslem garrison in the early 12th century appears to have been 500 cavalry and 1,000 infantry, relieved four times a year according to William of Tyre. The Franks captured it in 1153, the Hospitallers assisting in its defence after 1177. Lost in 1187, it was one of the many fortified sites in this general area to have its defences dismantled on Saladin's orders by Saif ad-Din, for fear that the Franks might recapture them en route to Jerusalem following King Richard's victory at Arsuf; the others comprised Belmont, Belveer, Blanchegarde, Casal Maen, Casal des Plains,

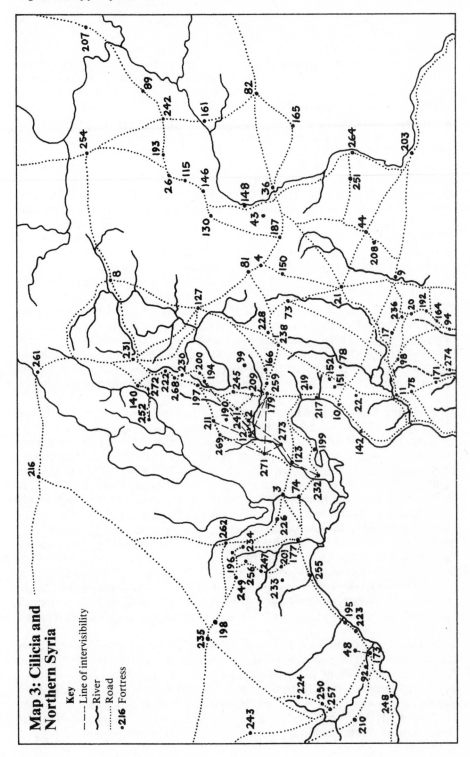

Map 3: Cilicia and Northern Syria

Key

— Line of intervisibility

—— River

.... Road

•216 Fortress

Chastel Arnaud, Le Galatie, Gaza, Jaffa, Mirabel, Ramla, Toron des Chevaliers and probably Bombrac and Ibelin. It was briefly reoccupied in 1192 when Richard spent four months rebuilding its walls. Dismantled again, it was recovered by treaty in 1240 and refortified on Richard's plan 1240-1241. It was again entrusted to the Hospitallers in 1243 and the citadel further strengthened in 1244. Finally lost in 1247 despite a strong garrison of Hospitallers, its fortifications were demolished.

20 Athareb (Cerep) Captured by Tancred in 1110 after his siege-engines had pounded its walls 'to pieces'. Refortified, it was surrendered to Ilghazi and Toghtekin in 1119. Recovered by treaty 1121 only to be lost again 1135. An allied Byzantino-Frankish force under Emperor John II recovered it briefly in 1138, but it was lost again, and finally, shortly after.

21 Azaz (Hazart, Hasarth, Hasar) Held briefly circa 1111-1113 and captured 1118 by Roger of Antioch with the aid of Leon I of Cilicia. It successfully withstood major sieges in 1124 and 1125 but fell to Nur ed-Din in 1150.

22 Baghras (Gaston, Castrum des Bachelers) Captured by Bohemond of Antioch circa 1099 and granted to the Templars circa 1137, this was a large fortress which in the mid-10th century had been garrisoned by 1,000 men. Apparently held briefly by the Byzantines in 1132, 1137, 1138 and 1142, and reverted to a secular fief until circa 1165, despite being reassigned to the Templars, who refortified it, in 1156. It was next held by the Armenians until about 1175 and thereafter returned to the Templars, to fall to Saladin after a prolonged siege in 1188, its garrison being understrength. Dismantled in 1190 at the approach of Duke Frederick of Swabia's German crusaders, the site was occupied and refortified by the Armenians either the same year or in 1191 and restored to the Templars in 1216. They abandoned it after the fall of Antioch in 1268.

23 Baldwin's Tower Allegedly a small hilltop fortress of the 12th century but probably a fortified farmhouse with a single small tower, situated in a position commanding 'Robber's Gorge', in Frankish called Le Vallis de Cursu (Valdecours) or 'The Valley of Running' in reference to fleeing from brigands.

24 Banyas (Belinas, Paneas) A fortified Moslem town built 1106-1107, Banyas was handed over to the Syrian Assassins by Toghtekin of Damascus in 1126. They in turn handed it over to the Franks in 1129. Lost in 1132 to Toghtekin's grandson Ismail but recovered by an alliance with Damascus in 1140. Part of the fortress was sold to the Hospitallers in 1157 but was sold back the same year. Lost in 1164. A Frankish siege by King Amalric I was bought off by Nur ed-Din's widow in 1174. Dismantled 1219.

25 Beaufort, Belfort Built by King Fulk circa 1139-1140. After Hattin it did not fall to Saladin until 1190, being dismantled in 1219 for fear the Franks might retake it. Recovered by treaty 1240, it was sold to the Templars by Julian of Sidon in 1260 and fell to Baibars after heavy bombardment in 1268. He repaired its walls and installed a large garrison.

26 Behesni An Armenian fortress probably annexed by the Franks with Raban and Kesoun in 1116 and lost to Sultan Masud of Rum 1150. Held by the Armenians from the mid-13th century until lost to the Mamluks 1293.

27 Beirut (Baruth) A fortified town captured after a three-month siege in 1110 and lost to Saladin in 1187. It was recaptured during the German crusade of 1197 when its amir had begun to dismantle the walls in preparation for abandonment. Abandoned and lost to the Mamluks under the amir Shujai in

1291, its walls and citadel were razed.

28 Bel Hacem, Belhasan Probably of Moslem origin, this fortress was captured in 1128 but had to be besieged again in 1161 when its lord, Gerard of Sidon, was in revolt in alliance with Nur ed-Din. Lost in 1187, it was recovered by treaty in 1240, although apparently only briefly.

29 Belmont A small 12th century fortress assigned to the Hospitallers before 1168. Captured by Saladin in 1187 and dismantled in 1191 after his defeat at Arsuf, but apparently rebuilt by the Moslems at some time thereafter. Together with Belveer it had guarded the western approaches to Jerusalem.

30 Belveer, Belveir, Belvoir Another small 12th century fortress, situated at modern Qastal (undoubtedly derived from *Chastel*) only a mile and a quarter from Belmont. Assigned to the Hospitallers in the 1150s and lost in 1187, this was the Belvoir dismantled by Saladin in 1191.

31 Belvoir, Beauvoir, Coquetum, Coquet Built circa 1138-1140, sold to the Hospitallers in 1168 and strengthened in 1178. At the beginning of 1189 it was lost to Saladin, the Moslems dismantling it in 1219. Recovered by treaty in 1241 it was restored to the Hospitallers and refortified, to be finally lost in 1247.

32 Bethanie, St Lazarus A small tower keep built in 1143. Possibly held by the Knights of St Lazarus, it was lost to Saladin in the 1180s and demolished.

33 Bethgibelin, Bethgeblin, Gibelin Built in 1136 and assigned to the Hospitallers in 1137, the first fortress to pass into the hands of the Military Orders. Together with Blanchegarde and Ibelin it was built to guard against incursions from Egypt via Ascalon. Lost in 1187 and dismantled by Saladin. Recovered by treaty in 1240, restored to the Hospitallers and refortified. Lost after the Battle of La Forbie 1244.

34 Bethsan, Bessan Captured and fortified by Tancred in 1099. Both town and fortified citadel were abandoned by the Franks and sacked by Saladin in 1183, and even if the Franks did reoccupy it after his withdrawal Bethsan was certainly again in his hands after 1187, and he refortified it in 1192. It was sacked in 1218 during the Fifth Crusade and recovered by the Franks by treaty in 1240 to be lost again in 1260. Although raided as late as 1264, it was never again in Frankish hands.

35 Bethsur A small tower-keep. The area was given to the Hospitallers in 1136 and they probably built the tower. Lost in 1187, it was probably dismantled; certainly it is recorded in ruins in 1283.

36 Birejik (Bira) Apart from Acre and Antioch, and together with Marash and Samosata, this was probably one of the best-fortified towns in the mediaeval Levant. Of Byzantine origin, it was recaptured from the Turks by the Franks in 1098 and in 1104 given to the Armenians, from whom Count Baldwin II of Edessa took it back in 1117 after a siege of one year. Sold back to the Byzantines with five other Edessene fortresses in 1150. Lost to Timurtash of Mardin in 1151, it was refortified by Saladin's son Malik az-Zahir of Aleppo in the late 12th century.

37 Blanchegarde, Blanca Guarda, Alba Specula Built in 1142, one of the three castles constructed by King Fulk as a defence against Egyptian raids from Ascalon. The fortress, and its surrounding town, fell to Saladin after Hattin in 1187, and he had it dismantled following his defeat at Arsuf in 1191. Although recovered by King Richard in 1192, it was lost by treaty the same year. Recovered in 1241, also by treaty, it was lost for good after the defeat at La Forbie in 1244 and may never have been refortified anyway.

38 Bombrac, Bénibrac A 12th century fortress dependent on Ramla, probably built before 1150 and lost in 1187. Fairly certainly dismantled by Saladin in 1191 along with all the other ex-Frankish fortresses in this area, it was probably recovered by treaty in 1192, rebuilt, and lost in 1244.

39 Botron This fortress was captured circa 1104 and lost after Hattin in 1187. Recaptured ten years later it was razed by the Templars during a civil war of 1277, the town being lost to Qalaun in 1289 after the fall of Tripoli.

40 Le Bouquiau, Bacades, Bokehel A Moslem fortress captured by Baldwin III and lost in 1187. It probably had to be refortified after its recovery by treaty in 1241, and was lost for good circa 1266.

41 Bourzey Possibly the 'Rochefort' mentioned in some Frankish sources, this ex-Byzantine fortress was captured from the Turks in 1099. Lost to Saladin in 1188 and never recovered.

42 Buria, Burie An early 12th century tower keep capable of holding well over 500 people in times of need. Saladin sacked it during a raid of 1182 and captured it after Hattin in 1187. Recovered by treaty 1241, lost 1247, and again recovered in 1255. It was probably demolished by Baibars in 1263 like neighbouring Mount Thabor.

43 Burj ar-Risas An undefended town lost to the Moslems in 1151. On its recapture by Count Joscelyn III in 1156 the town was dismantled and a lead-reinforced citadel built from the rubble. Held only briefly by the Franks, it was lost in 1157 and its defences further strengthened by Nur ed-Din.

44 Buzaah A walled town. Roger of Antioch captured it briefly in 1119, and in 1138 Raymond of Antioch, in alliance with the Byzantines under John II, again held it. Thereafter it remained in Moslem hands, being held by the Assassins 1170-1176.

45 Caco A tower keep built before 1123 when a Frankish army mustered here, probably by Baldwin I. Probably assigned to the Templars before 1172 and certainly before 1187, when its garrison of about 40 brethren, together with that of Castrum Fabae, was wiped out by the amir Kukburi at the Spring of Cresson. Lost the same year, it was probably recovered by treaty in 1192 and lost in the 1260s. The Mamluks refortified it in 1267, Prince Edward of England's troops proving insufficient to recover it from them in 1271.

46 Caesarea, Cesaire, Tower of Straton A fortified town with Byzantine walls described as 'impregnable'. Captured 1101, it surrendered without a fight in 1187. Recaptured 1191 and refortified with the assistance of the Hospitallers 1217-1218, the defences being further strengthened by Louis IX in 1252. Lost briefly in 1220 and finally fell to Baibars in 1265, after which its fortifications were completely demolished.

47 Calansua An open town with a tower keep. Part of the town was early assigned to the Hospitallers, who possibly assisted in its defence after 1129. Lost in 1187, it was recovered by treaty in 1192 and held until 1265.

48 Camardesium, Camerdes An Armenian fortress granted to the Hospitallers by Leon II in 1210 and refortified.

49 Capharlet A pre-Crusade fortress whose 12th century history is unknown but probably followed similar lines to that of Merle. Its fortifications appear to have been strengthened in the second half of the 12th century. Probably held by the Hospitallers from 1213 and sold to the Templars in 1232, probably as a dependency of Château Pèlerin. Lost in 1265, it was recovered and restored to the Templars at some unknown date before 1291, when it was finally abandoned. Subsequently dismantled by the Mamluks.

50 Capharnaum A small 12th century fortress probably lost in 1187. When King Richard reached it in 1191 it was to find that the Moslems had laid it 'level with the ground'.

51 Carmel One of three small tower-keep forts built during the first half of the 12th century to defend the Frankish settlements of the Judaean Desert, the other two being Semoa and Teqoá. Constructed on the ruins of a large Byzantine church and settlement. Amalric I mustered his forces here in 1173 to dispute one of Saladin's invasions. Probably abandoned after the Battle of Hattin in 1187, Carmel was still in limited use under the Mamluks in the 13th century.

52 Casal Maen, Casal Moyen A 12th century fortress so-named because it stood halfway between Jaffa and Ramla. Presumably lost in 1187, Saladin dismantled its defences in 1191 following his defeat at Arsuf. King Richard spent 15 days restoring it 'to its old strength' during his advance towards Jerusalem the same year. It probably reverted to the Moslems by the treaty of 1192 but was possibly recovered as a result of the treaty of 1204 and held until 1244.

53 Casal des Plains A small tower keep captured in 1099 whilst deserted. Lost briefly in 1102, and lost to Saladin 1187. Its defences were dismantled in 1191. The site was reoccupied during King Richard's advance on Jerusalem the same year and rebuilt by the Templars, who had probably held it prior to its fall. Recaptured by the Moslems prior to the Battle of Jaffa, it reverted to Frankish hands by the treaty of 1192 but was dismantled by the Moslems before being handed over. It was refortified at the beginning of the 13th century and probably finally lost in 1244.

54 Casel Imbert, Castellum Ziph Captured 1104, fortified circa 1123 and lost in 1187. It was recaptured in 1191 and in 1232 was the scene of one of the battles of the Lombard War. Sold to the Teutonic Knights in 1256, it was lost in 1271.

55 Castellum Arearum, Casal Arearum A small early 12th century fortress, possibly a seigniorial seat, lost to Saladin in 1187. Probably recovered by treaty 1240 and finally lost in the 1260s.

56 Castellum Beleismum Small 12th century tower fortress, the history of which probably paralleled that of Castellum Arearum.

57 Castellum Feniculi, La Tour des Salines A fortified seigniorial seat of the early 12th century. Lost 1187, it was recovered in 1191 and finally lost to Baibars, who dismantled it, in 1265.

58 Castrum Fabae, La Fève Built on the Campus Fabae ('Plain of the Broad Bean') by the Templars before 1172 but exact date unknown. Lost after the defeat at Hattin in 1187, at which time its garrison was probably about 40 brethren. Probably recovered by treaty 1240, apparently assigned to the Hospitallers in 1262 and lost some time thereafter, possibly 1263.

59 Le Cave de Tiron A cluster of caves in the Lebanon Mountains fortified by the Franks circa 1133 and approachable only by steep paths and rope ladders. Lost to Shirkuh 1166. Recovered briefly in 1240.

60 Caymont, Caymon A seigniorial seat, probably built late in the first half of the 12th century and lost in 1187. Still in Moslem hands in 1191 when Saladin camped on the site (the castle having presumably been dismantled). In 1192 he restored it to the Franks, presenting it to Balian d'Ibelin. Refortified, it was probably lost for good in the 1260s.

61 Chastel Arnaud, Chastel Ernant, Castrum Arnaldi Apparently the foundations of this fortress were laid in 1106 but a Fatimid raiding party

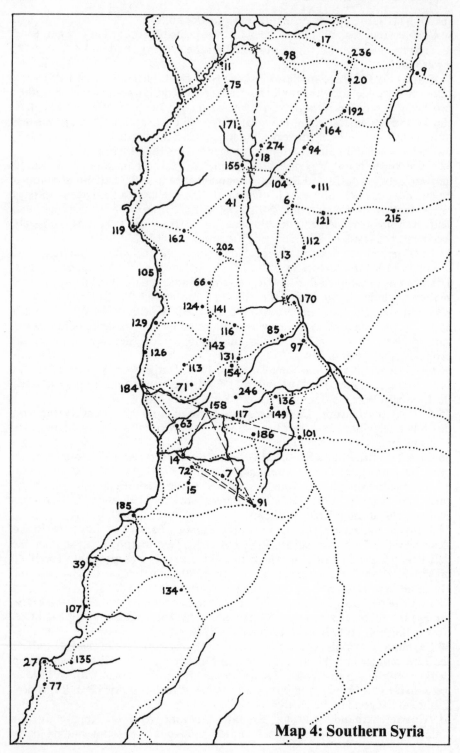

Map 4: Southern Syria

interrupted construction and massacred the workmen. The Patriarch of Jerusalem appears to have completed it, presumably on the original foundations, in 1133. Assigned to the Templars before 1150, it was lost following Hattin in 1187 and dismantled by Saladin's orders after his defeat at Arsuf in 1191.

62 Chastel Béroart, Castel Béroard, Castellum Beroardi Pre-Crusade Moslem site possibly refortified by King Fulk some time between 1137 and 1142 as part of his encirclement of Ascalon, although it may have been in Frankish hands earlier, possibly being named after a certain Béroard recorded in 1112. Nothing is known of this site for certain, and indeed it may not have been occupied at all during the Crusade era, although this seems improbable. Its position between Jaffa and Ascalon would suggest that, like them, it was lost in 1187 and any fortifications subsequently dismantled. The site was fairly certainly restored to Frankish hands by the treaty of 1241 and was probably refortified too; either way it would have finally fallen in 1244.

63 Chastel Rouge A substantial tower-keep fortress built within a Byzantine curtain-wall. T.E. Lawrence observed early this century that this was 'a fortress without a history', and this remains true today. Its history can only be guessed at; probably, like its neighbours at Safita, Tortosa and Coliath, it did not fall after Hattin, and it seems likely that it would have remained in Frankish hands for most of the 13th century, perhaps until the 1260s or 1270s. The Hospitallers may have held it at some stage.

64 Le Chastellet, Jacob's Ford Built in five months 1178-1179 in spite of a treaty that the site would never be fortified. After his offers of 60-100,000 dinars in exchange for its dismantling had been rejected, Saladin took the castle by force the year of its completion and razed its defences to the ground. Its Templar garrison had comprised 80 brother knights and their esquires and 750 foot-soldiers, plus servants and craftsmen.

65 Château Baudouin Lost to Toghtekin of Damascus in 1106 shortly before it could be completed, following the death of its builder Hugh de St Omer, Prince of Galilee, as he returned from a raid.

66 Château de la Vieille An ex-Byzantine fortress captured by Tancred, regent of Antioch, in 1111. Lost to a Turcoman adventurer in 1131 and recaptured 1136, later being assigned to the Hospitallers. Lost to Saladin 1188.

67 Château dou Rei, Châstiau dou Roi, Castellum Regis, Franc Château Captured and fortified circa 1104 and lost in 1187. Recaptured in 1192 and sold to the Teutonic Knights in 1220, it was finally lost to the Mamluks in 1265.

68 Château Neuf, Castellum Novum Built 1105-1106, part of the fortress was sold to the Hospitallers 1157 but was sold back the same year. Lost to Nur ed-Din in 1167 and presumably razed, it was recovered and rebuilt in 1178, only to be lost and dismantled again after Hattin in 1187. Recovered by treaty in 1240 it was lost for good in 1266. Baibars rebuilt it in 1267.

69 Château Pèlerin, Chastel Pèlerin, Castrum Peregrinorum A walled town, with a fortified citadel built by the Templars 1217-1218 with the assistance of the Teutonic Knights and European pilgrims (hence its name of Pilgrim's Castle). Virtually impregnable, it survived a six-month siege by Sultan al-Adil in 1220. It was the last Frankish stronghold to be abandoned on the mainland after the fall of Acre in 1291. Subsequently dismantled by the Mamluks.

70 Cité Bernard d'Etampes A fortress on the River Yarmuk captured 1118 and lost 1129. It was named after its lord.

71 Coible Captured 1117 or 1118 and lost to the Assassins, who strengthened its defences, in the early 1140s. Baibars' amirs seized it from them in 1271.

72 Coliath, Colea, La Colée Captured in 1118, this fortress was held by the Assassins for a while in the 1140s. Captured from the Franks and dismantled by Sultan al-Adil in 1207 it was still in ruins in 1212 but was recovered and rebuilt some time thereafter. In Templar hands by 1243 and probably dependent on Safita, it was lost and again dismantled in 1266.

73 Corice An Armenian fortress held by the Franks from 1117 until its loss to Nur ed-Din in 1150.

74 Cumbethfort Small Armenian fort south of Adana held by the Teutonic Knights from 1209.

75 Cursat Captured in 1132 and owned by the Patriarch of Antioch during the 12th century. It was one of the few fortresses that did not fall to Saladin in the years after Hattin, and its defences were strengthened in 1256. After 1268 it was held by its Frankish lord under Moslem suzerainty, before passing into Mamluk hands in 1275.

76 Damascus A fortified city in Moslem hands throughout this era, although briefly occupied by the Mongols in 1260.

77 Damour, Ahmid This site was probably of Moslem origin, refortified by the Franks early in the 12th century, when it was held by the Hospitallers (who called it Casal Damor). It fell to Saladin in 1187 and thereafter its history most likely followed that of nearby Beirut, its final loss probably likewise dating to 1291.

78 Darbsaq (Trapesac) Probably assigned to the Templars at the same time as Baghras, circa 1137. Lost to Saladin 1188, it was unsuccessfully besieged by the Templars in 1237 with the loss of 100 brethren. It was given to the Armenians by the Mongols during their invasion of 1261 but was surrendered to the Mamluks with Behesni and Raban by treaty in 1268.

79 Daron Built by King Amalric I in 1170 on the ruins of an older stronghold as a base for his operations against Egypt and assigned to the Templars. Lost in 1187. King Richard's English troops recaptured it in 1192 after a four-day siege, when its Ayyubid garrison comprised 360 men. Unable to himself spare it a garrison, however, Richard was obliged to dismantle its defences. The Moslems rebuilt it soon after as an outpost against the Franks.

80 Le Destroit, Casel Destreiz, Districtum, Pierre Encise, Petra Incisa A small fortress comprising a tower and rock-cut stables at 'the Defile' (Le Destroit) or 'Rock-cutting' (Petra Incisa) where the road from Acre to Jaffa traverses Mount Carmel, built after Baldwin I was wounded in ambush there in 1103. Later served as a small Templar outpost, dependent on Château Pèlerin after the construction of the latter in 1217-1218. It was abandoned and destroyed in 1220.

81 Duluk A fortified town captured in 1097 and sold to the Byzantines in 1150. Lost to Sultan Masud of Rum in 1151.

82 Edessa A fortified town of Byzantine origin which came into Frankish possession in 1098 and fell to Zengi of Mosul on Christmas Eve 1144. An Armenian conspiracy to restore the city to the Franks in 1146 resulted in it being briefly retaken by Count Joscelyn II. The citadel held out, however, and the insurrection was crushed by the Turks under Nur ed-Din. Thereafter Edessa remained in Moslem hands, Seljuks and Ayyubids contesting its ownership.

83 Efraon, Saint-Elie Small tower-keep fortress of the early 12th century, assigned to Joscelyn III in 1176. It reverted to the king in 1182 and was lost in 1187. Its Arabic name of Et Taiyiba means 'The Good', often substituted for place-names beginning with the prefix *Afr*, 'The Bad'.

84 Elyn A town at the head of the Gulf of Akaba captured and fortified by Baldwin I in 1116. A second fortress was built the same year on the small Ile de Graye. Both fell to Saladin's troops in 1170, although Elyn itself was briefly recaptured by Reynald de Châtillon, Lord of Oultrejourdain, during his piratical expedition of 1182.

85 Exerc, Eixserc Built by Tancred circa 1110 to guard against the Moslems of Shaizar. Surrendered to Zengi 1137 but apparently recovered some time thereafter. Bought by the Hospitallers in 1163 and thereafter fairly certainly a dependence of Krak des Chevaliers. Probably fell to Saladin after Hattin and was not recovered.

86 Fier, Figuier, Castle of Figs A small fortlet on the edge of the Judaean Desert probably built early in the 12th century and abandoned after the Battle of Hattin, 1187. In 1192 its Ayyubid garrison blew up its walls with Greek Fire in the face of King Richard's advance and abandoned the site.

87 Forbelet A small 12th century Hospitaller fortress dependent on Belvoir. Lost and burned in 1183. Its Arabic name of Afrabala means 'The Bad' or 'ill-omened'.

88 Le Galatie, Galatia Small 12th century fortress halfway between Ascalon and Blanchegarde. Lost in 1187 and dismantled by Saladin after his defeat at Arsuf in 1191. Richard camped here in 1192. Recovered by treaty 1241 but lost again after La Forbie in 1244.

89 Gargar (Roche-Jaune) A fortified Armenian town held by the Franks from 1117 until 1123, when Baldwin II surrendered it into Moslem hands. The Armenians retrieved it the next year in a surprise attack with just 50 men. Briefly garrisoned by Joscelyn II in 1136, but thereafter in Armenian hands.

90 Gaza, Gadres A Fatimid garrison town at the time of the First Crusade, its defences must have been dismantled at some time during the first half of the 12th century. Baldwin III rebuilt the fort 1149-1150 as his base of operations against Ascalon, assigning it to the Templars. It surrendered to Saladin by order of the Grand Master in 1187. Its defences were dismantled in 1191, and though recaptured by King Richard the same year and restored to the Templars, it was lost to the Franks forever by treaty in 1192, after which the Moslems refortified it and installed a substantial garrison. In 1260 it was briefly occupied by Mongol forces during Kitbugha's invasion.

91 Gibelcar Captured 1109, this fortress fell to Nur ed-Din circa 1165 (possibly 1167). Recaptured 1170, it was assigned to the Hospitallers. Saladin captured it in 1188 but it was recovered by treaty and restored to the Hospitallers in 1192. Finally lost to Baibars in 1271 after a two-week siege.

92 Govasse An Armenian fortress ceded to the Hospitallers in 1233.

93 Le Grande Mahomeria A tower keep guarding the possessions of the canons of the Holy Sepulchre, probably dating to the first half of the 12th century. Held by the Templars in the 13th century. Nothing more is known of this site except that it was built within a Byzantine curtain wall, apparently of stone looted from a Byzantine church. Neighbouring Ramalla (Ramelie) performed an identical function.

94 Hab (Hapa) Held by the Franks from circa 1098 until lost to Nur ed-Din in 1147.

95 Habis Jaldak (Cave de Sueth) A fortified series of caves similar to Akaf and Le Cave de Tiron. Captured in the first decade of the 12th century. Lost to Damascus in 1111, it was recaptured and refortified in 1118. Lost in 1182 to Faruk-Shah, governor of Damascus, but recovered by Raymond III of Tripoli the same year. Probably lost to Saladin in 1187.

96 Haifa (Cayphas, Caifas) A walled town captured in 1100, Haifa was surrendered without a fight in 1187. King Richard recaptured it in 1191 during the Third Crusade. Finally lost to Baibars in 1265, its defences then being demolished.

97 Hamah (La Chamelle) A fortified town in Moslem hands throughout this era, though briefly occupied by the Mongols in 1260.

98 Harenc Captured in 1098, this was an ex-Byzantine stronghold enlarged by the Franks. Lost to Nur ed-Din in 1149, recaptured 1157, and lost again and finally to Nur in 1164. Its defences were completely rebuilt by az-Zahir of Aleppo at the beginning of the 13th century, but that did not prevent the Mongols from sacking it in 1260.

99 Harunia An Armenian fortress built in the 8th century by the celebrated Caliph Haroun al-Raschid, hence the name. Granted to the Teutonic Knights and strengthened 1236. Still in their hands 1271.

100 Hebron, Saint Abraham An open town to which the Franks added a strongly fortified citadel in 1099 in order to control Bedouin incursions in southern Judaea. Lost after Hattin in 1187, it was raided by the Templars as late as 1242 but was never again in Frankish hands.

101 Homs, Hims A fortified town in Moslem hands throughout this era, though briefly occupied by the Mongols in 1260.

102 Hormoz A small 12th century castle close to Sela and Le Vaux Moise and probably dependent on the latter. It was one of the chain of seven castles strung out along the main highway to the Gulf of Akaba, the others being Kerak, Tafilé, Krak de Montréal, Sela, Le Vaux Moise, and Elyn at the head of the gulf. Lost to Saladin after Hattin, probably in 1188.

103 Ibelin, Ybelin, Ibenium Built in 1141 by King Fulk as one of a series of three castles designed both to protect the kingdom from incursions and to blockade Ascalon, the others being Blanchegarde and Bethgibelin. It was assigned to the Hospitallers 1143, lost briefly 1182 but recovered three months later, and then lost to Saladin 1187. Recovered in the 1240s, probably 1241, the date of its final loss is unknown. Its principal claim to fame is as the original home of Outremer's most illustrious family.

104 Inab (Napa) Captured 1098, briefly abandoned 1104-1105, and finally lost to Nur ed-Din following the Battle of Fons Muratus in 1149, one of Antioch's last fortresses east of the Orontes.

105 Jabala (Gibel, Gibellum) Captured by Tancred in 1109 and assigned to the Hospitallers some time before its loss to Saladin in 1188. Recaptured briefly by Templar and Hospitaller raiders in 1233.

106 Jaffa (Japhe, Joppe) A fortified town captured in 1099. It surrendered in 1187 and was dismantled by Saif ad-Din shortly before the Franks reoccupied the site in 1191, when King Richard spent seven weeks in rebuilding its defences. It was lost again in 1197 but recovered by treaty in 1204, and Teutonic Knights assisted in its defence after 1206. Lost in 1268 and dismantled.

107 Jebail, Jubail, Gibelet This fortified town was captured by Raymond de Saint-Gilles in 1104 and the castle added some time soon after. It fell to Saladin in 1187 but proved so strong that attempts to dismantle its fortifications were abandoned. Recaptured in 1197 and remained in Frankish possession until 1298, though under Mamluk suzerainty after 1289.

108 Jerash (Jarras) Built by Toghtekin of Damascus on an old Roman site in 1120, this fortress was captured and demolished by Baldwin II in 1121. Its garrison is recorded as 40 men.

109 Jerusalem (Hierosolyma, Iherusalem, Hierusalem) A fortified town and the capital of the kingdom after its capture in 1099. Its Fatimid garrison at that date included 400 Arab cavalry according to Albert of Aix, while Fulcher of Chartres records 500 Sudanese infantry being released after the city's surrender. In 1108 its Frankish garrison appears to have comprised 200 cavalry and 500 infantry. Its Roman walls were restored and strengthened in 1116 and 1177 and again in 1187 after its capture by Saladin. The walls were dismantled in 1219. Recovered by treaty 1229, it was again lost in 1239, when an-Nasir of Kerak dismantled more of its defences before it was recovered in 1240. The Templars partially restored the defences, but this did not prevent the city's fall to the Khwarizmians in 1244. Its walls were rebuilt by Sultan as-Salih in 1247.

110 Judyn, Iudin A small seigniorial fortress of the later 12th century close to Acre (and probably lost and recaptured at a similar date to that city). It passed to the Teutonic Knights in 1220 with Château dou Rei. They rebuilt the fort and probably held it until its fall. It was in ruins by 1283.

111 Kafarlatha Captured from the Assassins by 1110 (probably 1106). Lost after Ager Sanguinus 1119, it was recovered the same year and finally lost to Nur ed-Din 1147.

112 Kafartab (Capharda) Captured in 1099, this walled town repeatedly changed hands. Ridwan of Aleppo took it in 1104 after its garrison had fled, it was in Frankish hands again in 1106, lost again in 1115, recaptured and held 1119-1125, in Moslem hands again until 1126, and lost for good—to Zengi—in 1135. It was briefly recovered by the Byzantines under Emperor John II in 1138 but retaken by Zengi only two months later.

113 al-Kahf A fortified town in Moslem hands throughout this era. Sold to the Assassins in 1135, it fell to Baibars in 1273, the last independent Assassin stronghold in Syria.

114 Kerak, Krak des Moabites, Petra Deserti Built on the site of a Roman fortress in 1142 by Pagan le Bouteiller, lord of Montréal and Oultrejourdain, and enlarged by his immediate successors. Hospitallers assisted in its defence after 1152. Withstood two major sieges in 1183 and 1184 when held by the infamous Reynald de Châtillon, and only fell after a siege of more than a year that ended in 1188. Sultan al-Adil ordered its refortification in 1192 and further work was done under Baibars. The adjacent town was also fortified under the Ayyubids and Mamluks.

115 Kesoun (Crasson) A strong fortress annexed from the Armenians by treaty in 1116 and lost to Sultan Masud of Rum in 1150.

116 Kharibah A Moslem fortress captured in 1105 and lost to the Assassins 1136.

117 Krak des Chevaliers (Le Krak, Le Crac, Le Crat) Probably the best known castle associated with the Crusades, and certainly the most spectacular. Built by the amir of Homs in 1031 as a military colony for Kurds and called by the Moslems Hisn al-Akrad or 'Castle of the Kurds'. Krak des Chevaliers is a late name, and the Franks themselves knew it simply as Le Crac or Le Crat.

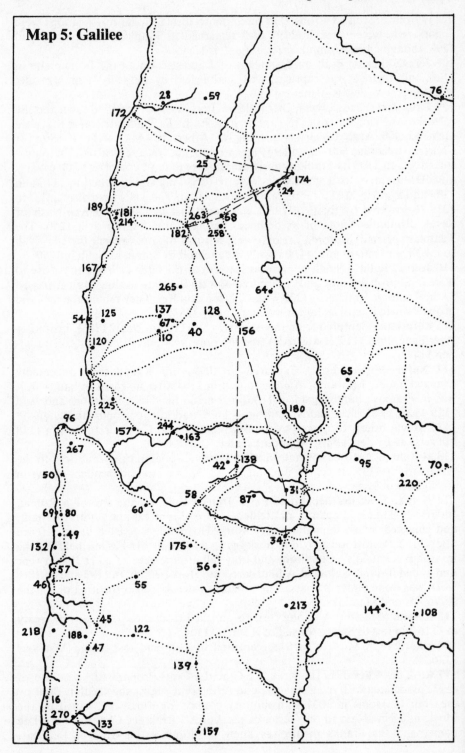

Map 5: Galilee

Captured 1110 and granted to the Hospitallers in 1142. Despite suffering earthquake damage in 1170 (which it did again in 1202), Krak was one of the fortresses that Saladin declined to attack after Hattin and consequently remained in Frankish hands. In 1211 its garrison is recorded as 2,000 combatants even in peacetime. Lost to Baibars in 1271, considerable repairs taking place under both he and Qalaun. A contingent from its Moslem garrison was present in the Mamluk army which defeated the Mongols at the Battle of Homs in 1281.

118 Krak de Montréal, Mons Regalis Built by Baldwin I in 1115. It surendered to Saladin after a prolonged siege which ended in 1189. The castle was dismantled by the Ayyubids but restored under the Mamluks.

119 Lattakieh (Laodicea) A fortified town with Byzantine walls and a small sea-fort. Captured in 1097 but occupied by the Byzantines 1098-1103 and 1104-1108. It was betrayed to Saladin in 1188 and remained in Moslem hands until it was captured and restored to the Franks by the Mongol Ilkhan Hulagu in 1260. After its walls were badly damaged by an earthquake in 1287 it fell to one of Qalaun's lieutenants, the very last Antiochene stronghold.

120 Lemezera, Somelaria Small 12th century fortress forming part of Count Joscelyn III's fief after 1179 until Saladin took it in 1187. Recaptured 1191, it was sold to the Teutonic Knights in 1228. Lost circa 1270-1280.

121 Maarrat an-Numan (Marra) A walled town captured in 1098 after its defences had been mined. Its Frankish garrison withdrew in the face of a Moslem invasion in 1104 but it was recovered in 1109. Lost briefly in 1119 after the Battle of Ager Sanguinus, it finally fell to Zengi 1135.

122 Malve, Munitio Malve A small fortress built by Baldwin I and lost in 1187. Joshua Prawer describes it as 'an unimportant outpost'.

123 Mamistra First captured by Tancred in 1097, this fortified town was frequently in Byzantine or Armenian hands. The Franks held it 1097-1099, 1101-1104, 1108-1131, briefly 1136 and 1143-1144, and finally in 1185.

124 al-Maniqah A Moslem fortress captured in 1118 and lost to the Assassins circa 1151.

125 Le Manuet, Manueth A small fortified site probably built in the early 12th century. Captured by Saladin 1187 but reverted to the Franks 1192. A tower and fortified storehouse were added by the Hospitallers after they had purchased the site in 1212. Baibars captured it in 1260 and converted it into a base for his attack on Safed (1264), but it was back in Hospitaller hands by 1270 when it was leased to the Teutonic Knights as a dependence of Montfort. It was still in Frankish hands in 1278, long after the fall of Montfort, but was fairly certainly lost soon after.

126 Maraclea Built by a certain Bartholomew on the coast between Buluniyas and Tortosa circa 1270 and garrisoned with 100 men. It was built in such a way that stones fired at it would roll harmlessly off its roof into the sea, and despite its smallness it was regarded as virtually impregnable; certainly it easily withstood a determined assault by Baibars in 1271. Shortly thereafter, however, the Count of Tripoli was obliged to order it to be dismantled, under threat of retaliatory Mamluk raids if he should refuse.

127 Marash A heavily fortified town, one of the best in the Levant, captured by Count Baldwin II in 1103. At first part of the Principality of Antioch, but transferred to Edessa circa 1126. It surrendered to Sultan Masud of Rum in 1149 and its garrison was massacred. Nur ed-Din took it in 1152 and granted it to his

Armenian ally Mleh. It remained in Armenian hands until its loss to the Mamluks in the 13th century.

128 Le Maron, Maronum, Meirun A small seigniorial fort built in the first half of the 12th century, probably circa 1105. Lost in 1187, it was recovered by treaty in 1229 and assigned to the Teutonic Knights. Lost before 1281, probably to Baibars in 1266.

129 al-Marqab (Margat, Castrum Mergathum) Captured 1118 and sold to the Hospitallers in 1186. This was one of the few fortresses that remained in Frankish hands after Hattin in 1187, being such a strong position that Saladin did not dare to attack it. Its garrison is recorded as 1,000 men in 1212, though this had apparently declined to 600 horsemen by the 1280s, an alternative source recording 200 cavalry and 500 infantry. Lost in 1285, the Mamluk garrison then installed by Sultan Qalaun comprising 1,000 infantry, 550 mamluks and 400 craftsmen.

130 Marzban An Armenian fortress in Frankish hands until lost to Sultan Masud of Rum in 1150.

131 Masyaf A fortified town in Moslem hands throughout this era. Held by the Assassins from 1140 to 1270, when it fell to Sultan Baibars.

132 Merle Built in the first half of the 12th century and assigned to the Templars before 1187, when it was lost. Recaptured and restored to the Templars at an unknown date in the first quarter of the 13th century, it was abandoned and lost in 1291. It had been dependent on Château Pèlerin after 1218.

133 Mirabel An open town with a fortified citadel that was built before 1122. Lost 1187 and dismantled in 1191 by Saif ad-Din on Saladin's orders after the defeat of Arsuf. The site was recovered by treaty in 1241 but no refortification appears to have taken place.

134 Le Moinestre, Le Monestre Ceded to the Franks by Toghtekin of Damascus in 1109 and lost to Nur ed-Din in 1167.

135 Mons Glavianus, Mont Glavien Built by Baldwin II in 1125, probably on foundations of Moslem origin. Lost in 1187 and probably dismantled.

136 Montferrand, Mons Ferrandus Captured 1115, this fortress was lost the same year but recaptured 1126. It remained in Frankish hands only until 1137, when it was surrendered to Zengi after a prolonged siege. The Moslems eventually dismantled it 1238-1239.

137 Montfort, Castellum Novum Regis, Starkenberg Built circa 1150 and lost 1187. It was recovered by treaty in 1192, then sold to the Teutonic Knights (who translated its name to Starkenberg) and virtually rebuilt 1228-1229. Lost in 1271 after a siege of only one week.

138 Mount Thabor A fortified monastery was built here by Tancred circa 1099. It was sacked in 1113 but reoccupied and presumably strengthened soon after. It withstood a major assault in 1182 but surrendered without a fight in 1187. The site was converted into a huge fortress by Sultan al-Adil 1210-1211 and unsuccessfully besieged by the Franks in 1218, after which al-Adil dismantled it as too vulnerable and not worth the cost of its upkeep. Restored to the Franks by treaty 1241 but lost six years later. Again restored in 1255 and this time assigned to the Hospitallers who carried out some refortification and installed a garrison of 40 knights plus supernumeries. Finally abandoned, again without a fight, in 1263 and its demolition completed by Baibars.

139 Nablus (Turris Neapolitana, Neapolis, Naples) An open town with a small tower keep built by Baldwin I, Nablus was captured in 1099 and remained in

Frankish hands until 1187. The town was sacked by a Templar raiding party in 1242 but was never again actually held by the Franks. Briefly held by the Mongols during Kitbugha's invasion of 1260.

140 Norpert (Castellum Novum, Château Neuf) An Armenian fortress granted to the Hospitallers with Silifke and Camardesium in 1210.

141 Ollaiqa (Laicas) A fortified town in Moslem hands throughout this era. Held by the Assassins circa 1170-1271.

142 Port Bonnel A 12th century fortress above the port, held by the Templars probably from circa 1137. Lost to Saladin 1188. Abandoned by the Moslems on the approach of the German crusaders in 1190 and occupied by the Armenians 1191 and intermittently for the next few years. It was finally regained by the Templars circa 1211-1213. Abandoned by them following the fall of Antioch 1268.

143 al-Qadmus Briefly held by the Franks 1129-1131. It was recaptured by the amir of al-Kahf in 1131, who sold it to the Assassins the next year. Thereafter an Assassin stronghold until 1272.

144 Qalat ar-Rabad Built at al-Ajlun by one of Saladin's amirs circa 1184 and enlarged 1214-1215. Its name means 'The Castle with the Suburb'.

145 La Quarantaine, Quarantene, Quarantana A 12th century Templar fortress built atop Jebel Quruntul and incorporating a network of subterranean hermits' caves, used to store arms and provisions. Recorded in 1172 by the German pilgrim Theoderich, who states that the Templars 'can have no stronger fortress'. Lost in 1187 and never recovered.

146 Raban An Armenian fortress annexed with Kesoun in 1116 and lost to Sultan Masud of Rum in 1150.

147 Ramla (Ramle, Rames) A walled town captured in 1099 but lost after the Frankish defeat at First Ramla during the Fatimid counter-attack of 1102, its defences at that time apparently being in sore need of improvement. Recovered in 1103 and lost to Saladin in 1187, who dismantled its defences in 1191 after King Richard's victory at Arsuf. Half recovered by treaty in 1192 and in its entirety in 1204, it was probably lost after La Forbie in 1244.

148 Ranculat A fortress of mixed Arab and Armenian origin captured 1098. Lost, and recaptured, by Baldwin II in 1116. When the remnants of the County of Edessa were abandoned in 1150 it was sold to the Armenian Catholicos, remaining his residence until its fall to the Mamluks in 1292.

149 Raphania A Moslem fortress abandoned in the face of the First Crusade but reoccupied thereafter. The Franks captured it circa 1104 but lost it again 1105. Recaptured in 1126, having been only briefly recovered in 1115, it was surrendered to Zengi in 1137.

150 Ravendel Captured by Baldwin of Boulogne in 1097 during his advance to Edessa. Sold to the Byzantines in 1150, who lost it to Nur ed-Din 1151. Fortifications strengthened by Saladin.

151 Roche Guillaume, Rocca Guillelmi Like Roche Roussel captured circa 1102 and assigned to the Templars circa 1137. Possibly besieged by Saladin in 1188 but remained in Templar hands. Seized by the Armenians 1204 but returned to the Templars soon after. Finally lost to the Mamluks 1299, probably the Templars' last Armenian possession.

152 Roche Roussel, La Roche de Roussel, Roche de Roissol Captured circa 1102 and granted to the Templars circa 1137. Apparently not lost to Saladin after Hattin, despite the loss of neighbouring Darbsaq. Seized by the Armenians 1204 but returned soon after, to be abandoned after the fall of Antioch in 1268.

153 Rouge Cisterne, Turris Rubea, Castrum Dumi, Maldouin Very few details available except that this was 'a strong castle' four miles east of Jerusalem built by the Templars before 1172 and captured empty by Saladin during his advance on Jerusalem in 1187, its garrison probably having been wiped out at Hattin. It would have been recovered by treaty in 1192 and was probably finally lost in 1265. Burchard of Mount Sion speaks of it in 1283 as if it still stood.

154 ar-Rusafa A fortified town in Moslem hands throughout this era. Held by the Assassins from the early 1140s until 1271.

155 Rugia, Chastel Rouge Captured by Raymond de Saint-Gilles in 1099 and used as a mustering point for Antiochene armies during the 12th century. Lost some time after 1132, probably 1149, and unsuccessfully besieged in 1157. Recovered circa 1159 and lost to Saladin in 1188.

156 Safed (Saphet) Built circa 1102 and refortified by King Fulk circa 1138-1140. Sold to the Templars in 1167. Lost to Saladin in 1188 and dismantled 1219, it was recovered by treaty and restored to the Templars in 1240. Refortification took place 1240-1243, at which time its peacetime garrison is recorded as 50 brother knights and their esquires, 30 brother sergeants, 50 Turcopoles, 300 'operators of the military engines', 820 labourers and 400 slaves, '1,700' (1,650?) men in total which increased to 2,200 in time of war. Surrendered in 1266 after a 16-day siege by Baibars, who had its Templar garrison executed. He subsequently strengthened its defences.

157 Le Saffran A small 12th century Templar tower keep. Captured by Saladin's nephew Taqi ad-Din a day before Acre in 1187, it was Saladin's camp immediately after the Frankish capture of the same city in 1191. Probably recovered by treaty 1192 and lost 1263.

158 Safita (Chastel Blanc) Built before 1112 on the site of an earlier Byzantine fortress, and assigned to the Templars before 1152, this fortress was partly demolished during a foray by Nur ed-Din in 1171. Refortified, it was one of the few Frankish strongholds to hold out against Saladin after the Battle of Hattin and its defences were further strengthened in 1202. It was surrendered to Baibars, by order of the Grand Master, after a brief siege in 1271. Its garrison at that time is recorded as 700 men.

159 Saint-Gilles A small early 12th century tower keep probably named after Raymond de Saint-Gilles. Lost to Saladin during his march on Jerusalem after Hattin in 1187.

160 Saint John's Ford Small but well-fortified 12th century Templar fortress on the River Jordan north of the Dead Sea, lost in 1187.

161 Samosata Unsuccessfully attacked by Baldwin I of Edessa in 1098, this fortified Turkish-held town became subject to the Franks the same year and passed into their hands soon after. Sold to the Byzantines in 1150, it fell with Birejik to Tirmurtash of Mardin in 1151.

162 Saone The largest in extent of all the known crusader fortresses. Of Byzantine origin, it was probably captured 1098 and a keep added by circa 1130. Passed to the Hospitallers at some time thereafter. Fell to Saladin in 1188 after just three days, when the Moslems found one of the most accessible stretches of wall undefended. Refortification took place under both the Ayyubids and Mamluks.

163 Saphoria, Sephorie Date of construction unknown. It fell to Saladin soon after Hattin in 1187, was recovered by treaty in 1240, and was assigned to the

Templars before 1251. Lost in 1263.

164 Sarmin (Sermin) A walled town captured in 1099. Its Armenian population handed it over to the Turks in 1104, but it was recovered by Tancred, regent of Antioch, in 1105. It had to be recovered by the Franks again in 1119 following its loss to the Moslems after the Battle of Ager Sanguinus. Finally lost to Zengi 1135.

165 Saruj (Sororgia) An open town with a large, strongly fortified citadel. Captured in 1098 and lost to Zengi in 1145.

166 Sarvantikar An Armenian fortress held by the Franks until 1135, when it was lost to Leon I. It was regained in 1185 but certainly lost again by 1194. Thereafter in Armenian hands until 1299.

167 Scandelion, Scandalion, Scandalium Built on an older site by Baldwin I in 1117 to blockade Tyre, a town wall being constructed at a somewhat later date. In Frankish hands until the demise of the Frankish states in 1291.

168 Sela Like Hormoz, a small castle close to Le Vaux Moise, its history probably following the same course. Lost to Saladin in 1188 or 1189.

169 Semoa A small frontier fort of tower keep construction built in the first half of the 12th century amidst the ruins of an earlier Byzantine settlement. Probably abandoned immediately after Hattin in 1187.

170 Shaizar (Chezar) A fortified town in Moslem hands throughout this era.

171 Shughr Bakas A double castle, surrendered to Saladin in 1188 and never recovered. Heavily rebuilt by the Moslems in the 13th century.

172 Sidon (Seete, Sagette, Sagitta, Saietta) A fortified town captured by Baldwin I with the assistance of King Sigurd of Norway in 1110, Hospitallers assisting in its defence after 1162. Captured and dismantled after Hattin in 1187, its ruins were recovered ten years later, although pockets of Moslems remained in the suburbs until 1204. Château de Mer, an offshore castle, was added 1227-1228, and Louis IX rebuilt the walls in 1253 after the town had been sacked in a Damascene raid. Sacked by the Mongols in 1260, Sidon was sold to the Templars the same year. Following the fall of Acre in 1291 the Templar garrison held out in Château de Mer in the face of a Mamluk assault under the amir Shujai, but abandoned the fort and sailed away to Tortosa as the situation worsened. The Mamluks then razed its defences.

173 Silifke (Saleph) After constantly changing hands between Armenia and the Byzantine Empire in the 12th century, this fortress was granted to the Hospitallers in 1210 and held by them until 1224, when they sold it back to the Armenians. Enlarged in 1236.

174 Subeibe (L'Assebebe) Built between 1129 and 1132. Shams al-Mulk of Damascus took it in a single day in 1135, but King Fulk recovered it by treaty in 1140. Finally lost to Nur ed-Din in 1164. Dismantled in 1219, considerable rebuilding took place under the Mamluks in the 13th century, possibly under the auspices of Baibars. It was briefly held by the Mongols in 1255.

175 Taanoch A small tower keep of the 12th century. Lost 1187, recovered by treaty 1240, and finally lost in the 1260s.

176 Tafilé, Tafilet Small 12th century castle probably built by Baldwin I or Baldwin II, part of the chain of seven controlling Oultrejourdain. Lost in 1188.

177 Tarsus This walled town was the chief city of the Cilician plain. It was captured by Tancred in 1097, who had to surrender it to Baldwin of Boulogne the very next day. Baldwin installed a garrison of 300 men. It was back in Byzantine hands by 1099, thereafter being spasmodically held by the Franks

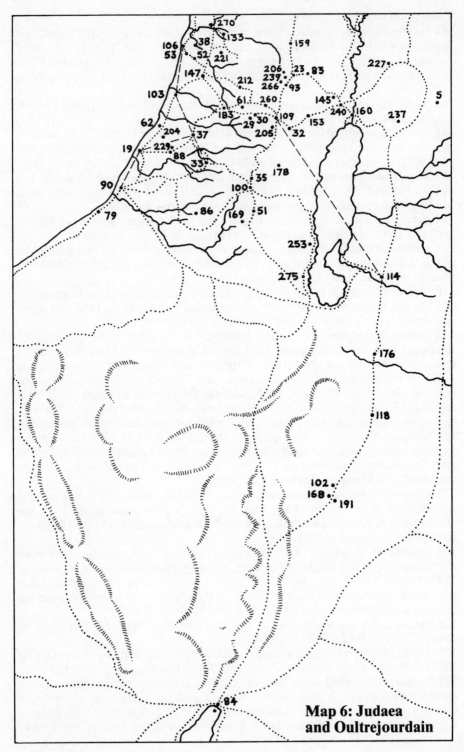

**Map 6: Judaea
and Oultrejourdain**

1101-1104, 1108-1131, 1143-1144 and circa 1182-1183. The Armenians held it undisturbed thereafter, although it was sacked by the Mamluks in 1266.

178 Teqoá, Thecoa, Thecua Third of the trio of small tower keeps constructed to control the Judaean Desert, built by King Fulk circa 1140 (probably 1139) and abandoned in 1187 after the Battle of Hattin.

179 Tell Hamdun Ceded to the Franks by the Armenians in 1185 and possibly held by the Hospitallers. Recovered by the Armenians only a few years later, it was lost to the Mamluks in 1266.

180 Tiberias (Thabaria, Thabarie) Captured by Tancred in 1099. It was Saladin's siege of this fortified town in 1187 that was the direct cause of the confrontation at Hattin, and it fell the day after the battle. It was recovered by treaty in 1240 but lost for good only seven years later, soon after its citadel had been rebuilt. The Mongols held it briefly in 1260.

181 La Tor de l'Opital A small outlying Hospitaller tower keep, probably of mid-12th century origin, amidst Tyre's orchards, defending the approaches to the city. Likely to have remained in Frankish hands until the fall of the kingdom. It had a close neighbour of unknown name.

182 Toron, Thoron Built by Hugh de St Omer, Prince of Galilee, in 1105, and refortified circa 1150. It fell to Saladin after a two-week siege in 1187 and was dismantled in 1219. Recovered by treaty in 1229 and refortified, it was lost to Baibars in 1266. The history of a small fortress of uncertain name sited at neighbouring Qalat ad Dubbe, more than likely dependent on Toron, most probably followed the same course.

183 Toron des Chevaliers, Toronum Militum Built by the Templars some time between 1150 and 1170, this fortress fell to Saladin in 1187 and was dismantled late in 1191 following his defeat at Arsuf. If was recovered by the treaty made between Frederick II and Sultan al-Kamil in 1229 and refortified circa 1241. Lost following the defeat at La Forbie in 1244.

184 Tortosa (Tartous) A fortified town captured and held between 1099 and 1100 during the First Crusade and recaptured by Raymond de Saint-Gilles in 1102. Nur ed-Din sacked it in 1152, and it was assigned to the Templars, who rebuilt and enlarged the castle, immediately after. In 1230 its garrison probably comprised about 200 horsemen and 1,000 infantry. It was lost in 1291. The island of Ruad two miles offshore, given to the Templars in 1301, held out as late as 1303. Although sources differ as to whether or not they had time to 'build' a proposed castle there its garrison, resident on the island at its fall, was 120 brethren and 500 Syrian archers (Maronites or Turcopoles). Probably there was a castle on Ruad already and the Templars had planned only to strengthen it.

185 Tripoli A fortified town that surrendered to the Franks in 1109 after a blockade by land and sea that had continued since 1103, when Raymond de Saint-Gilles had constructed the fortress of Mons Pelegrinus or Château Pèlerin (Mount Pilgrim) to control the land approaches to the city. Tripoli was saved from Saladin in 1188 by the timely arrival of a Sicilian fleet and was only finally lost in 1289, Mons Pelegrinus itself being undefended at that time.

186 Tuban Captured 1109. A Hospitaller fortress acquired in 1180 and dependent on Krak des Chevaliers. Lost to Baibars in 1266 and destroyed.

187 Turbessel A fortified town captured by Baldwin of Boulogne with Armenian assistance in 1097. Sold to the Byzantines 1150 and lost to Hassan of Menbij in 1151 after a siege of several months, the Byzantine garrison being starved into submission.

188 Turris Rubea, Turriclee, Tour Rouge A small 12th century tower keep built by the Templars and held by them until 1189, when it fell to Saladin. Probably recovered by treaty in 1192, it does not appear to have reverted to the Templars, instead being assigned to the Hospitallers in 1248. Probably lost the same year as its close neighbour Calansua, 1265.

189 Tyre, Tire A fortified town with walls that in the 1170s the traveller Ibn Jubayr reported as proverbial in their strength. Captured 1124, it was saved from Saladin in 1187 by the timely arrival of Conrad of Montferrat, who took over the city's defence. The walls were strengthened and a citadel added in 1210. It was finally abandoned in 1291 after the fall of Acre.

190 Varan An Armenian fortress granted to the Hospitallers in 1214.

191 Le Vaux Moise, Li Vaux Moyse Built by Baldwin I in 1117 and strengthened by Pagan le Bouteiller 1142, this was one of the three principal castles responsible for controlling Oultrejourdain, the other two being Kerak and Krak de Montréal. It was briefly occupied by Moslem forces in 1144 or 1145 but otherwise remained in Frankish hands until its conquest by Saladin circa 1188.

192 Zerdana (Sardone, Sardanaium) A fortified town surrendered to the Franks by treaty in 1110. Lost in 1119 following the Battle of Ager Sanguinus, its lord, Robert the Leper, being executed shortly after when captured following the Battle of Hab. Dismantled in 1120 but recovered by treaty and refortified the next year. Lost to Zengi in 1135.

The following additional castles are largely sites about which insufficient information was available to justify their inclusion in the main gazetteer; this is not to say that such information does not necessarily exist, merely that my own research failed to uncover it. Nevertheless, many of them were of considerable importance. Most of the additional sites listed here for Map 3 are Armenian, in Armenian hands for most of this era. There were a minimum of 72 castles in Armenian hands by Leon II's reign (1187-1219), 49 of which were 'of the first order'. *Kale,* incidentally, is Armenian for castle.

193 Adiyaman (Carbanum).
194 Ak Kale.
195 Ak-Kale (Bonbilico).
196 Anahsa-Kale (Rodentos, Butrentum).
197 Andirin.
198 Asgouras (Essers).
199 Ayas (Layas, Laicum).
200 Azgit.
201 Babaron, Sempad's Castle.
202 Balatunus.
203 Balis.
204 Beitderas.
205 Bethafava.
206 Bethal, Bethalla.
207 Bibol.
208 Bir.
209 Bodrum.
210 Bragana.
211 Bucak.

212 al-Burj.
213 Burj el Malih.
214 Burj Qibli.
215 Burj Sibna.
216 Caesarea.
217 Calamella, Canamella.
218 Castellum Rogerii Langobardis.
219 Castrum Nigrinum.
220 Cavea Rohob.
221 Chola, Cola.
222 Cokak.
223 Corycus (Le Courco).
224 Dagpazari.
225 Doc.
226 Durak.
227 Es-Salt.
228 Frenk Kale.
229 Geladia.
230 Gheiben (Gaban).
231 Gogison (Coxon).

232 Gokvelioglu.
233 Gosne.
234 Gouglag.
235 Heraclea.
236 Hisn ad-Dair.
237 Husban.
238 Islahiye.
239 Jafenia.
240 Jerico.
241 Kadirli, Kars.
242 Kahta.
243 Karaman (Laranda).
244 Khirbet el Badawiye.
245 Kum Kale.
246 Lacum.
247 Lampron.
248 Liman Kale.
249 Loulon.
250 Maghva.
251 Manbij.
252 Maran.
253 Masada.
254 Melitene.
255 Mersin.

256 Molevon (Mons Leonis).
257 Mut.
258 Noire Garde.
259 Osmaniye.
260 La Petite Mahomerie, Parva Mahomeria.
261 Pinarbasi, Comana (Plastencia).
262 Pozanti.
263 Qalat ed Dubbe.
264 Qalat Najm.
265 Raheb.
266 Ramelie.
267 Saint Johan de Tire.
268 Schoghagan (Château de Geoffroi).
269 Sis (Sisium).
270 Le Toron aux Fontaines Sourdes, Surdi Fontes.
271 Tumlu.
272 Vagha, Vakha.
273 Yilan Kale, Shah-Meran Kale.
274 Zur.
275 Zuweira al Fawqa.

Chapter 14

Aspects of a Crusade campaign for the wargamer

As will be obvious enough by now, this book is in no way intended as a guide to novice wargamers; there are already plenty enough such books in existence. It should come as no surprise, therefore, that in this chapter I do *not* intend to set out a complex array of instructions and rules covering the setting up and running of a campaign. That subject would require a volume in its own right and has been more than adequately dealt with in several, notably in Tony Bath's *Setting up a Wargames Campaign* (Wargames Research Group, 1973) and *War Games Campaigns* by Donald Featherstone (Stanley Paul, 1970). Anyone who has not already done so *must* purchase and/or read a copy of Tony Bath's book in which, as he admits himself, the emphasis tends to be on ancient and mediaeval campaigning. It is therefore ideally suited to subtle adaptation for our period. What I intend to actually concentrate on here are those aspects of campaigning which are either unique to, or of particular import in, Crusading warfare, with suggestions for both umpire and players as to how they might be best dealt with in the context of a wargame campaign.

For any campaign it is obviously essential that each of the protagonists should first have a particular goal. As we have seen elsewhere in this book, the aim of the Moslems was to capture as much territory and as many towns and castles as possible, and if in so doing they could goad the Franks into ill-considered battle all the better. The Franks, on the other hand, more often assumed a defensive stance, interfering with the Moslems' sieges, dogging their movements and blocking their lines of advance but at the same time wherever possible avoiding battle.

Inevitably avoidance of a decisive battle was nevertheless frequently impossible, particularly if there were Western leaders in the Frankish army, who were notorious for their rashness. The liklihood of the Franks indulging in rash actions in a wargame campaign would depend on the personalities involved, who can be based either on historical prototypes or invented characters with personalities established by following Tony Bath's suggestions on characterisation in his book. I should emphasise here that characterisation of all the leaders, even down to individual Templar officers or Moslem amirs, is *imperative* for a workable and enjoyable Crusade campaign, personality being a key factor in mediaeval Levantine conflicts. The index of any book on the Crusades will supply you with a wealth of names for your characters.

Most campaigns would usually involve no more than a single major engagement, after which the losers would, if routed, disperse, although a withdrawal in good order would keep the army intact. The victor might or might not continue on his proposed course depending on his own losses and whether or not the enemy was still in the field; such a decision would have to be made on his own assessment of the situation. Moslems, incidentally, would fight at their best on a Friday, the Moslem sabbath, and the campaign umpire might be justified in adapting dice results somewhat in their favour on morale tests. The same is *not* true of Christians fighting on a Sunday, although the presence of the sacred relic of the True Cross in their ranks could be regarded as an excuse for giving a plus one to all Frankish morale tests.

The armies must by necessity assemble at well-watered sites, the orchards and gardens of the larger cities being frequently used for the purpose of feeding and watering a mustering army. The Franks most often mustered their forces at Jaffa, Acre, Saphoria, Gaza, Ascalon, Tripoli, Antioch or Rugia, though basically any of the larger towns were ideal for this purpose. Moslem armies invading from Damascus usually tended to muster at Damascus itself or to the east of Lake Tiberias, while armies from Egypt assembled either at Ascalon or near Cairo, an additional mustering point for the latter in the mid-13th century being at al-Salihiyya in the north-east of Lower Egypt.

Water being so vital to armies operating in the Levant, it would be wise for all springs, wells and oases to be marked in advance on the campaign master-map, with agreement by all parties on which can support an encamped army and for how long (in relation, obviously, to the size of that army). All players have access to this data. Roads follow the best watered routes so should be adhered to wherever possible. In broad terms travel by major road was half as fast again as travel by minor road, which was twice as fast as travel cross-country, ie, a ratio of 3:2:1. All off-road movement is subject to penalties of a quarter per cent losses in men and one per cent losses in horses and livestock per month, these rates doubling in the winter. Off-road movement in the desert is deemed impossible except for Bedouin and Turcoman tribesmen. Rates of movement can be estimated as being at the following speeds (by major road in the case of land forces), subject to weather conditions:

	miles per day
Berid couriers	120
Frankish couriers (for one day only)	60
All-cavalry force with baggage	15
All-cavalry force with no baggage	20
Mixed cavalry/infantry force with baggage	10
Mixed cavalry/infantry force with no baggage	15
All-infantry force with baggage	10
All-infantry force with no baggage	15
Turcoman or Bedouin raiders	30
Ships under sail	60
Galleys under oar	20

Winter conditions would slow down ships and couriers by half and all other land forces by three-quarters, but it should be borne in mind that in winter activities would be localised to Syrian and Egyptian waters only, ie, there would be no movement to or from the European mainland. Even under ideal conditions the above speeds might not be attained; King Richard's advance down the coast from Acre to Jaffa in 1192, a total of 81 miles, took 19 days, an average of only about $4\frac{1}{4}$ miles a day. In fact on some days his army covered only two or three miles (travelling in the relative cool of the morning), while as many as eight days were spent resting in camp. Phil Barker suggests in *Alexander the Great's Campaigns* (Patrick Stephens, 1979) that at least one day in ten should be a rest day, but Richard's itinerary would seem to indicate that rest periods might be as frequent as one day in three, although admittedly in his case a good few of these rest days were actually used to unload stores from the offshore fleet. Later Mamluk armies would march for longer periods and then rest for several days at a time.

Since, as we have already observed, the Franks relied to a great extent on drawing manpower from their castles to make up a field army, the Frankish player, on mustering his forces, should hand in to the umpire a list of those towns and fortresses from which he has drawn elements of their garrisons, stating numbers and troop-types. If the Frankish army is subsequently severely defeated in the field, the Moslem player is therefore likely to find many of the local castles undermanned, although elements of the defeated Frankish army taking refuge in such forts will obviously help to restore the garrison to its requisite strength. Frankish castle garrisons were provided by mercenaries so need to be allowed for in one's budgets.

Sieges feature prominently in crusading warfare, and an ingenious set of rules for deciding sieges 'by calculations rather than having to fight them on the table' is contained in Tony Bath's book. I would certainly recommend these to anyone, although one or two slight modifications may be necessary before they are perfectly suited to the Crusade era. For instance, no Levantine fortress of the 12th or 13th centuries was big enough to qualify for Tony's category of '1st Class Fortress' with an unlimited garrison strength, although castles such as Krak des Chevaliers and Safed nevertheless warrant the top 'strength points' rating of 150; so it seems that the best solution would be to combine his 1st and 2nd classes to give a strength value of 150 points and a maximum garrison of 200 figures (4,000 men at the standard ratio of 1:20, although no castle garrison of this era ever exceeded about 2,200 men). Secondly, there need to be two classes of walled town, a 1st Class with a defensive value of 100 points and a 2nd Class valued at 40 points. The 1st Class would comprise only a very select group of cities comprised of Acre, Aleppo, Antioch, Birejik, Cairo, Damascus, Damietta, Edessa, Jerusalem, Marash, Samosata, Tripoli and Tyre, with no limit on the size of their garrisons. Otherwise Tony's rules cover every aspect of a siege including treachery, assault, breaches and morale, though one other amendment I would suggest is that the besieged garrison may attempt to surrender in exchange for safe conduct at any point during the siege. Mind you, surrender is inadvisable if the character represented by the player to whom you must submit has a reputation for treachery!

The alternative to using calculations and dice to decide a siege is to actually fight it out on the wargames table, building a section or the whole of the castle in question plus siege entrenchments and engines. An ideal medium for the construction of a scale castle is provided by the Linka system, manufactured by Thomas Salter Ltd, Glenrothes, Fife. This involves casting units of stonework in rubber moulds, from which you can then produce virtually any shape of castle you might require. The system's only disadvantage is that the moulds are flat and it is therefore impossible to cast round towers. Nevertheless, impressive results can be achieved. Siege engines are produced in plastic by Atlantic and in metal by several wargame figure manufacturers (see Appendix A), or can be made from card and balsa. A useful series of articles by Terry Wise on how to build siege equipment for the wargame table appeared in *Airfix Magazine* between May and November 1971, and these are worth trying to get hold of.

Any player wishing to strengthen his defences during the course of a campaign by the construction of a new castle must first muster enough men for the purpose, and for the sake of argument I would suggest that the minimum number should be some 1,000, paid at one dinar or bezant per month. For each ten per cent more men up to a total of 2,000 the castle can be built five per cent more swiftly. Unless one wishes to transform the whole campaign into an exercise in logistics it is simplest to assume that the necessary building materials are available locally; one exception to this ruling should perhaps be the desert regions. The smallest fortresses of all, the unfurnished tower keeps used by the Franks as refuge during raids and capable of holding about 500 people in an emergency, would take two weeks to build. Small castles capable of holding 1,000 souls would take four months, larger castles with permanent garrisons of up to a thousand (such as Le Chastellet) six months, and the largest castles of all, with garrisons of over 1,000 (such as Safed), would take two to two-and-a-half years to construct. Using Tony Bath's system these qualify respectively as Weak Forts, Strong Forts, 3rd Class Fortresses and amended 1st/2nd Class Fortresses.

Partially completed castles attacked during construction would have a defensive value directly comparable to their degree of completion. For example, a 3rd Class Fortress attacked two months after the commencement of building, ie, when it is one third completed, would have a defensive value of one third of its full strength points of 60, therefore 20 points. The cost of building a castle, incidentally, was astronomical. Le Chastellet, which I have called a 3rd Class Fortress, cost some 60,000 to 100,000 dinars to build, while Joinville tells us that when Louis IX refortified Jaffa a single gatehouse and a portion of wall, which Joinville himself guessed might have cost 500 and 300 livres respectively, cost the colossal sum of 30,000 livres tournois, equivalent to *60,000* bezants!

Siege equipment was similarly very expensive. The cost of actually building a belfry in 1219 was 2,000 silver marks (over 1,300 bezants), while Joinville records that a belfry built during the Seventh Crusade comprised timber 'valued at 10,000 livres and more' (ie, 20,000 bezants). Compare this to the cost of building a ship, 14,000 bezants at the time of the Eighth Crusade. So if you are going to build a fortress *or* indulge in a siege, first make sure you can afford to.

Establishing the incomes of individual mediaeval Levantine states is difficult or, more accurately, impossible. The following figures are therefore almost entirely my own, aimed at a balanced wargame campaign rather than entirely accurate historical reconstruction. The annual incomes derive principally from direct or indirect land revenue—directly in the form of rents and produce, indirectly in the form of taxes on people, produce and industry. Either way the loss of land meant loss of revenue. The revenue of fiefs and iqtaat belong to the fief-holder anyway, and you can establish the value of each individual fief by dividing the total income of infeudated land by the number of knights or askaris it supports (for which see Chapters 3 and 4). Fief-holders dispossessed by enemy action are no longer obliged to serve their lords unless alternate fiefs, either in cash or land, are found for them elsewhere. Annual incomes of individual regions within a state can fluctuate by ten per cent if there is a poor harvest, by 25 per cent if there is pestilence or drought, and by as much as 50 per cent if the region is fought over repeatedly throughout the campaigning season.

Revenue can be increased by levying extraordinary taxes for the Holy War, or *Jihad,* the nature of which is left to the player's discretion, but no more than once in any single year; it is up to the umpire to decide on the population's reaction, which will depend on how odious the taxman's proposals are in relation to current circumstances. The Franks may in addition borrow cash from the Military Orders, who acted as bankers, at moderate interest rates. Usury was actually anathaematized, so the interest on such loans would be calculated beforehand and added to the sum borrowed—ie, a loan of 500 bezants at five per cent interest would be entered in the records as a loan of 525 bezants and repaid accordingly.

All parties start out with a cash reserve equal to half a year's non-infeudated income, which is kept in the state treasury in the capital. This will be lost if the city is captured. It is worth noting in this context that the Kingdom of Jerusalem was nearly always close to bankruptcy as a result of its huge military expenditure, and when Jerusalem *did* fall in 1187 there was not even as much as 30,000 dinars to be found in the royal treasury. The booty from other captured towns can, of course, boost one's finances and it would be wise to establish the 'loot' value of all towns and villages prior to the commencement of the campaign, basing the figures on relative size and population. Some towns will yield the additional prizes of large armouries, royal mints and so on.

Unfortunately not a single original source or modern authority that I have consulted in the course of my research has even attempted a guess at what Outremer's annual revenue might have been, yet alone given any worthwhile figures. However, for our purposes the Kingdom of Jerusalem can be said to have a gross income of two million bezants (about 2,400,000 dinars) in the 12th century, of which one-and-a-half million would have been spent on its military resources, with about 750,000 bezants tied up in fiefs (excluding those held by the Military Orders), 340,000 bezants-worth of which comprised the royal demesne. The balance of 750,000 is available for fortifications, bribes, hiring of mercenaries and the like. Tripoli could be said to have a military budget of 300,000 bezants with 180,000 in fiefs, Antioch a million bezants with 500,000 in fiefs, and Edessa 800,000 bezants with 450,000 in fiefs.

These incomes would be boosted from time to time by pecuniary aid from Western Europe which, as we saw in Chapter 3, could be considerable. To represent such gifts in the context of a campaign I would suggest that the player representing the King of Jerusalem should roll two ordinary dice at the beginning of each of the 'summer' months (May-October), any double meaning that such a gift has arrived from the West. Using a pack of cards he must then draw a single card which will denote the size of the gift; a two means a gift of 1,000 bezants, three a gift of 10,000 bezants, four 20,000, five 30,000, six 40,000, seven 50,000, eight 60,000, nine 70,000, ten 80,000, jack 90,000, queen 100,000, and a king means the jackpot of 250,000 bezants. An ace indicates a gift in men rather than money: the ace of hearts represents 20 knights and 100 crossbowmen, the ace of clubs 60 knights and 200 crossbowmen, the ace of diamonds 80 knights and 300 crossbowmen and the ace of spades 100 knights and 500 crossbowmen. Such mercenaries serve for 12 months but can obviously be retained thereafter if the king continues to pay them, either from his own resources or further money gifts.

Unsophisticated as this method is, I have found it works comparatively well, although it is wise to keep track of which contingent's 12 months expires when; otherwise you may find half your army dispersing right in the middle of a campaign as I once did! Obviously, you can develop on the system as much as you like; in the 13th century, for example, the cash figures would need to be reduced but in addition there would be a regular gift during each of the summer months from both the Pope and the King of France. Tripoli and Antioch too could receive such gifts, but only at about a tenth of Jerusalem's level. Crusaders and pilgrims receive no pay at all, incidentally, other than from their own lords who accompany them, so do not need to be covered by the Frankish player's budget. Their numbers and leaders need to be agreed upon prior to the commencement of the campaign, although their actual time or arrival could be left up to the umpire or some sort of chance card system. Once again, it would be between May and October.

The Military Orders had their own revenues for military expenditure, but it is even harder to establish what these may have been. Certainly in 1168 the Hospitaller Grand Master Gilbert d'Assailly put his Order in debt to the tune of 100,000 bezants by hiring too many mercenaries, and we know that the Hospital provided 500 knights and 500 Turcopoles for King Amalric's Egyptian campaign of that year. Allowing for the pay of their castle garrisons it seems likely that the Temple and Hospital in the Kingdom of Jerusalem each had half a million bezants per annum for military expenditure in the 12th century, though in effect their resources were virtually unlimited. The Hospitaller Convent of Tripoli can be said to have 200,000 bezants (Krak des Chevaliers alone being worth an annual income of some 40,000), and the Templar Convent of Antioch 300,000 bezants. The Hospitallers of Antioch and Templars of Tripoli have 100,000 bezants each, as does the Convent of the Teutonic Knights for the whole of Outremer.

Fatimid Egypt appears to have had an annual military expenditure of some five million dinars in the first quarter of the 12th century, which was still much the same under the Ayyubids; Saladin, for instance, assigned 4,653,019 dinars to military expenditure in 1189, of which 3,462,096 was paid out to the regular mamluks in iqtaat while the balance was used for incidental military expenses such as paying mercenaries and ghazis and improving Cairo's defences. For wargame purposes, then, we can say that the Egyptian treasury has five million dinars gross for military expenditure of which all but a million and a half is tied up in military fiefs in which, of course, the bulk of the revenue goes to the holder. The Syrian city-states had considerably smaller annual revenues, probably something on the following lines:

	Iqtaat	Additional military expenditure	Total income
Aleppo and Northern Syria	1,125,000	375,000	1,500,000
Damascus	562,500	187,500	750,000
Diyar Bekr	450,000	150,000	600,000
Hamah	375,000	125,000	500,000
Harran	225,000	75,000	300,000
Homs	225,000	75,000	300,000
Mardin	450,000	150,000	600,000
Mosul	937,500	312,500	1,250,000
Shaizar	187,500	62,500	250,000

Unlike the fiefs of Frankish knights, iqtaat can be withdrawn from their holders, although this reduces the strength of the relevant askar (see Chapter 4) on a directly proportional basis. For example, if the player representing the governor of Mardin decides to reclaim 45,000 dinars-worth of iqtaat (ie, ten per cent), then his annual allowance for additional military expenditure is bumped up by that figure while his provincial askar of 1,000 men is reduced by ten per cent to 900 men. Similarly, more iqtaat can be granted out as long as there is the cash to support them. One thing to note: reducing the number of iqtaat results in unemployed professional soldiers—100 in the example given—among whom rebellion may break out if there are further grounds for disaffection. That decision must be the umpire's, although the characters of the dispossessed amirs need to be taken into acount. The amount of money available for additional military expenses may not seem considerable, but if should be borne in mind that most Turcoman, Bedouin and Kurdish tribesmen were paid with loot taken on campaign rather than with cash.

Losses of equipment on campaign can be partially made up for from equipment looted from the battlefield—assuming you are the victor. I would go along with Tony Bath's suggestions here in that 60 per cent of the victor's missiles and all but five per cent of his equipment can be retrieved from the battlefield, while 50 per cent of the equipment scavenged from the enemy dead and prisoners is considered fit for re-use. Moslem victors will in addition capture ten per cent of the horses of all killed or captured Frankish horsemen, Frankish victors capturing the substantially higher figure of 50 per cent. The vanquished lose in addition ten per cent of all equipment if they withdraw in good order, or considerably more if they rout (see Chapter 8). Moslem armies campaigning *jaridatan* (ie, without baggage) have less equipment to lose anyway, and in battle they count as having no heavy troops. If the Frankish player is fortunate enough to surprise a Moslem army on the march the same ruling applies, for the Moslems only donned their armour when there was an immediate prospect of fighting. Montgisard in 1177 is a classic example of such a surprise attack and its consequences. Good scouting is therefore essential on both sides, and the umpire may assume that an army will always have scouts a few miles ahead.

Spies were sewn thick in both Christian and Moslem camps and contemporary chroniclers leave us with a distinct impression that very little could be kept secret for very long. The best Moslem intelligence service was that of the Fatimids, reputedly so efficient under the vizier al-Mamun (1121-1125) that from the very moment when an Assassin left distant Alamut his every movement was known and reported. Baibars inevitably had the next most reliable service, which operated under the guise of the berid, or post office, where, as we have seen, his postmen actually doubled as spies. The chief of intelligence was the Postmaster General, the *Amir el-Berid* or *Sahib diwan al-insha.* He had deputies in Damascus, Aleppo, Hamah, Kerak, Tripoli and Safed.

Most of the Franks' spies were renegade Moslems, Arabic-speaking Syrians (including Turcopoles), and Bedouin, probably all coming under the control of the *mathesep,* or chief of police. The *Itinerarium* records such spies in action in the affair of the great caravan in June 1192, telling us how 'Bernard, the king's scout, came up with some other spies, who were all natives of the land. They were clad in Saracen garb and came from the direction of Egypt, differing in no respect, so far as appearance went, from the Saracens. Thus they were able to study the Saracen positions at ease and keep the king informed thereon. No one spoke the Saracen tongue better than they, one of them having formerly received 100 silver marks from King Richard for his service in this way'. However, it is worth noting that Richard would not trust the report of one of these spies because he 'belonged to the land' (ie, was a native of the district). He therefore sent out a Bedouin and two Turcopoles 'whom he had dressed up so as to look like Bedouins' to verify the facts. These, eluding some Saracen scouts who attempted to intercept them, walked nonchalantly into the Turkish camp, satisfied themselves about the accuracy of the first spy's information, and then reported back to Richard, all in the space of one night.

It is worth noting, incidentally, that while Bernard's men had been spying in the Moslem camp, a Moslem spy in the Frankish camp had been simultaneously keeping Saladin equally well informed of Frankish movements! Also, the frequent use of the word 'scout' in the *Itinerarium*'s account indicates that such men performed a double function.

I have yet to find a satisfactory way of representing spies in a wargame campaign—after all, so much depends on the cunning and resourcefulness of the individual. However, in the context of a Crusade campaign things are somewhat simpler. As I mentioned earlier, there were so many spies around (especially if one includes disaffected natives, traitors, and so on) that it was as good as impossible to keep a secret for anything more than a few days. Therefore, as long as a player has one of his spies in the right place at the right time—be it the enemy encampment or a particular port or city—then he will know within reason of any major military or political decision agreed on in that place. Mind you, the extent and accuracy of his information must be at the discretion of the umpire; it will be substantially correct, but at the same time the umpire should do his best to make it obscure where possible, further confusing the issue by occasionally giving very accurate data instead. In addition a single dice throw will denote the number of days to elapse before the spy can be assumed to have discovered the relevant secret: a six on the dice means that the spy has his information the very same day, while throws of one to five indicate lapses of as many days.

Movement of spies and the despatch of their reports should be governed by the rules set out in Tony Bath's book, my only addition to these being that agents can carry a single carrier pigeon about their person, the speed of which would be as set out at the beginning of Chapter 9. However, before his spy sets out the player in question *must* state the cot from which the pigeon has come and to which it will therefore return, this information to be given to the umpire. Remember, these are *homing* pigeons, not radio-controlled.

Assassins are a slightly different kettle of fish. Chapter 6 should have given you a good idea of their potential, and it can be seen that it would be best if a player with no scruples could take the part of the Old Man of the Mountain! The Ismailis had secret followers in most towns who assisted them on their missions, so we may take it for granted that, although the successful completion of an Assassin's journey is subject to the same rules as the movements of a spy, his orders can be automatically assumed to have reached him *wherever* he may be. Once he has received his orders to strike then his victim has to throw a single dice: a six will save him and a four or five means he is wounded, but any other score means he is dead. If a four or five is scored then a second dice must be thrown; a one, two or three indicates that he is mortally wounded and will die within three days (this giving him enough time to choose his successor and advise his heir and generals of whatever plans he may have had); while four, five or six indicate a slight wound preventing movement for two weeks.

An Assassin is automatically assumed killed or captured when he has made his 'hit', another dice roll here (a six is required again) indicating that he has been captured. Yet another roll of the dice is now called for: a one or two means he dies under 'interrogation', having revealed nothing; a three, four or five means that the names he has given during interrogation may, or may not, include those of the actual instigators of the crime; and a six means that the name(s) given are actually those of the real instigators. Obviously only the umpire must know whether the information is true or not, so he rolls the dice and then extracts the relevant details from the player representing the Old Man of the Mountain. A captured Assassin therefore has the rare pleasure of implicating, before he dies, as many of his enemies (or friends!) as he likes.

Three last points on the Assassins. The first is that though the Old Man may, if he so wishes, ally with or sell his services to any player he chooses, he *must* present the umpire with a sound motive. The second is that the success of assassination attempts on officers of the Military Orders are at the umpire's discretion. Finally, the umpire would be wise to limit the Assassins' activities in some way, perhaps by stipulating a maximum number of murders that can be committed in a single year, or by restricting the number of fidais at the Old Man's disposal. Otherwise you may find that every ruling house in the land has been wiped out before the end of even the first campaigning season!

Appendix A

The availability of wargame figures

A wargamer's choice of figures is very much a matter of personal taste; what is an attractive figure to one person may be thin, fat, overlarge or badly proportioned to another. This appendix is therefore basically restricted to listing all the manufacturers that I know of who produce figures relevant to the Crusades, with a few remarks about their general appearance, where—I confess—I have occasionally allowed my personal opinion to come to the fore. I am grateful to most of the manufacturers listed here for supplying catalogues and samples. In particular I am indebted to Neville Dickinson of Minifigs for producing moulds and casting figures from his forthcoming Crusades range especially for use on the cover of this book, many months in advance of his original schedule.

Please note that neither I nor the publishers can accept any responsibility for the standards of service or quality of product which any of these companies may provide. Nor can we guarantee the up-to-date accuracy of the addresses given.

Advance Guard (Miniatures) Limited, *114 Crawford Street, Motherwell, Strathclyde, ML1 3BD.* 15 mm. Although at the time of writing I have yet to see any samples, Advance Guard's advertising lists two ranges specifically intended for Crusade wargaming, these being their 'Armies of Islam' (six infantry, six cavalry and two command packs) and 'Armies of Christendom' (five infantry, three cavalry and one command pack).

Asgard Miniatures, *15 Furlong Avenue, Arnold, Nottingham.* 25 mm. Norman and Mediaeval ranges comprising 31 figures at the time of writing. The Mediaeval figures are more appropriate to the 13th century and include Knights Templar and knights on barded horses. An Arab range has been planned for some time but as I write has yet to appear. Unusually for this scale, cavalrymen and their horses come moulded together in one piece. Spearmen have open hands and spears are supplied in the form of lengths of stiff wire on which points need to be hammered. Asgard figures are 'large' 25s and nicely detailed.

Castile Miniatures, *20 Rankin Street, Carluke, Lanarkshire.* 25 mm. 'Feudal 1066-1300' and 'Islamic' ranges. At the time of writing the latter comprises only nine figures but Castile intend to cover Islamic armies extensively in the future. The Feudal range includes a Turcopole, and Teutonic Knights are also available. Spearmen and crossbowmen largely have their weapons moulded separately, and various packs of spare weapons and shields are available. Excellent figures, very attractive and somewhat slimmer than those of many other manufacturers.

Citadel Miniatures, *Newark Folk Museum, 48 Millgate, Newark, Nottingham-*

shire. 25 mm. A '1200 AD Mediaevals and Vikings' range manufactured under licence in this country for Ral Partha, the American company. This includes Byzantines, Mongols, various European types, some of them 14th century, and 'Moors' (North African or Andalusian types). Citadel themselves have a Dark Ages range which includes Arabs, Normans and 10th-12th century Byzantines. Both the Ral Partha figures and Citadel's own are crisp, extremely detailed castings with bags of character and Citadel's Byzantines are among my personal favourites.

Dixon Miniatures, *Ash Grove, Royles Head Lane, Longwood, Huddersfield, West Yorkshire, HD3 4TU.* 25 mm. A small range of Dark Age Arabs, also a comprehensive Mongol range including a superb Bactrian camel complete with *naker* drums and drummer, and a range of Asiatic cavalry of which several are usable as 11th-13th century Turkish cavalry. A 'Medieval' range has started to appear at the time of writing. These are again 'large' 25s, although scale varies slightly from figure to figure.

Frei Korps 15, *30 Cromwell Road, Belfast 7, Northern Ireland.* 15 mm. At the time of writing Frei Korps' AM range includes a wide variety of Frankish and Moslem figures such as Negro archers, Knights Templar, Seljuks and Normans. Spaniards and Moors of the Reconquista are also available. Future plans include 11th-13th century Armenians and Georgians, plus late Byzantines and siege equipment. These are finely detailed 'large' 15s. Some of the cavalrymen come separately from their horses.

Greenwood and Ball Limited (Garrison), *Unit 27, Bon Lea Trading Estate, Thornaby-on-Tees, Teesside.* 25 mm. Norman, Ghaznavid Turk and Mongol ranges. As Garrison's catalogue says, the Ghaznavids can be used with Saracen armies, four actually being Arabs while others are suitable for use as Seljuk Turks. The Mongol range includes another nice camel-drummer. Excellent figures, finely detailed and well proportioned. Garrison horses are arguably the very best available in 25 mm.

Hinchliffe Models Limited, *21 Station Street, Meltham, Huddersfield, HD7 3NX.* 25 mm. A small Mediaeval range of which the infantry are the best. The four knights are 13th century types rather than the 11th-12th century that the lists claim, while the three Saracen figures in this range are rather Eastern-looking and better suited to the role of 13th-14th century Ilkhanid Persians. An extensive Late Byzantine range is also available, comprised of 17 figures including a Varangian, a Norman cavalryman, and Asiatic auxiliaries. In their '25 mm Equipment Range' there is a superb 30-piece belfry kit, an additional kit providing layers of hide coverings. Catapults are available too. Well detailed 'large' 25s again. Wire spears.

Lamming Miniatures, *254 Wincolmlee, Hull, Yorkshire, HU2 0PZ.* 25 mm. Norman, Byzantine and Mediaeval ranges. The latter is comprised largely of 14th-15th century types but includes some earlier figures suitable for the Crusade era. Several Moslems also appear in the Mediaeval range. One of the novelties of Lamming figures is that many of them have separate heads and arms, as well as individual weapons and shields. Twenty-one different weapon packs are also available including crossbows, swords, maces and axes. A small mediaeval equipment range includes catapult and ballista. Robust figures which paint up very nicely, the horses being amongst the best available.

Mike's Models, *38 Queen's Road, Brighton, Sussex, BN4 4RQ.* 15 mm. Norman, Ghaznavid and Arab ranges. At the time of writing a range based on

Armies of Feudal Europe is about to go into production, apparently to comprise nearly 200 figures, this to be followed by a range based on *Armies and Enemies of the Crusades* which should be available by the time this book is published. Clean castings embodying considerable character, although faces are not always clear. Horses and riders are supplied separately.

Miniature Figurines Limited (Minifigs), *1/5 Graham Road, Southampton, Hampshire, SO2 0AX.* 15 mm and 25 mm. Even as I write Minifigs are cutting the masters for a comprehensive range of 25 mm Crusade figures, again based on *Armies and Enemies of the Crusades,* the figures shown on the dust-jacket of this book being the very first castings. These are excellent miniatures with separate shields and, in many cases, separate lances and swords too. The range should eventually comprise some 60 figures including knights of the Military Orders, Bedouin, Syrian Christians, Byzantines and assorted Turks, Arabs and Franks. Minifigs also have an 'Alexander Nevski' range which includes some suitable figures, a small Mongol range, and a Dark Ages range which includes Normans, Arabs and 10th-11th century Byzantines. There are also several siege engines available. A 15 mm Crusades range is also on the cards. Excellent figures and clean castings with well detailed faces and armour.

Peter Laing, *'Minden', Sutton St Nicholas, Hereford, HR1 3BD.* 15 mm. 'Feudal and Dark Ages' range which includes both Saracens and Norman-style Frankish cavalry and infantry. A variety of equipment is also available, including an ox-cart, mangonel and crew figures, ladders, battering rams, trebuchets, ballistas and a 12-part belfry. The 'Ancients' range includes 6th-7th century Byzantines, some passable as 11th-12th century types in this scale.

Vulcan Miniatures, *Wargame Publications (Scotland) Limited, St George's Buildings, 5 St Vincent Place, Glasgow, G1 2DH.* 25 mm. Shortly before this book went to press Vulcan's advertising announced a range of figures to include Normans and Late Byzantines, some of the latter apparently suitable as 12th-13th century types.

Warrior Miniatures, *44 Candleriggs, Glasgow, G1 1LE.* 25 mm. Very small Norman and 13th century ranges, the latter comprising just two figures, both of indeterminate provenance. A range of some 50 Crusades figures based on *Armies and Enemies of the Crusades* is planned to start appearing some time during 1980. Well proportioned figures, if sometimes a little 'flat'.

Appendix B

The classification of troops under WRG rules

Abbreviations used in weapons column: *Ax*—Heavy axe, *B*—Bow, *HD*—Heavy dagger, *J*—Javelins, *L*—Lasso, *LS*—Light spear, *LTS*—Long thrusting spear or cavalry lance, *M*—Mace, *Sa*—Sabre, *Sh*—Shield, *Sw*—Sword, *Xb*—Crossbow. *R* or *I* in the fourth column denotes whether the troops are regular (ie, drilled) or irregular.

	Class	Type	R or I	Weapons
Franks				
Western or Syrian Frankish knights	B[1]	HC/EHC[2]	I	LTS,Sw,Sh
Western or Syrian Frankish mounted sergeants	B or C	HC or MC	I	LTS,Sw,Sh
Western or Syrian Frankish infantry	C	HI[3]	I	LTS,Sw,Sh or B/Xb,Sw
Mercenary Frankish knights	C	HC/EHC[2]	I	LTS,Sw,Sh
Mercenary Frankish mounted sergeants	C	HC	I	LTS,Sw,Sh
Mercenary Frankish infantry	C	HI[3]	I	LTS,Sw,Sh or B/Xb,Sw
Pilgrims	D	MI	I	B/LS,HD
Arrière-ban levies	D	MI	I	LTS,HD,Sh
Brother knights of the Military Orders	A	HC/EHC[2]	R	LTS,Sw,Sh
Brother sergeants of the Military Orders	A or B	HC	R	LTS,Sw,Sh
Turcopoles	C	LHC[4]	I[5]	LS,B,Sw,M,Sh
Cilician Armenian cavalry	B or C	HC	I	LTS,Sw,Sh
Cilician Armenian infantry	C	MI or LHI	I	LTS,Sw,Sh or B,Sw
Maronite cavalry	B or C	HC or MC	I	LTS,Sw,Sh
Maronite infantry	C	LMI	I	B,Sw,Sh
Syrian Christian knights	C or D	HC	I	LTS,Sw,Sh
Syrian Christian infantry	D	MI,LHI or HI	I	LTS,Sw/HD,Sh or B,Sw/HD

Moslems

Mamluk cavalry[6]	B or C	LC[7] or HC[8]	R	LS,B,M,Sw,Sh
The Royal Mamluks and the *al-Halqa*	A	LC[7] or HC[8]	R	LTS/LS,B,M,Sw, Sh
Non-mamluk Arab/Kurd cavalry	C	MC or HC	I	LTS,Sw,Sh
Non-mamluk Turkish cavalry	C	LC[7] or HC[8]	I	LS/J,B,Sa,M,L,Sh
Turcoman or Khwarizmian cavalry	C	LC[7]	I	LS/J,B,Sa,M,L,Sh
Turcoman infantry	C	LMI	I	LS/J,Sw,Sh *or* B,Sw
Bedouin cavalry	C	LC or MC	I	LTS,Sw,Sh
Bedouin infantry	C	LMI	I	LTS/B,Sw,Sh
Syrian levy infantry and town militiamen	C or D	MI or LMI	I	LTS,Sw/HD,Sh *or* B,Sw/HD
Sudanese Guard infantry	B	MI or HI	R	LTS/B,Sw,Sh
Sudanese ghulam infantry	B or C	MI	R	LTS/B,Sw,Sh
Regular infantry other than Sudanese	C	MI,LMI or HI	R	LTS,Sw,Sh *or* B/Xb[9],Sw/HD
Ghazi volunteers	C[10]	Any category	I	As for respective troop type
Assassins	B[10]	Any category	I	As for respective troop type

Byzantines

Heavy infantry	C	HI or LHI	R	LTS,Sw,Sh
Other infantry	C or D	MI,LMI or LI	R or I	B,Sw,Sh *or* LTS/ LS/J,Sw,Sh *or* Xb,Sw
Varangian Guards	A	SHI or HI	R	Ax,LS,Sw,Sh
Vardariots	A or B	LC[7] or HC	R	LS/J,B,Sa,M,Sh
Turkish mercenaries (Cumans, Patzinaks, etc)	C	LC[7] or HC[8]	I	LS/J,B,Sa,M,L,Sh
Heavy cavalry	B or C	EHC or HC	R or I	LTS,Sw,Sh
Light cavalry	C or D	LC	R or I	LTS/B,Sw,Sh

Mongols

Heavy cavalry	A,B or C	EHC or HC	I	LTS,B,Sa,M,Sh
Light cavalry	C	LC[7]	I	LS/J,B,Sa,M,L,Sh
Georgian cavalry	B or C	LC or HC	I	LTS,B,Sa/Sw,M, Sh

Notes

1 There may be a case for making some Western Frankish troops irregular fanatics, therefore A class troops. This is particularly true of the late 12th and

13th centuries.

2 Knights would count as HC up to circa 1175, and as EHC thereafter. Also, from circa 1190 a small number might be mounted on armoured horses and would therefore count as SHC. It should be noted, incidentally, that Frankish HC charged in close order even if they thereafter fought in loose formation. In WRG's forthcoming 6th Edition rules such EHC and SHC become EHK and SHK respectively, 'K' standing for 'knight'.

3 From circa 1225 a good proportion of Frankish infantry could actually be classified as SHI.

4 This category, Light Heavy Cavalry, does not exist in WRG's system, but without it it is impossible to successfully classify Turcopoles. I would define them, using WRG's style of phraseology, as comprised of men in partial metal or quilted armour mounted on unprotected horses, fighting in close, loose or dispersed formation as needs dictated, moving at a trot and charging at a gallop. They were often mustered alongside the Frankish knights and sergeants.

5 Turcopoles in service with the Military Orders would count as Regular.

6 For the sake of this assessment these include non-mamluk horsemen incorporated into mamluk units.

7 Some Turkish and Mongol light cavalry wore felt, leather or quilted armour, or occasionally even mail or lamellar.

8 By the middle to late 13th century in Egypt and Syria, and from the very beginning of this era in Rum, Persia and further East, some Turkish heavy cavalry might be equipped as EHC or SHC. These would nevertheless have been relatively few in number.

9 The crossbow only began to appear frequently in use among Syrian Moslems in the mid-12th century. Contemporary sources seem to indicate that those who used it should be classified as LHI. Some infantry were also armed with heavy two-handed axes, eg, the Mamluk Tabardariyah regiment.

10 Some of these would count as fanatics, therefore A class, but fanaticism was largely out of fashion amongst Moslems by the Crusade era.

Select bibliography

Translations of original sources

On the whole these are not easy to come by, even in large libraries, but to really get the 'feel' of the period they are essential reading. Don't be put off by the idea that, as original sources, they will be dull and academic—many are immensely readable, particularly the works of Ambroise, Usamah and William of Tyre.

Archer, T.A.: *The Crusade of Richard I, 1189-1192,* 1888.

Berry, Virginia G.: *De Profectione Ludovici VII in Orientem* (Odo de Deuil), 1948.

Gabrieli, Francesco: *Arab Historians of the Crusades,* 1969.

Gibb, H.A.R.: *The Damascus Chronicle of the Crusades* (Ibn al-Qalanisi), 1932.

Hill, Rosalind: *The Deeds of the Franks and Other Pilgrims to Jerusalem* (Gesta Francorum), 1968.

Hitti, P.K.: *An Arab-Syrian Gentleman of the Crusades* (Usamah ibn Munqidh), 1929.

Hubert, Merton Jerome: *The Crusade of Richard Lion-Heart* (Ambroise), 1941.

Krey, A.C. and Babcock, E.A.: *A History of Deeds done Beyond the Sea* (William of Tyre), 1943.

McNeal, E.H.: *The Conquest of Constantinople* (Robert de Clari), 1936.

Marzials, Frank: *Memoirs of the Crusades* (Geoffrey de Villehardouin and Jean Sire de Joinville), 1908.

Ryan, Frances Rita: *A History of the Expedition to Jerusalem, 1095-1127* (Fulcher of Chartres), 1969.

Sewter, R.A.: *The Alexiad of Anna Comnena,* 1969.

Stewart, Aubrey: *The History of Jerusalem* (Jacques de Vitry), 1896.

Wilson, C.W.: *Life of Saladin* (Beha ed-Din), 1897.

Modern works

This list only includes books which are available in English. Some of them are prohibitively expensive, while others are old and therefore hard to obtain. Nevertheless, they represent the 'cream' of the subject and cover all social, military and institutional aspects of the Crusade era. I apologise for the inclusion of one of my own works amidst such august company, but basically with the exception of Dr Smail's work and Terry Wise's *Wars of the Crusades*

(1978) it is the only book I know of that deals with Crusading warfare and military organisation. It *is* the only one that supplies detailed information on the dress and equipment of all the protagonists.

Baldwin, M.W.: *Raymond III of Tripolis and the Fall of Jerusalem,* 1936.

Beeler, John H: *Warfare in Feudal Europe 730-1200,* 1971.

Benvenisti, Meron: *The Crusaders in the Holy Land*, 1970.

Boase, T.S.R.: *The Cilician Kingdom of Armenia*, 1978.

Campbell, G.A.: *The Knights Templar, Their Rise and Fall*, 1937.

Gibb, H.A.R.: *Studies in the Civilization of Islam*, 1962.

Glubb, John Bagot: *The Course of Empire*, 1965; *The Lost Centuries 1145-1453*, 1967; *Soldiers of Fortune: The Story of the Mamlukes*, 1973.

Heath, Ian: *Armies and Enemies of the Crusades 1096-1291*, 1978.

Johns, C.N.: *Palestine of the Crusades: A Map of the Country on Scale 1:350,000 with Historical Introduction & Gazetteer,* 1938.

La Monte, John: *Feudal Monarchy in the Latin Kingdom of Jerusalem*, 1932.

Lane Poole, Stanley: *Saladin and the Fall of the Kingdom of Jerusalem*, 1898.

Lewis, Bernard: *The Assassins: A Radical Sect in Islam*, 1968.

Mayer, H.E.: *The Crusades*, 1972.

Mayer, L.A.: *Saracenic Heraldry: A Survey*, 1933; *Mamluk Costume*, 1952.

Nicolle, David: *Early Medieval Islamic Arms and Armour*, 1976.

Oman, C.W.C.: *A History of the Art of War in the Middle Ages,* 1978.

Prawer, Joshua: *The World of the Crusaders*, 1972; *The Latin Kingdom of Jerusalem,* 1972

Richard, Jean: *The Latin Kingdom of Jerusalem* (two volumes), 1979.

Riley-Smith, Johnathan: *The Knights of St John in Jerusalem and Cyprus c. 1050-1310,* 1967.

Rodgers, W.L.: *Naval Warfare under Oars*, 1967.

Runciman, Steven: *A History of the Crusades* (three volumes), 1951-1954.

Setton, K.M.: *A History of the Crusades* (four volumes at present), 1969-1977.

Seward, Desmond: *The Monks of War—The Military Religious Orders*, 1972.

Simon, Edith: *The Piebald Standard: A Biography of the Knights Templars*, 1959.

Smail, R.C.: *Crusading Warfare 1097-1193*, 1956; *The Crusaders in Syria and the Holy Land,* 1973.

Verbruggen, J.F.: *The Art of Warfare in Western Europe during the Middle Ages,* 1977.

On the wargaming side I would strongly recommend (and have already done so!) that you should read, or better still buy, a copy of Tony Bath's *Setting up a Wargames Campaign*, published by the Wargames Research Group. The WRG also publish what is certainly the most widely used and probably the best, if most hotly debated, set of rules for Ancient and Mediaeval table-top battles, their *Ancient and Medieval Wargames Rules 3000 BC to 1490 AD*, currently in its fifth edition. No wargame rules are specifically available for naval battles of this period, but those for the classical era cover most eventualities.

Articles of general interest are also to be found in *Slingshot*, the bi-monthly journal of the Society of Ancients. Membership of the Society is a 'must' for all Ancient and Mediaeval wargamers, and interested parties should write to the Treasurer, Michael Wasilewski, at 100 Woodhouse Road, Finchley, London, N12 0RL.